# *On Being a Person*:
## *A Multidisciplinary Approach to Personality Theories*

∞∞∞∞∞∞∞∞∞∞∞∞∞∞∞∞∞

*Edited by* Todd H. Speidell

*Wipf and Stock Publishers*
Eugene, Oregon

Wipf and Stock Publishers
199 West 8th Ave., Suite 3
Eugene, Oregon 97401

*On Being a Person:*
*A Multidisiplinary Approach to Personality Theories*
Edited by Speidell, Todd H.
©2002 Speidell, Todd H.
ISBN: 1-59244-104-1
Publication Date: December 2002

# Table of Contents

**Introduction**
*Todd Speidell* (Webb School of Knoxville)          5

**Chapter One: Aristotle, The Biblical Drama, and the Meaning of Personhood**
*Mary Stewart Van Leeuwen* (Eastern University)     15

**Chapter Two: Personhood, Spiritual Formation, and Intersubjectivity in the Tradition of the Desert Fathers and Mothers**
*Robert A. Watson & Michael W. Mangis*
(Wheaton College)                                   34

**Chapter Three: Psychology Before Psychology: Philosophical, Theological, and Scientific Roots of Modern Psychology**
*Trey Buchanan* (Wheaton College)                   55

**Chapter Four: Self and Other in Kierkegaard**
*C. Stephen Evans* (Baylor University)              72

**Chapter Five: Theodicy, Autonomy, and Community: The Nature of Personhood in *The Brothers Karamazov***
*Ralph C. Wood* (Baylor University)                 88

**Chapter Six: John Macmurray as a Philosophical Basis for Harry Guntrip's Object Relations Theory**
*Trevor M. Dobbs* (Pacific Oaks College)            106

**Chapter Seven: Discovering a Dynamic Concept of the Person in Object Relations Psychology and Karl Barth's Theology**
*Daniel J. Price* (First Presbyterian Church, Eureka, CA)
                                                    125

**Chapter Eight: The Social Ecology of Human Personhood: Implications of Dietrich Bonhoeffer's Theology for Psychology**
*Ray S. Anderson* (Fuller Theological Seminary)     146

## Table of Contents

**Chapter Nine: Attachment: Bowlby & the Bible**
*Robert C. Roberts* (Baylor University)                174

**Chapter Ten: Beyond Bowlby: Attachment Dynamics
in Family, Church, and Classroom Relations**
*Roger Newell* (George Fox University)                200

**Chapter Eleven: On Becoming a Person of Character:
Cognitive, Behavioral, and Developmental-Contextual
Perspectives**
*Kaye V. Cook et al.* (Gordon College)                217

**Chapter Twelve: Family Systems Epistemology: The
Evolution of a Perspective on Persons and Relationships**
*Cameron Lee* (Fuller Theological Seminary)                243

**Appendix**                296

# Introduction

## Todd H. Speidell
Webb School of Knoxville

What is "psychology"? Contemporaries too often limit the study of psychology to the modern, empirical study of the person that began in the 19th century. Simply survey a variety of texts in "personality theories" and you would conclude that psychology is a modern invention.[1] One must look to the history of psychology to discover that psychology is an ancient practice of reflection on what it means to be a person. "Our definition of psychological thought," Robert Watson rightly asserts, "must hold not only for our present day but for the past as well. Psychological thought has always centered on three fundamental questions: (1) How do I know the things I know? (2) How do I feel the things I feel? (3) How do I do the things I do?"[2]

This age-old concern with knowledge, emotion, and behavior assumes a unity of mind and soul (cf. that the Greek etymology of "psychology" denotes the "word" or "reason" [*logos*]

---

[1] The one exception that I discovered was the classic Calvin Hall and Gardner Lindzey's *Theories of Personalities* (NY: John Wiley & Sons, 1957), which admits that a "comprehensive" or "adequate account" of personality theories "must surely begin with conceptions of man advanced by the great classical scholars . . . and with the contributions of dozens of thoughtful individuals . . . who lived in the intervening centuries and whose ideas are still to be detected in contemporary formulation" (1f.). Unfortunately, this text just as quickly as the rest races to Sigmund Freud, qualifying its task as "limited" but not meeting its own criterion of an "adequate account." Salvatore Maddi's *Personality Theories: A Comparative Analysis* (Prospect Heights, IL: Waveland Press, 1996), 6th ed. notes the recent trend towards research in the field of personality theories as disparaging comprehensive accounts of personality as "the leftovers of a previous, pre-scientific age in psychology," leaving "the whole person quite lost from view" (viii). Maddi unfortunately truncates theories of "personality" to an examination "of behavioral processes, without recourse to any mysterious notions of the supernatural or free will" (7).

[2] Robert I. Watson and Rand B. Evans, *The Great Psychologists: A History of Psychological Thought*, 5th ed. (NY: HarperCollins, 1991), 20.

of both "mind" and "soul" [*psyche*]). The biblical concept of salvation, furthermore, includes a sense of healing the whole person, not merely of "saving one's soul."[3] Modern psychology unfortunately tends to limit the study of *psyche* to mind, which some contemporary theorists have reduced further to nothing but brain activity.[4]

Personology, or personality psychology, properly studies persons as embodied souls and minds, not merely as minds that can be reduced to bodies. What, then, is a "person"? All psychological theories presuppose a vision or philosophy of human life, a common acknowledgement prior to the emergence

---

[3] The notion of a "soul" separate from the "body" derives from a Platonic dualistic reading of the Bible, since it was Plato who conceived of liberating the soul from the body, over and against the Bible's and Aristotle's holistic understanding of the person.

[4] See *Whatever Happened to the Soul? Scientific and Theological Portraits of Human Nature*, eds. Warren Brown, Nancy Murphy, and Newton Malony (Phila.: Fortress, 1998)—and the title of the book poses an apt question for some of the contributors to the book! The book rightly argues against a dualistic separation of body and soul, on the one hand, and a reductive physicalist monism on the other hand, in favor of what is called a "nonreductive physicalism" type of "monism" (xiii). A few of its authors, however, demonstrate more care and nuance than others. Warren Brown, for example, confuses a correct critique of dualism as the *separation* of soul and body with the more extreme denial that "soul" even has "*distinctive* existence, awareness and agency" (99, emphasis added). In the conclusion to the book, he states more bluntly, "humans are what you see; that is, there is not another invisible, nonmaterial part of the individual that must be factored into the formula of understanding" (228). Warren Jeeves' discussion of the book's nonreductive physicalist viewpoint is more subtle: the mind and brain are "inner and outer aspects of one complex set of events which together constitute human agency." A relation of "logical complementarity," then, suggests a "duality of aspects rather than duality of substance" (89). Ray Anderson similarly suggests that "soul" is "a distinctive aspect of the human person," denoting "the inner core" or "spiritual dimension" of the embodied self (177). Pitting monism against dualism, Anderson further suggests, is itself a dichotomy. Instead, there is a tension of "the unity of the body/soul duality of the person" (186, including n. 25). I prefer the term "holistic," which still allows for distinguishable aspects of personal existence, instead of "monistic," which does not adequately challenge the dichotomous nature of the monism vs. dualism debate.

of psychology as an empirical science.[5]  Is a person an immaterial substance only contingently related to the body (as the dualistic philosophies of Plato and Descartes suggest)? A soul-less body (as Hume reasons) or an evolved animal (as Darwin, Freud, J. B. Watson, and B. F. Skinner think)?  A person in relation to others (as John Macmurray and object relations psychology propose)? It is the purpose of this book to pursue the fundamental question of human life: What does it mean to be a person?

Can one have knowledge of persons? "[W]e can know more than we can tell," declares biochemist-philosopher Michael Polanyi.  We can recognize a human face in a large crowd, he illustrates, even though we cannot tell precisely how we can specify this personal or tacit knowledge.[6]  "You cannot formalize the act of commitment," he continues, "for you cannot express your commitment non-comittally."[7] Knowledge is "a process of knowing . . . towards a deeper understanding of what is already known"—the "hidden presence" of what is "ready to be found."[8]

It is important not to misunderstand what Polanyi means by "personal knowledge," and he is worth quoting at length:

> Here then is a brief hint in answer to the great question which I had set aside: namely, whether knowledge, admittedly shaped by the knower, can be determined by him as he thinks fit.  A passionate search for the correct solution of a task leaves no arbitrary choice open to the

---

[5] Consider this unfortunate definition of "personality theories" in the *Encyclopedia of Psychology* (Ed. Raymond J. Corsini): "In essence, a theory of personality is a set of *unproved speculations* about aspects of human behavior. *Established facts* are often lacking in scientific work, but theories offer guidelines that serve in the absence of more precise information" (New York: John Wiley & Sons, 1994), Vol. 3, p. 54; emphasis added. A less dualistic and simplistic definition of "personality psychology" may be found in (another) *Encyclopedia of Psychology* (Editor in Chief Alan E. Kazdin): "Personality psychology is the scientific study of the whole person.  The central aim of the field of personality psychology is to provide a scientific account of human individuality" (New York: Oxford, 2000), Vol. 6, p. 124.
[6] Michael Polanyi, *The Tacit Dimension* (Garden City, NY: Doubleday Anchor, 1967), 4f.; *Knowing and Being* (Chicago: Univ. of Chicago, 1969), 133f.
[7] Polanyi, *Tacit Dimension*, 25.
[8] Polanyi, *Knowing and Being*, 132; *The Study of Man* (Chicago: Univ. of Chicago), 1959, 35.

seeker. He will have to guess, but he must make the utmost effort to guess right. The sense of a pre-existent task makes the shaping of knowledge a responsible act, free from subjective predilections. And it endows, by the same token, the results of such acts with a claim to universal validity. For when you believe that your discovery reveals a hidden reality, you will expect it to be recognized equally by others. To accept personal knowledge as valid is to accept such claims as justified, even though admitting the limitations imposed by the particular opportunity which enables the human mind to exercise its personal powers. This opportunity is then regarded as the person's calling—the calling which determines his responsibilities.[9]

Whether in natural sciences or social sciences ("personality theories" being a subset of the latter), personal knowledge "shapes all factual knowledge." One's "passionate participation in the act of knowing," then, overcomes a simplistic dualism between subjectivism and objectivism and implies "personal obligations to universal standards."[10]

Persons, in other words, may truly, even if not fully, be known. A commitment to know other persons guides the purpose of this anthology. Belief seeks understanding, as St. Augustine counseled in the 4th century C.E.—a unity of faith and knowledge corrupted by Locke's disjunction of faith and knowledge in the 17th century C.E.[11] We all make commitments to what we tacitly know; the goal of this book is to articulate various theories of personality in order to invite the reader to reflect on his or her basic

---

[9] *The Study of Man, 36.*
[10] Polanyi, *Personal Knowledge: Towards a Post-Critical Philosophy* (Chicago: Univ. of Chicago, 1962), 17. Polanyi suggests three criteria: (1) "certainty" or "accuracy"; (2) "systematic relevance" or "profundity"; and (3) "intrinsic interest," the first two being "inherently scientific" and the third "extra-scientific" (ibid., 135f.). The personal, he states, "is neither subjective nor objective" insofar as personal knowledge and individual passions acknowledge a reality independent of oneself (ibid., 300).
[11] Faith is assurance but "not knowledge; persuasion and not certainty . . . a persuasion of our minds, short of knowledge . . ." (quoted in Polanyi, *Personal Knowledge*, 266). Polanyi then immediately comments: "Belief is here no longer a higher power that reveals to us knowledge lying beyond the range of observation and reason, but a mere personal acceptance which falls short of empirical and rational demonstrability."

assumptions about human personhood.[12] Listening to different traditions of psychology will illumine one's personal viewpoint on being a person.

∞∞∞∞∞∞∞∞∞∞∞∞∞∞∞∞

The approach of this text will be *multidisciplinary*: psychologists, philosophers, theologians, and ethicists grappling with what it means to be a person. This volume will not attempt to provide a comprehensive history of psychology but will instead focus on selected representatives of various paradigms of psychology: from the first systematic psychologist, Aristotle, through psychology's development as an empirical science, and to recent developments in family systems theory. It will especially emphasize a *social-relational-spiritual* view of the self: namely, human relations to God and to others are essential to humanity.[13] It will also eschew both dualistic and monistic understandings of personhood in favor of a *unitary* or *holistic* view of the person.[14]

This text will engage the reader in philosophical assumptions about human nature. I have produced this text to complement the coverage of religious, philosophical, and scientific personologists found in Leslie Stevenson and David L. Haberman's *Ten Theories of Human Nature*, although this text may be used on its own, especially in courses concerned with philosophical and religious roots of modern psychology. Stevenson's book helpfully uses the following four-fold form of analysis,[15] which leads one to analyze his or her basic assumptions about human nature (philosophically adventurous readers may wish to refer to the Appendix, which provides continua along which one may plot personality theorists; others may profitably

---

[12] "Our believing," suggests Polanyi, "is conditioned at its source by our belonging" (ibid., 322).

[13] As Torrance writes, "I believe it is in a radical renewing of our personal and inter-personal structures that comes from communion with God, that we are to look for a healing of the deep splits which have opened up in our modern civilization. But this means that what we need is the recovery of *spiritual being*, being that is open to personal reality and not imprisoned in its own self-centeredness." T. F. Torrance, *Reality and Scientific Theology* (Edinburgh: Scottish Academic Press, 1985), 196.

[14] See n. 4 (above).

[15] Leslie Stevenson and David L. Haberman, *Ten Theories of Human Nature*, 3rd ed. (NY: Oxford, 1998), 9.

ignore the Appendix and simply keep Stevenson's typology in mind throughout this book):

1. **"a background theory about the world"**—i.e., one's viewpoints on the nature of the universe, such as belief in the existence of a personal God and a corresponding spiritual dimension to life or belief that the universe is essentially material in nature and religious faith is illusory.

2. **"a basic theory about the nature of human beings"**—e.g., whether created in the image of God or essentially a product of society, free or determined, etc.

3. **"a diagnosis of what is wrong with us"**—e.g., sinful, alienated, neurotic, low self-esteem, etc.

4. **"a prescription for putting it right"**—i.e., remedies for human ills, such as salvation, liberation, enlightenment, psychotherapy, etc.

The following chapters of this anthology are arranged in chronological order of the personality theorists discussed in each chapter:

**Ch. 1**: Dr. Mary Stewart Van Leeuwen (Prof. of Psychology and Resident Scholar, Center for Chirstian Women in Leadership, at Eastern University) discusses Aristotle as the father of modern psychology. Unlike his teacher Plato, who relied on reason alone, Aristotle upheld the unity of rational and empirical methods, anticipating modern psychology's commitment to empirical observation. Furthermore, the Judeo-Christian understanding of personhood conceives of a unity of the self—an "embodied soul"—in relation to God. The Bible presents the human person as created, fallen, and redeemed. Mary Stewart Van Leeuwen's essay originally appeared in her book *The Person in Psychology: A Contemporary Christian Appraisal* (Grand Rapids: Eerdmans, 1985), pp. 36-56, and is used by permission of the author.

**Ch. 2**: Drs. Robert A. Watson and Michael W. Mangis (Asst. & Assoc. Professors of Psychology, respectively, at Wheaton College, Ill.) argue that the contemplative desert tradition of the third, fourth, and fifth centuries, as exemplified in the lives and sayings of the desert fathers and mothers, contains rich lessons for those who seek to integrate psychotherapy with Christian faith. In this article, they explore the frameworks of the desert monastic life that provide contemporary insights for the relationship between individual persons and community. They also examine the praxis of the desert fathers and mothers regarding soul-care and spiritual formation and discuss lessons from this tradition for the life and practice of contemporary Christian psychologists. They close with lessons from their experiences as licensed clinical psychologists seeking to apply these lessons to their practice. Their publications include Watson, R. A., & Mangis, M. W., "The Contribution of the Desert Tradition to a Contemporary Understanding of Community and Spiritual Intersubjectivity," *Journal of Psychology and Christianity*, 20.4 (2001), 309-323, and this essay is reprinted in this volume (with minor revisions) by permission of the authors and publisher. .

**Ch. 3**: Dr. Trey Buchanan (Associate Professor of Psychology at Wheaton College, Ill.) examines a fundamental question of this volume, What is psychology? He argues that there are both points of continuity and discontinuity between pre-modern and modern psychology. The prehistory of modern scientific psychology in theology and philosophy may be seen in the age-old quest to "know thyself," which gradually but distinctively evolved into a specialized human science. Nevertheless, he contends, the modern study of empirical psychology should not be divorced from the larger question and diverse answers to the enduring exploration of what it means to be a human being.

**Ch. 4**: Dr. C. Stephen Evans (University Prof. of Philosophy and Humanities at Baylor University) presents a controversial thesis on Soren Kierkegaard, the father of existentialism: He is not the arch-individualist he is reputed to be. His understanding of the self does emphasize the individual standing before God, but this relation to God protects the self against individualism and fosters love of others. Evans' essay originally appeared as "Who Is the Other in *Sickness Unto Death?*: *God and Human Relations in the Constitution of the Self*" in *Kierkegaard Studies* (Berlin: Walter de Gruyter, 1977), and is used by permission of the author.

11

# Introduction

**Ch. 5**: Dr. Ralph C. Wood (University Prof. of Theology and Literature at Baylor University) proposes that one's answer to the problem of evil very much shapes one's concept of personhood. In a discussion of Dostoevsky's *The Brothers Karamazov*, Wood presents the atheistic answer to the problem of evil as requiring a godless autonomy, while the Christian response entails communal love. The problem of evil is not a mere theoretical question to be resolved intellectually. It is an immensely practical matter that must be dealt with in one of two ways: either according to an individualist notion of personhood based on autonomous freedom, or else through the communal conviction that we become persons only through a suffering mutuality grounded in the Gospel.

**Ch. 6**: Dr. Trevor Dobbs (Psychoanalyst and Prof. of Marriage and Family Therapy at Pacific Oaks College) analyzes John Macmurray's philosophy as a basis for the object relations school of psychology. Persons are persons in relation, contends Macmurray, not isolated individuals; "personhood" is constituted by relations that are preeminently personal. Dobbs' essay exemplifies one of the premises of this book: schools of psychology have latent philosophical assumptions and worldviews that need to be unearthed.

**Ch. 7**: Dr. Daniel J. Price (Pastor of First Presbyterian Church of Eureka, CA) perceives a convergence between Karl Barth's theological anthropology and dynamic views of the person in the natural and human sciences, especially in the British object relations school of psychology. The relational dynamic in psychology and theology that Price proposes as a common ground for theological anthropology and the human sciences also implies a unitary view of the person as embodied souls. Price's treatment of parallels in theology, psychology, physics, and the Bible nicely demonstrates the multidisciplinary perspective of this volume, and his emphasis on the unitary nature of the person also underscores the holistic emphasis of this volume. His essay is reprinted here (with minor revisions) by permission of *Perspectives on Science and Faith* and appeared in volume 45, no. 3 (September 1993): 170-81. For a fuller treatment of this essay, see Daniel J. Price, *Karl Barth's Anthropology in Light of Modern Thought* (Grand Rapids, MI/Cambridge, U.K.: Wm. B. Eerdmans Pub. Co., 2002).

**Ch. 8**: Dr. Ray S. Anderson (Senior Prof. of Theology & Ministry at Fuller Theological Seminary) argues that psychological discussions of "personality" fall short of a richer theological concept of "personhood" as created, fallen, and redeemed by God in the totality of our lives as personal, social, spiritual, and physical beings. Anderson draws upon the martyred theologian Dietrich Bonhoeffer to buttress his view and to unpack implications for the relation of sin and pathology, as well as for ethics. Anderson's understanding of the person as an embodied self in relation to God and others comports well with the holistic emphasis of this volume.

**Ch. 9**: Dr. Robert C. Roberts (Distinguished Prof. of Ethics at Baylor University) compares and contrasts John Bowlby's concept of attachment with that of the Bible. While Bowlby and the Bible both emphasize attachment as a positive good—over and against individualistic notions of the self that pervade modern American culture and psychology—the Bible also broadens one's perspective on attachment. The Bible, unlike Bowlby, includes a concern for proper attachments to things and to God, who creates us for relationship and leads us to relate to him as an attachment figure. Roberts' essay, which shares a concern of this volume for recovering theological resources for understanding personhood, originally appeared in Robert C. Roberts and Mark R. Talbot, eds., *Limning the Psyche: Explorations in Christian Psychology* (Grand Rapids: Eerdmans, 1977), and is used by permission of the author and the publisher.

**Ch. 10**: Dr. Roger Newell (Assoc. Prof. of Religious Studies, George Fox University) reflects on his pastoral supervision experience with British psychotherapist Brian Lake as a way of presenting Lake and Dorothy Heard's development of John Bowlby's attachment theory. He explores implications for caregiving and careseeking in family, church, and classroom contexts.

**Ch. 11**: Dr. Kaye V. Cook (Prof. of Psychology at Gordon College and a licensed clinical psychologist) writes with two of her undergraduate students, Daniel Larson and Maren Oslund, to argue that character is essential to personal and psychological wholeness. After reviewing and evaluating behaviorist and social-cognitive models, Cook et al. present a developmental-contextual paradigm as a more adequate alternative for conceptualizing the moral and spiritual aspects of the self. This essay, relating the psychological to the ethical and theological dimensions of human life, illustrates the multidisciplinary approach of this volume.

**Ch. 12**: Dr. Cameron Lee (Prof. of Family Studies, Graduate School of Psychology, Fuller Theological Seminary) examines the changing nature of family therapy. Just as notions of what constitutes "family" have evolved in recent times, so too ideas of "family therapy" have changed. The original family systems conception to treat persons not merely as individuals but as persons embedded in relationships still shared a modernist conception of the therapist as an expert diagnostician. A postmodernist view, by contrast, questions therapists' power and objectivity and understands therapists as collaborative partners with clients. The epistemological focus of this essay exemplifies the kind of philosophical analysis and critique to which this volume is committed.

oooooooooooooooooooo

**Works Consulted**:

"Persons" and "Psychology" in *The Encyclopedia of Philosophy*, Gen. Ed. Paul Edwards (New York: Macmillian, 1967).
"Persons" and "Psychology, Theories of" in *Routledge Encyclopedia of Philosophy*, Gen. Ed. Edward Craig (New York: Routledge, 1998).
"Personality Psychology" and "Psychology" in *Encyclopedia of Psychology*, Ed. In Chief Alan E. Kazdin (New York: Oxford, 2000).

**Acknowledgements:**

From Webb School of Knoxville: Katherine Walker and Keegan Luttrell designed the cover of this book, and Jim Manikas, David Pierce, and Stephanie Helwig provided technical assistance. My Personality Theories class (Fall 2002) helped proofread the essays of this volume. Megan Boyce, Jeremy Fournier, Kim MacLennan, and Vedran Oruc were especially careful and thorough in weeding out errors. My faculty colleague Dr. David Haines helpfully criticized my introductory essay.
Also, Dr. Ray Anderson (Fuller Theological Seminary), Dr. Kaye Cook (Gordon College) and Dr. Cameron Lee (Graduate School of Psychology, Fuller Theological Seminary) provided invaluable advice on contributors and various other aspects related to this project. Finally, Jon Stock, Jim Tedrick, and Stephanie Randels of Wipf & Stock Publishers made possible the publication of this book.

# Aristotle, The Biblical Drama, and the Meaning of Personhood

*Mary Stewart Van Leeuwen*
Eastern University

## *Aristotle: The Father of Modern Psychology*

If in terms of amount of influence Democritus and Protagoras can be considered grandparents of modern psychology, and Plato perhaps a great-grandparent, Plato's pupil Aristotle (384-322 B. C.) can be considered an even closer relative. As the de facto founder of the fields that psychology now labels sensation, perception, and cognition, he is virtually a parent of modern psychology. Many of the basic assumptions of these fields trace their heritage directly back to Aristotle, whose thinking (revived in the sixteenth century) had so much to do with the emergence of modern science generally.

Aristotle concurred with Plato in rejecting a simplistic materialism as the ultimate explanation of reality, but he rejected his teacher's insistence that a true understanding of that reality could be achieved only through the use of a priori reason. Rather, said Aristotle, ideas are the abstracted forms of real, material entities, and consequently matter and abstract form are always tied together in the only world to which we have direct access. Rejecting a view of science based on either purely innate or purely empirical knowledge, Aristotle instead combined the two. What he called a "demonstrative proof" in science, although syllogistic in character, included as its minor premise an empirical observation from nature. For Aristotle, then, the tool of science was not reason alone but rather a combination of empirical observation *plus* reason—or, more specifically, the four-step method of observation, classification, intuitive abstraction, and finally deduction.[1] It is

---

[1] The basic source for psychologists is Aristotle's *De Anima*, although his psychological theorizing also appears in his *Logic*, *Ethics*, *Poetics*, and *Rhetoric*. His theory of science appears particularly in the *Posterior Analytics*. Pertinent parts of these have been extracted and arranged by Richard P. McKeon in *Western Psychology*, pp. 47-67.

these aspects of Aristotle's philosophy of science, resurrected almost two millennia later, that helped to launch the scientific revolution in Europe and that continue to hold an important place in the methodological assumptions of science even today.

Although scholars see varying degrees of continuity between Plato's and Aristotle's writings, they are generally agreed that one central Aristotelian doctrine concerning man is almost totally his own. This is the so-called "teleological principle," according to which the understanding of human beings is to be sought in an implicit purpose that gradually reveals itself in their development. At first hearing this seems like a religious—even a quasi-Christian—doctrine: "Thou has made us for Thyself," wrote Saint Augustine some seven centuries later, "and our hearts are restless till they find their rest in Thee." In these words he expressed the Christian conviction that human purpose is best summarized as reconciliation with God, and praise and enjoyment of him thereafter. But like Plato, Aristotle was largely indifferent to the place of any deity in human affairs, even though he postulated a supreme being who alone was Pure Form and no part material. Aristotle's teleology held rather that there was an inherent purposiveness in nature itself and in every process and organism that partook of nature. In his emphasis on the course of human unfolding toward innately predetermined adult goals, Aristotle provided an organizing principle for the development psychology that emerged as a formal part of psychology in the twentieth century.

In his *De Anima* ("About the Soul"), Aristotle developed his interpretation of human nature. Persons as such are indeed a part of the physical world, but their essences, or souls, belong to the category of pure form. Moreover, in keeping with the teleological principle, the soul's true purpose can be seen to unfold more and more during the course of a lifetime. That purpose, in line with Plato's thinking, was that human conduct should be guided by reason. In *De Anima* Aristotle sees psychology as the discipline that explores not only the formal (i.e. rational) essence of the soul but also its various earth bound attributes. The former, wrote Aristotle, can be understood only by the use of reason itself. But the latter, he maintained, could be ascertained by systematic observation of real human behavior—an anticipation of modern psychology's commitment to empiricism.

What, then, did Aristotle conclude from his observations about the attributes of human beings in their earthly existence? Essentially that they were animals—but *rational* animals. That is, like other animals they were seen to possess the appetites and physical structures essential to growth and reproduction as well as the sensory and motor equipment necessary to monitor and move about in their environment. But in addition, Aristotle maintained, through their uniquely human powers of reasoning, persons could transcend their animal limitations and understand the laws of pure reason as found in the discipline of logic. Nevertheless, they must still do this by relying upon their bodies, which must contend with the limitations as well as the assets of functions like perception, memory, and imagination. Accordingly, Aristotle devoted much attention to each of these topics.

It was Aristotle who first suggested that the five senses are the "gateways to the mind," and his theory that these five senses are coordinated by a higher-order "common sense" is one basis of psychology's present-day distinction between sensation and perception. He referred to memory as the capacity that enables us to retain the impressions of the senses, and imagination as that which permits us to recombine these impressions into new ideas. He also postulated certain principles of association—such as similarity, contrast, and closeness in time and space—to account for the fact that one idea can suggest another. It should be noted that Aristotle did not equate these simple mental functions with transcendent human reason but rather saw them as natural phenomena that were amenable to systematic empirical inquiry. In studying them he made his most lasting contribution to the systematic psychology that is taken for granted today.

. . . [T]wo further points may be made concerning Aristotle's influence on psychology. The first is that his distinction between peripheral senses and higher-order central reasoning continues to play an important role in cognitive psychology, which still assumes that the raw input of the senses is reworked and organized in the mind, even though the latter is still usually held to be a purely material entity. But psychologists continue to debate the question (which is as old as Aristotle) about how *closely* what we call thinking depends on mere sensory input and how much is the result of independent activity in the brain. For example, B. F. Skinner, who is a staunch materialist, ties thinking very closely to input from the empirical world that feeds into it via the senses, whereas Piaget, who is more of a rationalist, attributes much more creative independence to the mind itself. It is often an Aristotelian identification of the independently rational mind with the image of God in persons that makes theorists like Piaget seem more acceptable to Christians than someone like Skinner. But this is an assumption that has its own limitations . . .

A related point concerns Aristotle's teleological principle and his suggestion that human beings best reflect their inherent purpose in the final unfolding of adult rationality. I have already pointed out that developmental psychology follows this assumption of a natural unfolding of behavior toward a mature ideal, and that abstract reasoning is often considered the best expression of that ideal. But Aristotle's concept of mature rationality (like Plato's) included *wisdom* and *virtue* in addition to the capacity for theoretical abstraction—something that cognitive-developmental psychologists easily forget. It is possible, then, that in our continuing reverence for the mind, we are overlooking aspects of human purpose that are at least as important. How might the developmental drama of the Bible regarding creation, fall, redemption, and the final goal of history alter our perspective toward the idea that reason and the material benefits that it brings in its wake represent the developmental goal of human existence? Let us explore some possible responses to that question now.

*The Biblical Drama and the Meaning of Personhood*

> The concept of the exceptional position of man is to be derived less certainly from the "principal passages" . . . than from the overall impression made by the entire OT [Old Testament], where God's precepts and commands apply only to man, where the divine revelation is given only to man, where man alone is responsible for his decisions, and where man alone can be sinner or "righteous."[2]

> The emergence of Christianity must be counted as an occurrence whose importance to psychology is matched, if at all, only by the Hellenic epoch.[3]

> Let us review briefly . . . ancient conceptions of the person and their implications for psychology . . . [T]he ancient Mesopotamians had developed a clear sense of both the *power*

---

[2] Fritz Maass, *"Adham,"* in *Theological Dictionary of the Old Testament*, ed.
G. Johannes Bottemeck and Helmer Ringgren, trans. John T. Willis (Grand Rapids: Eerdmans, 1974), 1:85.
[3] Daniel Robinson, *An Intellectual History of Psychology* (New York: Macmillan, 1981 ), p. 111.

and the *personal nature* of their gods. In some contexts the powers of these gods were considered available, upon petition, to their loyal followers; in other contexts the gods were actually considered to be spiritual expressions of the different aspects of human functioning. But either way it was understood that the gods were personal beings, willing under the right circumstances to engage in dialogue with human underlings who were in some respects like them.

By contrast, both Hinduism and Buddhism have insisted on the *impersonal* nature of a single, metaphysical force and hence the illusory nature of human personality and the desirability of transcending it to attain unity with this impersonal "soul of the universe." The result has been an implicitly "abnormal" psychology, focusing on human existence and thought processes largely as indicators of various levels of bondage to an undesirable worldly life.

When we come to post-Socratic Greek thought, we find Plato locating the bridge between human and divine realms within human reason itself, best developed in an elite class of "philosopher-kings" who strive to transcend the deceptive world of appearances in order to explore the eternal and stable world of pure ideas. To Plato this meant that all of scholarship, including psychology, was to be a rational enterprise, little concerned with empirical observation, the results of which were considered idiosyncratic and hence largely unreliable. To Aristotle, however, human beings were more clearly creatures of two legitimate realms, one material and the other immaterial. While the human soul's ultimate nature and purpose centered on pure reason, and had to be studied by abstraction from the empirical, much else that was human—including many psychological functions—could be regarded as natural and could be essentially understood through empirical observation subsequently refined by rational classification and deduction aimed at ascertaining what teleological principles were at work.

The reader should by now understand that a particular culture's *anthropology*, or theory of human nature, intimately determines its psychological *epistemology*—that is, its assumptions as to how the details about human beings and their unique functions can best be studied. Democritus believed that the universe and the human beings within it were reducible to a common set of atomic elements. We should not be surprised, then, that he and his intellectual heirs have thought of psychology as ultimately being a branch of the natural sciences, and have insisted that the only valid way to study human thought and behavior is to look for causal laws of a deterministic sort. By contrast, Plato (and to some extent Aristotle) regarded the human psyche as transcending the physical and thus requiring for its understanding a very different approach than the one recommended by Democritus—requiring, for instance, an approach based on the understanding and application of the rules of logic that were themselves regarded as metaphysical ideals.

*Evolutionism in Modern Psychology*

. . . [M]odern psychology seems to vacillate somewhat uneasily between these two positions—between a view of human thought and behavior as ultimately material in nature and hence reducible to causal laws, and a more rationalistic position that seems to accord the human mind a greater degree of independence from the physical order and appeals to a set of logical rules for its understanding. It might be more accurate, however, to say that naturalism in psychology has tended to swallow up the rationalist position appealing to a third and more recent tradition—namely, evolutionism. Rooted in the eighteenth-century idea of progress and refined by Darwin's work in the nineteenth century, this point of view asserts that all human structures and functions—including those that seem the most mentally creative and independent—are the result of natural selection acting on genetic diversity.

Briefly summarized, evolutionism holds that members of any species of animal living in a state of nature will show great genetic diversity in their makeup, a diversity that makes it likely that some individuals will have characteristics enabling them to adapt in a superior way to their environment. Such individuals are consequently the most likely to survive and produce offspring—that is, their genes are most likely to be naturally selected. When invoked as a total anthropology by psychologists, evolutionism concludes that "the characteristics and abilities that make us *Homo sapiens* have been shaped by natural selection. We are what we are because we have survival value—not just as individuals, but as a species . . . We are the largely accidental result of particular environmental pressures acting on the available genetic material."[4] By such an account there is nothing mysterious

---

[4] Gardner Lindzey, Calvin S. Hall, and Richard F. Thompson, *Psychology* (New York: Worth, 1975), p. 31.

or metaphysical about our possession of extraordinary abilities that seem to separate us from other species: we would not have survived, multiplied, and altered our world so successfully if the chance genetic mutations underlying such abilities had not been sufficient to compensate in intelligence, linguistic ability, and social tendencies for what we lack in mere brute strength. As expressed by another psychologist, "We are Homo sapiens, the self-named wise one, due to a large degree to our well-developed brains, our opposable thumbs, the fact that we walk upright, and our ability to communicate through the use of arbitrary symbols."[5]

Such an anthropology need not be naively optimistic about human nature. On the contrary, most contemporary adherents of evolutionism conclude that we carry many compromises and even defects as part of our random genetic inheritance, and that these will persist provided only that they do not reduce our fitness to have offspring.[6] Moreover, the occasional writer of a psychology text will be a self-conscious enough Popperian to concede that evolutionary theory, especially as applied to human abilities and institutions, is open to falsification like any other scientific theory and therefore should not be taken as dogma.[7] For the most part, however, evolutionism has become the basic anthropology of Anglo-American psychology. "In Genesis we read that God created the world, including man," runs an opening chapter in a highly respected psychology text. "But the creation of man and woman, their idyllic life in the Garden of Eden, and their banishment from this paradise for eating the forbidden fruit are regarded by most people today as lovely myths, rich in symbolic and moral significance." By contrast, the writer continues, "Darwin's theory of evolution is quite rightly called the greatest unifying theory in biology. It provides a framework for the relatedness of all living creatures . . . [and accounts for] the countless ways in which man's genetic make-up affects his behavior."[8]

---

[5] Guy R. LeFrancois, *Psychology* (Belmont, Calif.: Wadsworth, 1980), p . 37.

[6] See, for example, Edward O. Wilson, *Sociobiology: The New Synthesis* (Cambridge: Harvard University Press, 1975), and *On Human Nature* (Cambridge : Harvard University Press, 1978).

[7] See, for example, LeFrancois, *Psychology*, p. 37.

[8] Lindzey, Hall, and Thompson, *Psychology*, p. 29.

*The Christian Response*

How is the Christian student or Christian observer of psychology to react to the claims of rationalism, naturalism, or evolutionism within the discipline? By way of an introductory summary, the following should be noted. First of all, over against naturalism and evolutionism, Christianity points to the possibility of an immaterial part of ourselves that survives death. Relatively little is said about this in Scripture, however, because much more emphasis is placed on the final resurrection of whole persons, including their bodies. Second, this points to a biblical emphasis on the unitary nature of the self in opposition to the atomism that began with Democritus and continues in psychology even today. For although souls may be "separable" from during an intermediate state (after death but prior to the resurrection), this is perhaps best seen as a temporary aberration: both at creation and at the final resurrection the norm is clearly an embodied soul, functioning as a whole person rather than as an uneasy alliance between material and immaterial functions. This, of course, puts the Christian view of persons at odds with Platonic dualism as well. Third, the biblical view of persons sees them as irreducibly in *relationship*—first with God, then with the physical world and with other persons. Human freedom and individuality are important because they are God-endowed; indeed, these are grounds for asserting that the very concept of the individual person arose only with Christianity.[9] Yet human freedom is not absolute or unqualified but rather is exercised in the context of our inborn dependence on God and the physical world he upholds, and of our equally inborn interdependence on each other. This Christian notion of irreducible interrelationship contrasts with all movements in psychology that rest on individualistic assumptions . . .

But within this network of relationships, finally, the Bible sees persons as accountable stewards over the rest of creation, answerable to God for their activity in all spheres of life—natural, social, artistic, political, and so on. Although qualified, our

---

[9] See, for example, Robinson, *An Intellectual History of Psychology*, chap. 4; and Max Muller and Alois Halder, "Person Concept," in *Sacrementum Mundi*, ed. Karl Rahner (New York: Herder and Herder, 1969), 4: 404-19.

freedom enables us to act intentionally and purposefully, at least much of the time; yet this very freedom is accompanied by moral responsibilities that are unique to persons. With these anticipations of what the Bible means when it speaks of persons—immortality, unity, relationality, and responsibility—let us look in more detail at the biblical world view of which personhood is the central feature. The reader should, of course, bear in mind that I make this examination not as a systematic theologian but as a psychologist looking for the biblical themes that are most pertinent to a contemporary appraisal of psychology.

## *The Biblical World View: Both a Theory and a Drama*

In a little book entitled *Seven Theories of Human Nature*, philosopher Leslie Stevenson suggests a set of useful guidelines for understanding past and present attempts to answer the question, What is Man? Implicitly or explicitly, says Stevenson, a complete theory of human nature will include four features: a background theory about the nature of the universe, a theory about the essential nature of human beings, a diagnosis of the present human condition, and a prescription for the ills diagnosed.[10] Let us begin our review by using Stevenson's fourfold classification.

A biblical view of the universe begins with the assertion of the opening lines of Genesis: "In the beginning God created the heavens and the earth." That is to say, the God whom Christians acknowledge is not just one of many objects in the universe but rather the originator of the entire enterprise. Neither is he to be identified with "everything that exists," after the manner of pantheistic religions such as Hinduism and Buddhism. For "although in some sense present everywhere and all the time, He is also beyond or outside the world of things in space and time."[11] But if the God of the Bible is thus inaccessible by any of the empirical methods of science, this does not mean that he is a mere abstraction or a totally impersonal entity. As the creator of the universe he is all-powerful, and yet at the same time he is a personal being who loves his creation, and especially his human creatures, with an intense and intimate concern.

---

[10] Stevenson, *Seven Theories of Human Nature* (New York: Oxford University Press, 1974). The seven theories surveyed by Stevenson are those of Plato, Freud , Lorenz, Sartre, Skinner, Marx, and Christianity.
[11] Stevenson, *Seven Theories of Human Nature*, p. 36.

In addition, and also in opposition to the thinking of much of the ancient world, God is portrayed in Scripture as having a high view of his material creation. Matter and organic processes are not to be despised as being of a lower order than intellectual and spiritual concerns, but rather used with thanks and careful stewardship as gifts from him. Finally, to say that "God created the heavens and the earth" does not mean that he wound up the universe like a clock and then withdrew to let it run—and run down—on its own, as the deist of the eighteenth and nineteenth centuries supposed. On the contrary, the world and its inhabitants are dependent on him moment by moment for their continued existence. Christ "reflects the glory of God . . . , upholding the universe by his word of power," says the writer to the Hebrews at the opening of that epistle, and Christians confess that nothing in the universe exists except by God's continuing purpose, or at least by his permission.

But having affirmed that God himself is no mere impersonal entity but a personal being involved with his creation, it is perhaps wise to balance this abstract doctrine with a picture that captures his personal nature and involvement somewhat more completely. Let me suggest, in keeping with a number of other Christian scholars, that Christianity is not only a theory but also an unfolding historical drama with a definite beginning, climax, and ending. Of this ongoing drama God is the author, director, and producer all at once, and consequently no less involved for seeming to be offstage for most of the performance. Paul Tournier's image of God as both composer and conductor of a symphony may also be helpful, because it captures the idea of a director continually in contact with the players before him.[12]

*The Original Human Creation.* The images of God as author and director of a play or composer and conductor of a symphony also help us to understand the contours of a Christian doctrine of persons. For it is said that we are "made in God's image," and therefore like him in ways not shared by the rest of the material and organic world. Clearly the players on the stage or in the orchestra pit are much more like their director than they are like the props they handle or the instruments they play. But what is the nature of this similarity? What does it mean to say that we are "in God's image," especially when this phrase occurs only

---

[12] Tournier, *The Meaning of Persons* (London: SCM Press, 1957).

rarely in the Bible and receives very little elaboration?[13] Are *all* persons "made in God's image" in some way that distinguishes them from, say, animals, or is the image confined to those who acknowledge God through Jesus Christ? Or are even Christians only incomplete imagers of God, still "seeing through a glass darkly," as Paul put it in his letter to the Corinthians. Is it even possible that some non-Christians are better imagers of God than some Christians in certain ways, and if so, how?

Theologians have debated such questions for many years now, and their importance to Christians in psychology would seem obvious. But despite persistent controversy over the fine details, this much seems both scripturally clear and historically consistent in Christian theology: God's original will and achievement was the creation of male and female human beings who occupied an intermediate place in the creation. Formed of "dust from the ground," they were as fragile and earthbound as their animal neighbors, needing food, sleep, air, and self-propagation as much as any other living thing. Yet human beings were apparently made to be more than merely complex living for *things*, for we are told in the creation accounts of Genesis 1 and 2 that God himself bestowed upon them "the breath of life," making them living beings in a way not accorded to other creatures. These beings, physically vulnerable while on earth, were nonetheless meant to live forever in relationship with God and each other. Moreover, both creation accounts speak of God as giving human beings a special kind of control over the rest of creation: to name its animals; to "fill the earth and subdue it"; to "till . . . and keep" the Garden; to "have dominion . . . over every living thing that moves upon the earth." Thus it seems that a significant way in which persons originally "imaged" God was as accountable overseers of his creation, endowed with the capacities, the curiosity, and the relative freedom to carry out that mandate.

Human beings, then, were created to be both continuous and discontinuous with the rest of creation, and the tension between these two states must clearly be reflected in any Christian

---

[13] Aside from the Genesis 1:27 passage, only three others refer specifically to the concept of persons made "in the image of God": Genesis 9:6 ("Whoever sheds the blood of man, by man shall his blood be shed; for God made man in his own image"); 1 Corinthians 11:7 ("For a man ought not to cover his head, since he is the image and glory of God"); and James 3:9 ("With [the tongue] we bless the Lord and Father, and with it we curse men, who are made in the likeness of God").

appraisal of contemporary psychology. Given that we are indeed creatures of flesh and blood, such an appraisal cannot exclude some examination of man behavior that appeals to the theories and methods used to study nonhuman entities. Nor does it preclude the possibility as many "theistic evolutionists" have suggested, that human beings, by God's *fiat*, did evolve from lower species but at a particular point in this process were set apart as God's special "imagers," or representatives.[14] But it does mean that neither naturalism nor evolutionism will suffice as the foundational anthropology for the Christian psychologist.

Central to the Christian's understanding of human nature is a conviction regarding the person's ongoing relationship with God, a relationship that was intended to be of both a providential and a covenantal sort. That is to say, any temptation to human arrogance was precluded by a sense of continuing dependence on God (shared with the lowest of creatures and inanimate objects) as the very source of life and meaning. Human self-debasement—the opposite error—was precluded by the fact that God had called men and women into partnership with him, and thus endowed them with dignity and purpose. But it was a partnership, a covenant, sealed with a condition: eternal, satisfying fellowship with the Creator in return for a modest behavioral token of their dependence upon his ultimate authority. While the exact historical details may be debated by biblical scholars, this much seems clear from the biblical record: men and women were not to use their autonomy and dominion to legislate the nature of good and evil; this prerogative belonged to God alone.

We know this much, then, about our original relationship to God: first, he stamped us with the "seal" or "image" of accountable dominion over the earth; and second, we were to exercise this stewardship as his covenant partners according to norms set by him alone. In all of this, the most critical feature—what one personality theorist would call the "core tendency" of human beings[15]—seems to be our openness, our

---

[14] See, for example, the following: Bernard Ramm, *The Christian View of Science and Scripture* (Grand Rapid Eerdmans, 1954); Edmund J. Ambrose, *The Nature and Origin of the Biological World* (New York: John Wiley, 1982); and Robert B. Fischer, *God Did It, But How?* (La Mirada, Calif: CalMedia, 1981).

[15] Salvatore R. Maddi, *Personality Theories: A Comparative Analysis*, 4th ed. (Homewood, Ill.: Dorsey Press, 1980).

responsivity to God. By nature we were made to be in touch with him, and by voluntary obedience to serve him.

*The Diagnosis.* I have sketched the essentials of a biblical view of the universe and of human beings within it. But I pointed out earlier, with Leslie Stevenson, that no fully orbed theory of human nature has ever stopped there. On the contrary, all acknowledge that something is not ideal about the present human condition, and all attempt to explain what that "something" is . . . the ancient Mesopotamians concluding that their offenses against natural and political deities were the source of human unhappiness. In Hindu and Buddhist thought . . . overattachment to material and temporal modes of existence was seen to be the cause of human woe. To Plato it was disharmony among the three parts of the soul and a refusal to put reason before ambition and appetite that brought trouble to individuals and societies alike. So what is the Bible's response to the question "Where did things go wrong?"

The heart of the matter, according to Scripture, lay in the willful misuse of the very freedom and dominion that God gave to human beings as his stewards. Not willing to leave "the knowledge of good and evil" to God alone, our first ancestors preferred to violate the modest behavioral code, the keeping of which had been a token of their voluntary acknowledgment of God's lordship. The result was an immediate and permanent distortion of the shalom—the right and peaceful ordering—of the original creation. Self-consciousness of a shameful and defensive sort invaded the human mind. The formerly natural fellowship with God was replaced with a sense of guilt and fear toward him. The harmonious relationship between husband and wife took on highly ambivalent overtones. From that time on, neither earth nor the human womb would yield its fruit without hard work. Most tragic of all, the inevitability of death descended upon humanity: "In the sweat of your face you shall eat bread till you return to the ground, for out of it you were taken; you are dust, and to dust you shall return" (Gen. 3: 19).

To return to our dramatic metaphor, the human fall represents a tragedy. For to be a tragic hero, a person must originally have been of some importance—man or woman of substance, tempted by circumstances, to be sure, yet still personally responsible for choosing evil. "Our tragedy," wrote Pascal in the seventeenth century, "is that of a fallen nobleman." And yet one must not ignore the circumstances that made that disobedience possible. I do not agree with Stevenson that "it is not necessary for Christians to postulate some kind of personal devil to express the idea of a cosmic fall."[16] C. S. Lewis seemed to be much closer to the mark when he wrote,

> One of the things that surprised me when I first read the New Testament seriously was that it talked so much about a Dark Power in the universe-a mighty spirit who was held to be the Power behind death, disease and sin. The difference is that Christianity thinks that this Dark Power was created by God, and was good when he was created and went wrong. Christianity [says] that this universe is at war. But it does not think this is a war between independent powers. It thinks it is a civil war, a rebellion, and that we are living in a part of the universe occupied by the rebel.[17]

And so the plot of the biblical drama intensifies. We are indeed willful, accountable rebels against the God who made us—but at the same time we are naive, addicted followers of an archrebel, the origin of whose own sin in the cosmic realm remains a baffling mystery. We are free actors on the stage of life, able to hear yet choosing to ignore the promptings of author-director of the drama. Instead, we share with our primal ancestors the determination to let ourselves be strung up and manipulated like marionettes by a "dark power" who has, as it were, stolen the author's copyright and reinterpreted the script. Our wills, as Luther put it, are in bondage, and the results of this voluntary self-incarceration show up both in human character ("None is righteous, no, not one"; Rom. 3: 10) and in the imperfect state of the natural world, which is continually "groaning in travail" and "bondage to decay" (Rom. 8 :22, 21).

Seen in this light, it is true on one level to say that all psychology is "abnormal" psychology, if what we mean is that none of us functions as God originally intended us to. Indeed, when I quoted historian Daniel Robinson (at the beginning of the chapter) as saying that the emergence of Christianity may have surpassed the Greek epoch in its importance for psychology, I took this from a passage commenting on the efforts of the early church fathers—and in particular Augustine—to understand how the

---

16 Stevenson, *Seven Theories of Human Nature*, p. 41.
17 Lewis, *Mere Christianity* (London: Collins-Fontana, 1955), p. 47.

human will, paradoxically free yet bound, both apprehends and resists the voice of God. Robinson concludes that although Plato's dialogues "assert the existence of extrasensory, immaterial truths of a finer quality and graver meaning than any accessible to earthbound human beings," Christianity went even further:

> [Christianity] required not a philosophical life, but a religious one which, if neglected, led not to ignorance and its attendant unhappiness, but to sin and the ultimate retribution. It replaced [Plato's] true forms with the all-seeing vision of the timeless architect of all truth, an architect whose infinite love was carefully balanced against infinite justice. . . . This shift in emphasis provided early Christian scholarship with a decidedly psychological cast. The early Christian's problem about knowledge was not one of uncovering the truth, but of transmitting it, of readying the pagan mind for the light of faith. The problem thus conceived, Christian scholars inquired more deeply into the psychogy, as opposed to the purely rational factors, governing human conduct.[18]

Robinson goes on to point out that Augustine's *Confessions* were particularly indicative of this shift in orientation away from Greek metaphysics: "Where Socrates merely counseled against the rule of passion over reason, Augustine laid bare the genuinely personal and psychological dimensions of the conflict."[19] Herein lies the reason that Augustine has often been called "the first psychologist" and Freud "the godless Augustine." What both shared was a conviction about the passionate, irrational nature—however disguised and rationalized—of much human conduct, reduced to biological and interpersonal dynamics by Freud but interpreted by Augustine "in an unblushing, otherworldly idiom."[20]

*The Prescription.* We have said, in effect, that a "dark power" put into the minds of our remote ancestors the notion that they could be their own masters and invent for themselves some kind of dependable happiness outside of fellowship with God. Throughout history this inherent determination to run ourselves

---

[18] Robinson, *An Intellectual History of Psychology*, p. 123.
[19] Robinson, *An Intellectual History of Psychology*, p. 123.
[20] Robinson, *An Intellectual History of Psychology*, pp. 123-24.

on the wrong fuel, as it were, has been the cause of human misery. What, according to the Bible, was God's response to this act of human rebellion? Did he merely withdraw in a fit of pique, leaving us to flounder in the consequences of our own disobedience? Not at all. Right away, in several different ways, he began preparing us for the solution.

First of all, into the now distorted and co-opted human drama he inserted what theologians have often called "common grace"—that disposition or act of God that holds the spread of corruption in check, as Calvin defined it.[21] Or in C. S. Lewis's more modern idiom, "He left us with conscience, the sense of right and wrong; and all through history there have been people trying (some of them very hard) to obey it."[22] Although not sufficient to reverse the consequences of the Fall, this sense of right and wrong served and still serves to maintain a degree of order in human life, and also (if not totally crushed or ignored) to prepare men and women for a decisive and more complete return to God.

Second (Lewis intriguingly suggests), even in our puppet-like state as Satan's minions, God got through to us with "good dreams": "those queer stories scattered all through the heathen religions about a god who dies and comes to life again and who, by his death, has somehow given new life to men."[23] Thus both human conscience and human legend were allowed to grope back toward God's original intention and forward toward his final solution for human sin. Then, to cap it all off, he set up a species of "pilot plant," an experimental community. He selected one particular group of people, the Jews, and progressively revealed his ways to them over the centuries—not so that they might regard themselves as intrinsically superior to others or exempt from the fallenness common to all, but so that they might be the vehicle through which, at the right time, the Author himself would appear onstage and reorient the entire human drama. And this was the climax of the entire sweep of history: "Among these Jews there suddenly turns up a man who goes about talking as if he was God. He claims to forgive sins. He says that he has always existed. He says He is coming to judge the world at the end of time . . . . [And]

---

[21] Calvin, *The Institutes of the Christian Religion*, trans. Henry Beveridge (Grand Rapids: Eerdmans, 1957), 2.3.3.

[22] Lewis, *Mere Christianity*, p. 51.

[23] Lewis, *Mere Christianity*, p. 51. The only modern psychologist to suggest the existence of such a "racial memory" (although he gives it different content) is Carl G. Jung . . . .

the claim to forgive sins makes sense only if he really was the God whose laws were broken and whose love is wounded in every sense."[24]

It is as if the Author of the play suddenly joined the players onstage and began to add new lines conveying the true meaning of the script, which until then had been interpreted at best incompletely and at worst with deliberate distortion. Yet even then they misunderstood: they assumed that his agenda was a purely local one, aimed at restoring the Jewish nation to its former independence and military might. But in fact his aim was to break the spell of the original fall, giving to all persons—Jews and Gentiles alike—the possibility of a second chance. "We are told that Christ was killed for us, that his death has washed out our sins, and that by dying he disabled death itself. That is the formula. That is Christianity."[25] Or, as the Gospel of John puts it, "To all who received him, who believed in his name, he gave power to become children of God; who were born, not of blood nor of the will of the flesh nor of the will of man, but of God" (John 1:12-13).

*The Prognosis.* But what does all this mean for present, ongoing existence? Is Christ's atonement, once appropriated, merely an abstract assurance of freedom from ultimate judgment after death, or does it have practical implications for life on earth? Christian commitment claims to carry with it the power to enact its own prescription in individual and corporate life. "By this all men will know that you are my disciples, if you have love for one another," Christ said (John 1 3:35). Although it was a commandment, it was also a promise, delivered to the early Christians in the coming of the Holy Spirit at Pentecost—delivered so radically that it prompted non-Christian observers to marvel at the transformation that had taken place in such ordinary people (Acts 2-5 passim).

So the Christian prescription for the human condition indeed carries with it a powerfully positive prognosis. As persons appropriate Christ's salvation, both individual and corporate restoration begin to take place, with consequences spilling over into all areas of life. But even as Christians confess this is in faith and affirm it in experience, they add some essential qualifiers.

First of all, conversion brings with it the seed, not the full fruit, of restoration. To this end the quality of the human soil is

---

[24] Lewis, *Mere Christianity*, pp. 51-52.
[25] Lewis, *Mere Christianity*, p. 55.

relevant. The New Testament makes it clear that the inherent talents and burdens of individuals will condition their progress in the new life. In this sense at least, God is the supreme relativist: he judges persons not by standards of perfection (although without Christ this would indeed be the case) but rather by the quality of a person's efforts relative to innate and acquired gifts and struggles (Matt. 25:14-30). To put it another way, individual differences matter to God. Although persons share a common heritage both as an earthly species and as God recovered rebels, there is a wide variety of both special gifts and special limitations—a variety that ensures that the Christian life can never be reduced to a mere formula.

Second, whatever the nature of the soil, the motivations of the cultivator also influence the outcome of the harvest. God does not force sanctification on persons any more than he forces sin on them, and Scripture warns that there will be imposters within the church and even some who may deliberately reject the new life after they have tasted it (Heb. 10:23-3 1). Third, it seems that God puts limits on human progress in order to keep persons mindful of their continuing dependence on him. "We have this treasure in earthen vessels," Paul wrote to the early church, "to show that the transcendent power belongs to God and not to us" (2 Cor. 4:7). In other words, the building of the new heaven and the new earth is still in God's hands; Christians are not able to pull themselves up by their own bootstraps, however progressively strengthened they are becoming in Christ.

Finally, as Luther put it in a famous hymn, "Still our ancient foe / Doth seek to work us woe." To borrow Lewis's picture of the biblical drama as a cosmic battle, Christians live, as it were, between D-Day and V-Day. "Enemy-occupied territory: that is what the world is," wrote Lewis. "Christianity is the story of how the rightful king has landed, you might say landed in disguise, and is calling us all to take part in a great campaign of sabotage."[26] In other words, the decisive invasion, which marks the turning point of the war and of all history, has occurred. But there is still fighting to be done—with attendant casualties—before "the author walks onto the stage [and] the play is over."[27] And this too limits Christian progress in the new life, at least for the duration of earthly existence. There will be—indeed, there must

---

[26] Lewis, *Mere Christianity*, p. 47.
[27] Lewis, *Mere Christianity*, p. 64.

be—substantial healing, for this is the mark of the Christian church, without which the rest of the world will understandably give it no more attention than it will give any other theory of human nature. Yet, as preachers in the Reformed tradition so aptly put it, Christians live in the era of "the already, and the not yet." The turning point has occurred, but the strife is not yet completely over.

This chapter has focused on the Judeo-Christian concept of the person, especially those aspects of it that contrast significantly with prevailing assumptions in psychology. I have noted that the biblical drama speaks of the immortality of persons in their entire, embodied selves, even though a period of immateriality of the soul may intervene between death and the final resurrection. I have also noted that the biblical view of persons sees them as unitary (not fragmented), relational (not purely individual), and capable of responsible dominion within the limits imposed by their finitude and sinfulness. Moreover, the person who becomes a Christian makes the claim of being and continually becoming—a "new creation," capable of exercising progressively more of the "freedom within form" that was intended before the fall of humankind. Although this process is conditional (many other factors come into play), it is nevertheless real.

# Personhood, Spiritual Formation, and Intersubjectivity in the Tradition of the Desert Fathers and Mothers

*Robert A. Watson and Michael W. Mangis*
Wheaton College

*Introduction*

In recent years, conversations about the nature of the integration of psychology and Christianity moved beyond the traditional 'interdisciplinary' models and approaches.[1] At the same time, renewed interest in the wisdom of the Christian spirituality tradition regarding soul-care led integrationists to begin to rediscover distinctive Christian psychologies in the literature of the Church. Finally, recent integrative work expanded the horizon of the traditional psychologists' more-or-less exclusive focus on the individual person as unit of study and intervention to include communal contexts, including the role of the local church body in healing, spiritual formation, and transformation.

Recent conversations on the relationship between distinctively Christian approaches to psychological treatment and the soul-care and spiritual direction traditions point out the inadequacy of one to do the job of the other. In addition, the North-American Evangelical church's under-emphasis on spiritual formation is increasingly under scrutiny. As Dallas Willard aptly points out, "[Evangelicals] have counted on preaching and teaching, and knowledge or information to form faith in the hearer, and have counted on faith to form the inner life and outward behavior of the Christian."[2] Most Christian psychologists have witnessed the results in their clients of this emphasis on what Willard elsewhere calls "the gospel of sin management"[3]—an overemphasis on managing one's image to the spiritual community at the expense of one's interior development toward

---

[1] S. Bouma-Prediger, "The Task of Integration: A Modes Proposal," *Journal of Psychology and Theology*, 18.1 (1992): 21-31.
[2] Ibid., 254.
[3] *The Divine Conspiracy: Rediscovering our Hidden Life in God* (San Fran.: HarperSanFransisco, 1998).

maturity. Christian psychology is perhaps guilty of fostering an over-reliance on individualistically-oriented psychotherapeutic approaches to form emotional healing in the counselee and on healing to contribute to a more spiritually mature inward and outward life.

It is our hope in this essay to join the conversation of Christian psychologists looking to the history of the Church for wisdom regarding soul-care. We hope to contribute to a more clear and systematic understanding of spiritual formation and of the role of the church in healing, spiritual formation, and transformation of persons. We hope to participate in bringing forward to the 21st century Church the distinctively Christian psychologies developed within our tradition over the centuries. Specifically, we will examine the desert tradition of the third, fourth, and fifth centuries exemplified in the lives and sayings (i.e., the *Apophthegmata*) of the desert fathers and mothers.

In this essay we will focus on two questions, one broad and one specific: 1) What frameworks exist within the desert tradition that could provide contemporary models for exploring the relationship between individual person and community? and 2) What was the praxis of the desert fathers and mothers regarding soul-care and spiritual formation? We will examine these questions by first highlighting the desert tradition in historical and cultural context. Next, we will consider themes salient to contemporary discussions of spiritual formation and soul-care in the context of relationship and community. Finally, we will introduce the construct of Spiritual Intersubjectivity, borrowing from current psychoanalytic thinking on the nature of what promotes healing and transformation via therapeutic relationships. This way of viewing transformative processes will then be related to the types of relationships that characterized the desert fathers and mothers. Discussion of our own professional work will illustrate the application of these processes in the clinical or pastoral context.

*The Desert Tradition in Historical, Cultural, and Geographical Context*

By the end of the fourth century, an extraordinary movement of Christian men and women flowered in the Middle Eastern deserts around the Roman Empire. Many of the early desert fathers (e.g., St. Anthony) and mothers experienced the transition from the persecution of the church by previous Roman emperors to Constantine's sanctioning of Christianity as the state religion of the Empire in 313 A.D. The formal end of the persecution led these individuals not to settle into the new 'Christian' society, but to flee it:

> Society . . . was regarded (by the Desert Fathers) as a shipwreck from which each single individual man had to swim for his life . . . These were men who believed that to let oneself drift along, passively accepting the tenets and values of what they knew to be society, was purely and simply a disaster.[4]

Far from a type of 'schizoid contagion' or phenomena of pathological detachment, this flight from society was grounded in the conviction that the only real way to transform society was to be transformed themselves into the image of Christ. These individuals appear to have been a cross-section of their respective cultures: privileged and poor; former slaves and aristocrats; men and women; Romans, Egyptians, and Africans. The desert tradition has remained relevant and prone to re-discovery by the Church over the past seventeen centuries in large measure because of this radical commitment to the salvation and transformation of both individual and society. The individual and communal life structures that they developed were truly counter-cultural, and their relevance to Christian psychologists in a contemporary North American context is the point of this article.

The geographical center of this early monastic movement was in Egypt, though representatives of the desert tradition also lived in Syria, Asia Minor, and Palestine. The Egyptian desert provided the physical context for the development of three types of desert spirituality: the hermit (eremitic) life, the coenobitic life, and the group ascetic life.[5] The hermits of lower Egypt lived in the desert essentially in complete solitude. The most well known of these was Anthony, who is called 'The Father of Monks' and who lived for twenty years (from age 34 to 54) in solitude in the desert. After returning to the world for five years, he again retired to his hermitage in the desert for most of the rest of his life until his death 46 years later. Athanasius, Archbishop of Alexandria, wrote

---

[4] T. Merton, *The Wisdom of the Desert: Sayings from the Desert Fathers* (NY: New Directions Pub. Co., 1970), p. 3.
[5] B. Ward, *The Sayings of the Desert Fathers* (Kalamazoo, MI: Cistercian Pub., 1975), pp. xvii-xviii.

Anthony's biography, which became central in communicating to the church the essential components of desert spirituality. Of Anthony, Athanasius said,

> [H]is soul was free from blemish, for it was neither contracted as if by grief, nor relaxed by pleasure, nor possessed by laughter or dejection, for he was not troubled when he beheld the crowd, nor overjoyed at being saluted by so many. But he was altogether even as being guided by reason, and abiding in a natural state. Through him the Lord healed the bodily ailments of many present, and cleansed others from evil spirits. And He gave grace to Antony in speaking, so that he consoled many that were sorrowful, and set those at variance at one, exhorting all to prefer the love of Christ before all that is in the world.[6]

Henri Nouwen drew much from Anthony's life. Nouwen found, in the desert tradition a clear message "that we must be made aware of the call to let our false, compulsive self to be transformed into the new self of Jesus Christ . . . that solitude is the furnace in which this transformation takes place . . . that it is from this transformed or converted self that real ministry flows."[7]

The second type of desert spirituality, the coenobitic life, was centered in Upper Egypt, in close proximity to Thebes at Tabennesi. Pachomius (290-347) organized the first monastery where monks lived in community beginning in 320. What differentiated this form of desert spiritual life was its distinctively communal structure: the members lived in a compound with multiple dwellings, worked, ate, prayed, and worshipped together. The emphasis was on living in community or 'life together' (*koinobios*), united to each other in work and prayer.[8] Interdependence characterized the structure of relationships in these communities:

> One day Abba Pachomius himself told the brothers about this, which is a kind of vision: "I once saw a large place

---

[6] Athanasius, *Select Works and Letters*, in P. Schaff & H. Wace (eds.), *Nicene and Post-Nicene Fathers*, Series II (Vol. IV) (Grand Rapids: Eerdmans, 1984), p. 200.
[7] *The Way of the Heart: Desert Spirituality and Contemporary Ministry* (San Fran.: HarperSanFransisco, 1991), p. 8.
[8] Ward, *Sayings*.

with many pillars in it. And there were in the place many men unable to see where to go, some of them going around the pillars, thinking they had traveled a long distance toward the light. And a voice [resounded] from all directions: 'Behold! Here is the light!' They would turn back to find it, only to hear the voice again and turn back another time. There was great wretchedness. Afterwards I saw a lamp moving, followed by many men. Four of them saw it and the others followed them, each holding his neighbor's shoulder lest he go astray in the dark. And if anyone let go of the man in front of him, he would go astray with those following him. Recognizing two of them who had let go of their neighbor, I shouted to them, 'Hold on, lest you lose yourselves and the other.' And guided by the lamp, those who followed it came up to this light through an opening." He told these things to some brothers in private. And we heard it from them much later, along with the following interpretation: "This world is the dark [place, which is dark] because of error, each heretic thinking to have the right path. The lamp is the faith of Christ, which saves those who believe aright and leads to the kingdom of God."[9]

The group ascetical life is the third type of desert spirituality. In this model of monastic life, small groups of younger monks or nuns lived in relatively close proximity to their *Abba* or *Amma*—sometimes in the same 'cell' (dwelling), sometimes nearby.

The communities of men and women that reflect the desert tradition—ancient and contemporary—accommodate their cultural and historical milieu. They both recognize the reality of human contingency upon the other (and Other), as well as individual difference and particular calling. There is sensitivity to issues of 'goodness of fit.' At the same time, we can discern themes in the relationships of the desert fathers and mothers that may prove relevant to the relationship between individual and community in our own time.

---

[9] H. Feiss, *Essential Monastic Wisdom: Writings on the Contemplative Life* (San Fran.: HarperSanFransisco, 1999), pp. 48-9.

## The Spiritual Life—Themes in Desert Spirituality

Just as the desert monastics fled the distractions and illusions of established society, the renewed interest in spiritual formation and the spirituality of the desert among Western Christians seems corrective in nature. This return to contemplative origins has been stimulated by the Church's neglect of spiritual formation. When the Church becomes more concerned with the outward life than with the inward life of the believer—as the desert Abbas and Ammas felt it had—then some people will be called to eschew the distractions and excesses that enable such an outward focus. Such an over-emphasis on outward behavior can lead to what Willard calls Gospels of sin management. In such a gospel the goal of Christian maturity is to keep the outer life in order with little or no concern for the inner state of the heart. One is assumed to be holy of heart as long as holiness of behavior is evident.

Ironically, a focus on sin management rather than heart management creates a preoccupation with the thoughts and feelings of others. One's success, spiritually speaking, depends on how well one's behavior meets with the approval of one's religious community. This formula is quite in contrast to the teaching of the desert tradition in which the individual sought deafness to the praise and curses of others (i.e., 'dying to your neighbor') in the hope of attaining a purer inner life. The desert believers were known for their flagrant disregard for the opinions of others—even of their fellow monks—about their outward habits and appearance. The words of others were eagerly sought, however, toward the end of helping in the process of subduing the heart. No "word" from a brother or sister was to be rejected lest it prove useful for taming of the sinful heart.

These ascetic practices of the desert fathers and mothers have given them the reputation for being schizoid hermits, as much on the fringe of sanity as they were on the fringe of society. While this description certainly fits some of them the simplistic notion that desert spirituality is individualistic and isolationist must be abandoned after any serious study of these early monastics. Their strong rejection of the conventions and superficial excesses of society must not be confused with schizoid or antisocial flight from relationships. Their most profound teachings and practices revolved around the absolute centrality of relatedness in human spirituality and around the absolute necessity of encountering oneself in solitude in order to enter into that relatedness.

The contemplative and ascetic traditions of the desert may provide correctives to the western Church and to the integration of psychology and Christian faith. In that regard, the traditions of the desert fathers and mothers, captured in their recorded sayings, can provide a rich resource for the Christian psychologist. Although the sayings and practices of the desert tradition defy categorization, it is helpful to look at themes from this contemplative tradition.

*Solitude and Community.* Any understanding of desert spirituality must deal with the issue of solitude. Whether living as hermits or in monastic community the lives of the desert believers were tied together. It was understood that a rhythm between solitude and community was essential. Though the contemplative life is fostered in isolation, the teachings of the desert fathers and mothers acknowledge that spiritual maturity must also be purified in the crucible of community and must lead to action in the service of others. The monastic rules of communal life that were born in the cultural isolation of the desert, in fact, were then transplanted in religious communities where the inward and outward disciplines of solitude could be practiced even in the midst of the busiest city.

Diversity of spiritual and psychological temperaments was also acknowledged when it came to the balance of solitude and community, as noted in these words of Amma Syncletica:

> Not all courses are suitable for all people. You should have confidence in your own disposition. For many it is profitable to live in community; for others it is helpful to withdraw on their own ... Many people have found salvation in a city while imagining the conditions of a desert. And many though on a mountain, have been lost by living the life of townspeople. It is possible for one who is in a group to be alone in thought, and for one who is alone to live mentally with a crowd.[10]

---

[10] Ibid., p. 141.

## Robert A. Watson and Michael W. Mangis

In their teachings on the spiritual life, the desert Ammas and Abbas generally noted the need for such a balance between extremes. While their separation from the busy life of "the world" may seem extreme they would rightly note the typical contemporary person's extreme lack of solitude and separateness.

*Attachment and Detachment.* The call that led the contemplatives into the desert often led to the loosening of their attachments to the pleasures and worldly pursuits that characterize the lives of the non-monastics. Detachment from the things of this world, in fact, was the goal of life in the desert. At the end of his life, Malcom Muggeridge grasped the essence of the life-giving nature of the practice of the discipline of detachment:

> [I]n the wilderness, the world seems far away. No social life, no media, no occasion for bitterness or frustration. Just an arid haven of refuge, a dusty paradise. No votes to cast, women to seduce, money to accumulate, celebrity to acquire. All the habitual pursuits of the ego and the appetites are suspended. I love the wilderness because, when all these pursuits of mind and body have been shed, what remains . . . is an unencumbered soul, with no other concern than to look for God. And looking is finding. And finding, one may dare to hope, is keeping.[11]

In a very real sense, the desert contemplatives saw life in terms of attachments. To the extent that one collects attachments to things of this world, they believed, one develops a diminished capacity to attach to things that provide eternal significance. As St. Isaac of Syria notes, we become what we attach to:

> If something has become deeply united with your soul, you should not only regard it as your possession in this life, but believe that it will accompany you into the life to come. If it is something good, rejoice and give thanks to God in your mind; if it is something bad, grieve and sigh, and strive to free yourself from it while you are still in the body.[12]

Relationality, therefore, was not seen only as an

---

[11] *A Twentieth Century Testimony* (NY: Thomas Nelson, 1978), pp. 68-71.
[12] R. D. S. Chervin, *Quotable Saints* (Ann Arbor: Servant Pub., 1992), p. 147.

interpersonal issue but in terms of one's possessions as well. Casual possessing of things, or using people as things, leads directly to spiritual impoverishment. Through solitude and contemplation the desert Abbas and Ammas sought clarity of sight so that their souls could be released from attachment to things of this world and freed for stronger attachment to God. What they refused to see as their own possessions were, thus, viewed as God's possessions. The things of this world were, therefore, reframed as gifts from God to be used for his glory just as other people were to be received as brothers and sisters in Christ created in God's image. This commitment to relinquish attachments of all sorts committed the desert Christians to a path of regular dis-illusionment—an openness to having one's wish-fulfilling illusions challenged and the motives for the attachments exposed. Mourning losses of possessions—whether temporal or ideational—was woven into the desert experience.

*Hospitality and Confrontation.* With their emphasis on solitude and detachment, it is tempting to imagine the monastic communities founded on these principles to be rather harsh and uninviting. Stories of encounters with these desert monastics—both ancient and contemporary—paint a very different picture. Guests were and are received in these communities as if they may be angels.[13] A brother or sister, especially one with whom it is difficult to live, is to be treasured as a possible source of iron sharpening iron. As the following story illustrates, the desert believer took very seriously Christ's admonition to address the beam in one's own eye before meddling with the speck in the eye of another:

> A brother at Scetis committed a fault. A council was called to which Abba Moses was invited, but he refused to go to it. Then the priest sent someone to say to him, 'Come, for everyone is waiting for you.' So he got up and went. He took a leaking jug, filled it with water and carried it with him. The others came out to meet him and said to him, 'What is this, father?' The old man said to them, 'My sins run out behind me, and I do not see them, and today I am coming to judge the errors of another.' When they heard

---

[13] A. Jones, *Soulmaking: The Desert Way of Spirituality* (San Fran.: HarperCollins, 1985).

that they said no more to the brother but forgave him.[14]

Even contemporary pilgrims to monastic communities find a spirit of hospitality that is seldom equaled in other contexts. The emphasis on self-examination and slowness to correct another might lead to the criticism that desert spirituality made no room for appropriate confrontation of another's sin. Henri Nouwen, an articulate interpreter of desert spirituality to contemporary audiences, saw a unique form of Christian confrontation in the contemplative emphasis on authenticity:

> Receptivity and confrontation are the two inseparable sides of Christian witness. They have to remain in careful balance. Receptivity without confrontation leads to a bland neutrality that serves nobody. Confrontation without receptivity leads to an oppressive aggression which hurts everybody. This balance between receptivity and confrontation is found at different points, depending upon our individual position in life. But in every life situation we not only have to receive but also to confront.[15]

Nouwen's emphasis on this balance echoes the monastic call to healthy detachment. When one ceases to see others in terms of their usefulness for gaining praise or their potential threat as critics or judges then one is free to approach them out of true "disinterested" love.

> [I]n order to be of service to others we have to die to them; that is, we have to give up measuring our meaning and value with the yardstick of others. To die to our neighbors means to stop judging them, to stop evaluating them, and thus to become free to be compassionate. Compassion can never coexist with judgment because judgment creates the distance, the distinction, which prevents us from really being with the other.[16]

*Obedience, Submission and Freedom.* With such an emphasis on solitude, detachment, and dying to self and other, the

---

[14] Ward, *Sayings*, pp. 138-9.
[15] Nouwen, *Reaching Out: The Three Movements of the Spiritual Life* (NY: Doubleday, 1975), p. 99.
[16] Idem, *Way of the Heart*, p. 21.

desert tradition is open to the criticism of being excessively ascetic. In fact, many in the tradition ventured into extremes that mirrored the excesses of materialism and comfort in the dominant culture that they were fleeing. Excessive asceticism is by no means essential to a contemplative spirituality, however. Amma Syncletica pointed out the danger of asceticism in the monastic life when she said, 'As long as we are in the monastery, obedience is preferable to asceticism. The one teaches pride, the other humility.'[17]

Obedience was sought not as an end in itself but as a source of transformation. The desert tradition teaches us that we are to submit ourselves to the crucible of otherness. Encountering others only for their usefulness to us or for their similarity to us does not require us to change. Encountering the other as wholly other creates the 'heat' that softens the heart. When we encounter the other more as they are, and less as we would have them, we become open to dis-illusionment—the process of detachment of our projected desires from the other and our sense of entitlement that the other fulfill them. Transformation requires that we give others 'authority' over our spiritual formation and access to our hearts. This submission to another fallible human being is both the primary strength and the primary weakness of a desert monastic approach to spiritual development. The abuses carried out by some in the name of spiritual direction led to the near disappearance of the practice in all but the most cloistered monastic communities. The importance of baring one's soul to another for the sake of one's own formation, however, has led to a revival of the practice of spiritual direction and the consequent growth in the number of programs to train individuals in the art of spiritual direction.

*Speaking and Receiving.* As we have noted, there is no systematic understanding of the teachings of the desert fathers and mothers. There are common themes and emphases but one saying which espouses a certain belief or value might seemingly contradict another that encourages the opposite. As Ward points out, in fact, contemplative spirituality seeks always to see with new eyes. What was once fresh and life giving can become stagnant and oppressive:

---

[17] Ward, *Sayings*, p. 234.

The essence of the spirituality of the desert is that it was not taught but caught; it was a whole way of life. It was not an esoteric doctrine or a predetermined plan of ascetic practice that would be learned and applied . . . It is important to understand this, because there really is no way of talking about *the* way of prayer, or *the* spiritual teaching of the Desert Fathers. They did not have a systematic *way*; they had the hard work and experience of a lifetime of striving to re-direct every aspect of body, mind, and soul to God, and that is what they talked about. That, also, is what they meant by prayer: prayer was not an activity undertaken for a few hours each day, it was a life continually turned towards God. [18]

To guard against the stagnation that comes with routine and habit the desert fathers and mothers emphasized the practice of seeking a word. The one receiving the word would ask another brother or sister—usually an older and wiser one—to speak a word. The word was to be received without comment or question. Usually a phrase or simple image, the word was something to be contemplated, often for years, for its power to transform the life of the disciple. As Ward notes:

The key phrase of the *Apophthegmata* is, 'Speak a word, Father.' This recurs again and again, and the 'word' that was sought was not a theological explanation, nor was it 'counseling,' nor any kind of a dialogue in which one argued the point; it was a word that was part of a relationship, a word which would give life to the disciple if it were received. [19]

In the practice of receiving a word from one's brother or sister, the desert tradition offers its most radical corrective to a culture that wants to pick and choose what it believes and what it attends to. For the contemporary western mind this practice seems oddly archaic and even dangerous. In the age of postmodern suspicion in any sources of authority how could one simply submit to receiving, chewing on, and swallowing the "word" of another? In this tradition, faith was not placed, however, in systems or techniques but in the transformative power of the

---

[18] Ibid., p. xxi.
[19] Ibid., p. xxii.

human relationship. The "word" is not authoritative because of any human objectivity but because it is in the relational space that God's Spirit is the catalyst for transformation.

*'Spiritual Intersubjectivity': Mutual Transformation in the Context of Community*

   *Transformation occurs in the context of relationship.* Psychotherapy outcome research literature over the past two decades generated many questions and a few substantive conclusions. One clear finding pointed to the necessity of a positive therapeutic relationship for positive therapeutic outcomes. Contemporary psychotherapeutic systems with different theoretical foundations—particularly ones with constructivist leanings—focus more directly and explicitly on relational variables between therapist and client.[20]

   Within the contemporary psychoanalytic psychotherapy literature, the interaction of two subjects/subjectivities is not only unavoidable in the therapeutic encounter, but essential to transformation. The recognition that psychotherapy requires a 'two-person psychology' led to exploration of what is created when two persons encounter each other—an intersubjective space or matrix unique to the interaction of two (or more) psyches. This view of psychotherapy, relative to other 'modes of therapeutic action,'[21] is distinguished by the formation of a real (and also professional) relationship between two people characterized by mutuality and reciprocity. The therapist allows herself to respond to the interpersonal role pressures in the interaction and pays attention to the role pressures she exerts on the client as well. As such, psychotherapy involves careful participant-observation (primarily by the therapist, increasingly by the client)—particularly of intricate enactments of past maladaptive relational patterns. It is through the combination of new experiences and new understandings generated in the

---

[20] For example, J. D. Safran & Z. V. Segal, *Interpersonal Process in Cognitive Therapy* (NY: Basic Books, 1990); H. Levenson, *Time-Limited Dynamic Psychotherapy: A Guide to Clinical Practice* (NY: Basic Books, 1995); J. Greenberg, *Oedipus and Beyond: A Clinical Theory* (Cambridge, MA: Harvard Univ., 1992).
[21] M. Stark, *Modes of Therapeutic Action: Enhancement of Knowledge, Provision of Experience, and Engagement in Relationship* (Northvale, NJ: Jason Aronson Inc., 1999).

intersubjective field that transformation occurs in the client, but also in some ways in the therapist.

*Intersubjectivity (in practice) is not contemporary.* While intersubjectivity is a relatively new topic in the contemporary psychotherapy literature, often linked with the transition from modern to postmodern views of human relatedness, it is striking to encounter pre-modern notions that reveal levels of sophistication instructive to us today. The same understanding was essential to the desert tradition that now characterizes contemporary definitions of transformative relationships: that they involve a kind of permeability of heart and soul, a 'give-and-take' mutuality and reciprocity, and an openness to dwelling and being dwelt in by the other—a living intersubjectivity. Stewart describes this well:

> The basic insight of the desert . . . was that one cannot grow towards perfection through isolated, solitary effort: grace is mediated through one's neighbor, especially one's abba . . . If the devil was delighted by a monk's self-imposed isolation, surely this was because the opposite of isolation, encounter with another, was the way to salvation.[22]

*Dangers of 'manualizing' transforming relationship.* The living, dynamic nature of the individuals and the relationships they formed in the desert tradition became the context for the work of the Spirit within and between the members of the community. In an era and culture that wants to manualize approaches to 'treatment' of dis-ease, disorder, and even spiritual formation, the desert tradition offers a cautionary tale:

> The original, charismatic approach of the desert was not sure enough for later monks, who wanted written guidelines on how to deal with problematic issues. This began as early as the end of the fourth century, when the practical psychology of the desert fathers began to be systematized and labeled . . . The inescapable truth remained that insight and discernment lie in the gift of God rather than in books, but criteria began to appear for

---

[22] C. Stewart, "The Desert Fathers on Radical Self-honesty," *Vox Benedictina*, 8: 7-53.

how a spiritual father might be known . . . Despite Climacus' warning that the true teacher works through the 'energy of (God's) illumination rather than from notes on various writers, he provides a text which has been quarried for centuries by those who have undertaken this task either by chance or necessity.[23]

The lesson from the history of spirituality needs to be learned and relearned. Our era and cultural context appears to be one in which the focus is shifting back to the basic recognition that manuals and technologies can never capture the charisma and dynamism of the true transformative encounter. Crabb recently proffered a similar corrective:

> If you want to prepare for involvement in spiritual community, acknowledge that no amount of knowledge and skill and effort will make it happen, no more than a short person can will himself to be taller. Growth, both within us individually and in our relationships, is a mysterious work of the Spirit. No training program . . . will adequately equip anyone to develop spiritual community. Training has its place, but prayer is more the point. Humility *demands* prayer. Brokenness, the heartfelt admission that without Christ we can do nothing, *enjoys* prayer.[24]

*Characteristics of transforming telationship.* What use can contemporary mental health professionals make of the insights of the desert fathers and mothers? First, we would be wise to learn from them the risks associated with overly manualized, technologically-oriented approaches to soul-care. A balance between the development and utilization of 'tools' and technologies and careful participant-observation within the intersubjective matrix is essential—a balance between doing and being that relies ultimately on spiritual discernment.

> Tools can be used as either instruments of construction or destruction—as implements or as weapons. It seems to me that the therapist's fundamental orientation toward the other is critical to *being* a Christian therapist, because it

---

[23] Ibid., pp. 32-34.
[24] *Safest Place*, p. 128.

largely determines the way in which objectives, tactics, and methods of intervention are selected and implemented. The 'empirically validated treatment approaches' are ultimately valid only when they are used in the service of love rather than control.[25]

Second, two complementary 'postures' that characterized the transformative relationships of the desert provide direction for us today. On the one hand, a posture of accommodation (hospitality) makes the soul in need of care and transformation welcome. On the other, the unambiguous presence (confrontation with otherness) of the therapist facilitates the dis-illusionment necessary for seeing with new eyes.

*Accommodation (hospitality).* Accommodation (hospitality) creates and maintains the relational space within which the spiritual intersubjective matrix is formed and sustained. Within this space, Jesus' promise can be actualized: ". . . where two are more are gathered in my name, I am there in their midst." The desert fathers and mothers were acutely aware of their responsibility to accommodate those the Lord sent them for direction and healing:

> The old men of the desert received guests as Christ would receive them. They might live austerely themselves, but when visitors came they hid their austerity and welcomed them. A brother said, 'Forgive me, father, for I have made you break your rule,' but the old man said, 'My rule is to receive you with hospitality and send you on your way in peace.'[26]

Recent discussions of the nature of therapeutic neutrality argue for a less sterile, authoritarian posture by the therapist, and for a more mutual, reciprocal stance in which the therapist allows himself to be moved and affected by the client.

In addition, the expression of hospitality necessarily develops in ways consistent with the temperament and personal style of the care-giver:

---

[25] R. A. Watson, "Toward Union in Love: The Contemplative Spiritual Tradition and Contemporary Psychoanalytic Theory in the Formation of Persons," *Journal of Psychology and Theology*, 28 (4), pp. 282-92.
[26] Ward, *Sayings*, p. xxiv.

One monk was moved to question the difference between the monk who received visitors and the one who did not: the example he chose was his visit to the austere nobleman, Arsenius, and to the reformed robber, Moses. The former received him and sat down again to pray in silence, until the brother felt uncomfortable and left. Moses came out to greet him with open arms, and they talked all day with joy. That night the monk had a vision; he saw Arsenius in a boat with the Holy Spirit, sailing quietly along the river of life; and he saw Moses in a similar boat with an angel, and they were eating honey-cakes—so he knew that both ways were acceptable to God.[27]

*Unambiguous presence (confrontation with otherness).* As Nouwen noted earlier, receptivity without confrontation leads to a bland neutrality that serves nobody. All genuine transformation follows the paschal pattern: suffering leads to death that leads to new life and the giving of a new spirit.[28] In successful therapeutic relationships, the unambiguous presence of the other both raises the hopes, longings, and wishes of the other (transference) *and* disappoints and disillusions them. In the end, it is the individual, family, or community acceptance of what reality can and cannot fulfill that leads to real change because, short of the progressive 'destruction' of illusion and consequent mourning, one cannot discover 'externality'—the world as it is.[29]

It was said of Abba John the Dwarf, that one day he said to his elder brother, 'I should like to be free of all care, like the angels, who do not work, but ceaselessly offer worship to God.' So he took off his cloak and went away into the desert. After a week he came back to his brother. When he knocked on the door, he heard his brother say, before he opened it 'Who are you?' He said, 'I am John, your brother.' But he replied, 'John has become an angel, and henceforth he is no longer among men.' Then the other begged him saying, 'It is I.' However, his brother did not let him in, but left him there in distress until morning. Then, opening the door, he said to him, 'You are a man and you

---

[27] Ibid., pp. xxiv–xxv.
[28] Rolheiser, *Holy Longing*.
[29] D. W. Winnicott, *Playing and Reality* (London: Routledge, 1982).

must once again work in order to eat.' Then John made a prostration before him, saying, 'Forgive me.'[30]

*Clinical Application*

While it is tempting to try to provide a case example applying the principles derived from the tradition of the desert fathers and mothers, it would seem to us to work at cross-purposes with their way of being and relating. In fact, when we focused on how this tradition informs what we do with clients from a technical clinical standpoint, we were confounded. The relational and personal quality of this way simply does not lend itself to the 'experience-distant' evaluation of the client as object of study. When we began by looking at ourselves—specifically, the leading edge of our own spiritual formation—a way to provide examples became clearer. A spiritual intersubjective perspective assumes that God's current work in us cannot help but permeate the clinical interaction at some level and that God can use that unique intersubjective mix to transform both persons. At one level, this has been our ongoing lived experience teaching, writing, and being in close community together.

The leading edge of my (RW) spiritual growth is the progressive relinquishment of a kind of 'false-self' grandiosity[31] that relates to feeling overly responsible for the well-being of others. In fact, it involves the wish to heal others and, in some moments, is genuinely envious that healing ultimately comes from Jesus rather than from my own resourcefulness, insight, love, generosity, or skill. Indeed, I struggle with 'dying to my neighbor' and, in the intersubjective space, sometimes unconsciously exert role pressure on clients to become 'weak' so that I can 'save' them. This leads inevitably to a struggle for control since even clients with significant disturbance will fight for their freedom, autonomy, and dignity. This is the 'cyclical maladaptive pattern'[32] that I am most prone to enact with clients who have

---

[30] Ward, *Sayings*, p. 86.

[31] D. W. Winnicott, *The Maturational Process and the Facilitating Environment* (NY: International Universities Press, 1965); A. Miller, *The Drama of the Gifted Child* (NY: Basic, 1981).

[32] H. Levenson, *Time-limited Dynamic Psychotherapy: A Guide to Clinical Practice* (NY: Basic Books, 1995); H. H. Strupp & J. L. Binder, *Psychotherapy in a New Key: A Guide to Time-Limited Dynamic Psychotherapy* (NY: Basic Books, 1985).

complementary maladaptive patterns of relating.

In recent years, it is this interactional pattern to which God and my clients have inevitably drawn my attention. In this context my clients and I looked for what God was doing to transform us. This required a level of cautious self-disclosure that stretched beyond what is prescribed in traditional clinical training and practice. In general, this self-disclosure meant speaking the truth and being genuine even when doing so seemed risky. These moments generally involved the relinquishment of my attempts to control the other, protect myself from exposure or loss, or be the 'authority.' The *kenotic* (self-emptying) quality of these moments was as unmistakable as the presence of God's spirit and healing power that accompanied them. In fact, several of these spirit-infused moments followed fairly obvious clinical 'failures' on my part—significant breeches in empathy, lack of emotional presence to the other, and failures to maintain the frame of therapy. In sum, awareness that God is truly present in the intersubjective matrix and that He aims to free two people from their illusion-tainted patterns of relating creates the opportunity to participate in God's larger work—the building of His kingdom.

Similarly, my own (MWM) spiritual formation has required me to acknowledge the degree to which pride impacts my work as a psychotherapist. As I have owned my own "signature sin" of pride I have had to face my tendency to over-value self-reliance in myself and others. When clients manage their own difficulties or find my interventions helpful I am quite willing to invest in our relationship. When they ask for an emotional investment beyond what I am comfortable giving, however, I have sometimes labeled them "needy" or "dependent." If their requests seem especially intense, I have even bestowed the always useful tag of "borderline." By labeling and focusing on the defenses and pathologies of the client, I am able to rationalize my own emotional distance and self-protective detachment.

As I have embraced the truth of the intersubjective approach, however—especially through the radical self-honesty called forth by those in the desert contemplative tradition—I have learned from my most difficult clients what I need most in my own spiritual life. Their neediness raises my own personal anxiety that I might not be as self-sufficient as I would like to believe and portray. Their unwillingness to accept the boundaries and limitations that I impose is often not borne out of pathology but out of their accurate perception that I am being dishonest. By pretending to be sufficient to the task of caring for them I excite their hope of rescue but then disappoint them when I pull away. In innumerable situations I have had to accept, from my clients, the real feedback that it is my honest acknowledgment of inadequacy that they need. This was powerfully illustrated recently when a severe illness began to seriously limit my capacity to meet my own needs, let alone the needs of my clients. God's grace in allowing such a "thorn in my flesh" was radically revealed in the response of my most "dependent" and "clingy" clients. They intuitively sensed my own vulnerability and acknowledged it. My fear of their increased demands and neediness was not realized nor was my fear that they would become angry that I was not as helpful or insightful as they deserved. In fact, they seemed greatly comforted to have me acknowledge that I am afflicted with struggles like their own. As RW noted above, cautious self-disclosure did more to foster healing than my training had predicted.

As Christian mental health professionals we desire to reflect Jesus Christ to our clients. We both struggle to remember that we do not have to pretend that we are the "genuine article." In fact, we must strive to put off the desire to impersonate Christ and seek, instead, to imitate him, even to be increasingly transformed into his image. He is not accurately reflected in the dark and distorted mirror of our broken selves. Where there are cracks and distortions we must be the first to point them out lest we deceive ourselves and our clients and diminish Christ in the process. We have come to value and cherish our most difficult clients—the ones who call forth the most radical and unambiguous self-honesty.

*Conclusion*

It is tempting to try to draw one simple conclusion or summative statement of what the desert tradition has to offer to contemporary Christian psychology. If this tradition teaches us anything, however, it is that what may be a new and transformative truth for today will become stagnant and outdated tomorrow. Their corrective is in rejecting correctives, or else in seeking to avoid becoming settled enough to need correctives. With their focus on healing and transformative relationship as the center of spiritual formation they draw us away from systems and facile summaries. They call us to look carefully at every system and seemingly trustworthy conclusion, for therein lies the quickest route to the truth.

The very form of the apophthegmata arose from and leads

back into the heart of the desert quest. These monks staked everything on the effort to destroy illusion and deception. Their various disciplines were intended to help them cut through the noise of lives hooked on the deceptions, materialisms, and games which have characterized human beings since the Fall. The desert itself gave them a landscape which mirrored what they sought for their own hearts: an uncluttered view through clean air.[33]

As Stewart so compellingly notes, the desert tradition is one that seeks vibrancy and honesty. This will continually frustrate a culture (and church) that wants assurance that its image is polished and acceptable, that our desires and wishes will not consume us, and that it is entitled to comfort and gratification. The desert tradition calls us out of the Egypt of our idolatrous attachments, supports us through the wilderness of shedding illusions, and stirs our longings for the promised land.

---

[33] Stewart, *Desert Fathers*, pp. 7-8.

# Psychology Before Psychology: Philosophical, Theological, and Scientific Roots of Modern Psychology

*Trey Buchanan*
Wheaton College

Questions of origin are sure to arise when exploring the history of any contemporary cultural activity. Where did these ideas come from? Who was the "first" thinker to suggest such a concept? What conditions—both intellectual and social—gave rise to this way of understanding? While interesting questions to ponder, questions like these have derived, at least in part, from a *presentist* view of the past, one that assumes current ideas and practices can easily be found in previous historical contexts. This assumption appears necessary if we ask this question of the roots of modern psychology: What ancient and pre-modern thinkers possessed a psychological understanding of persons? If we define "psychology" to be the scientific study of behavior and mental events,[1] I would contend that *no one* had a psychological understanding of persons prior to the last hundred and fifty years. Such a definition, however, prevents us from exploring how psychology as a modern scientific discipline emerged within the Western cultural tradition of sustained self-reflection on what it means to be a person. Human beings have likely always reflected at some level on their own and others' actions and experiences. In fact, such an ability—not tool-making, language, or even reason—is currently touted among some cultural psychologists as the fundamental difference between us and other nonhuman primates.[2]

However, the ability to self-reflect is not the same entity as the modern discipline of psychology that has come to be a dominant force in Western culture. So how then should we try to explore the past for the existence of what became psychology?

---

[1] D. G. Myers, *Psychology*, 6th ed. (New York: Worth, 2001).
[2] M. Tomasello, *The Cultural Origins of Human Cognition* (Cambridge, MA: Harvard University Press, 1999).

55

Although our twenty-first century vantage point may move us to ask this question, great care is required not to unknowingly read our modern psychological concepts into the ideas of individuals like St. Paul, Augustine of Hippo, Thomas Aquinas, or René Descartes. The strong current of historical time should persuade us to bring as little as possible as we search for ideas that may have contributed to our own current notions of psychology. We can never look into the past completely detached from the present, but we do need to be aware of biases that we carry with us.

Given this historiographical warning, what is the best way to frame our search for the historical roots of modern psychology, whatever form they might take? At its broadest level, this chapter is grounded in two ideas central to this challenge. First is the acknowledgement that a type of "psychological" thought and practice—in the form of a sustained, self-reflective search to understand what it means to be human—has in fact existed throughout the Western tradition, from antiquity to the present. Widely diverse in its assumptions and purposes, I take the tendency of human beings to attempt to both ponder and ameliorate the condition of being human to represent Alistair MacIntyre's definition of a tradition as "a continuing argument."[3] Defined as such, intellectual discourse and social practices that encouraged self-reflection provide important points of reference for sketching a prehistory of psychology as a modern science. Given this definition, this "psychology before psychology" will be sought through the identification of broad historical trends that became central features of the field as it is currently configured.

The second idea is that the primary nature of this tradition experienced a slow but distinctive shift during the latter part of the second millennium (i.e., between 1500 and 2000 CE). As this chapter will argue, this shift was the result of a confluence of a set of relatively new ideas, cultural experiences, and social practices within which largely religious and theological concepts were replaced with ones largely secular and naturalistic. In a recent intellectual biography of Erik Erikson—himself deeply interested in the connection between history and psychology—Carol Hoare described this slow shift as a "trend line . . . in which scholars and the public have spent always decreasing time and effort gazing upward, as it were, to study premises about God and the Kingdom and ever more time gazing downward to study themselves and the

---

[3] A. MacIntrye, *Three Versions of Moral Inquiry: Encyclopedia, Genealogy, and Tradition* (Notre Dame, IN: Univ. of Notre Dame Press).

many objects scattered around them."[4]  This refocusing of cultural attention has been referred to as the secularization of Western culture, a process that has had a profound effect not only on how we live but also on how we understand ourselves.  Placing these two ideas together, this chapter will attempt to articulate how this shift changed the psychological tradition of Western culture.

These two ideas challenge us to see that while the presence of "sustained self-reflection" might move us to identify psychology among the ideas of the distant past, what we take to be psychological in our own day rests upon ideas, experiences, and practices that differ greatly from those we might regard as its originators or precursors.  While continuity does exist in what seems to be a deep human need to "know thyself," the way in which Western culture has set about heeding that maxim reveals remarkable variety.  As a coda to this story, I will end this chapter with some reflections about the current state of psychology and its relationship to current trends in theology, philosophy, and science.

### "Psychology" in Pre-modern Europe

In director John Madden's 1998 film *Shakespeare in Love*, one early scene depicts the Elizabethan dramatist mulling over the source of his writer's block with someone who appears to be a psychoanalyst.  Full of Freudian symbolism, sexual innuendo, and, of course, historical inaccuracy, it provides a clever juxtaposition of contemporary psychology with the pre-modern world of Western Europe.  This scene works in part because of its ability to transfer our modern understanding of people to a time and place that in many ways we would find foreign (and vice versa).

Although mental and emotional distress existed without a corresponding specialized profession of psychotherapy, it did not exist without a richly varied and deeply imbedded body of knowledge of what human beings were and what they needed to flourish.  What were the dimensions of this understanding?  In examining European culture prior to the nineteenth century, it is clear that while some if not most of the specific ideas about human beings widely held at that time no longer influence us, many of the broad conceptual and methodological roots of the modern human sciences did exist.  One of those roots pertinent to this collection of

---

4 C. H. Hoare, *Erickson on Development in Adulthood: New Insights from the Unpublished Papers* (NY: Oxford Univ. Press, 2002), 88.

essays is the relationship between religiously grounded notions of human nature and those connected more closely to philosophical commitments and scientific ideals. In fact, this relationship also finds its way into *Shakespeare in Love* when the playwright is later shown in immense despair over what he believes is his complicity in the murder of his chief literary rival, Christopher Marlowe; however, rather than sharing this with his therapist, we see him alone and in anguish kneeling before a chapel altar. In what ways were theological notions intertwined with other conceptions of what it meant to be human during this historical period?

If our modern conception of psychology has recognizable roots in the intellectual climate of pre-modern Europe (i.e., from roughly 1200 to 1600), it is likely to be found in the structure and curriculum of the early universities by the time of the Renaissance in the sixteenth century. These institutions existed primarily to train young men in the humanities and for careers in three professions: theology, law, and medicine. Like overlapping circles, questions dealing with what it meant to be human were considered the realm of each of these areas of learning. Classical liberal arts subjects like rhetoric, grammar, and logic formed the *studia humanitatis*, interconnected disciplines that reflected the ability of the mind, its expression, and above all the formation of character. Such a curriculum also pointed to the fundamental importance of the kind of sustained self-understanding that reveals historical continuity of a broad conception of "psychology." In fact, for most students in the Renaissance university, Aristotle's treatise on human beings *De Amina* (*On the Soul*) was set as the final text to be mastered before their university education was complete.[5]

In theology, thinkers like Thomas Aquinas (1224-1274) considered the nature of the human soul as part of a larger project of articulating Church doctrine by mining recently discovered texts by Aristotle that introduced the classical Greek philosophical tradition. Using the ideas of Aristotle and his most influential commentator, twelfth century Islamic scholar Averroes (1126-1178), Aquinas and other scholastics encountered a tripartite view of the human soul. Plants, animals, and human beings shared a vegetative soul, one that was seen in growth and reproduction. Animals and humans shared a sensitive soul, one that governed their sensory abilities and motor actions. Only human beings also

---

[5] R. Smith, *The Norton History of the Human Sciences* (NY: W. W. Norton, 1997).

possessed a rational soul, one that directed intelligence and thought. Although most theologians accepted this doctrine of the plurality of forms, Aquinas argued that the rational soul was not just another form but the center of what it meant to be human, the one substance that transcended the others and made human beings different from the rest of creation.[6] For a short time this view was officially condemned at Oxford University in 1277, reflecting the intense importance that theological conceptions of human nature held during the pre-modern period. Attempts to define the soul and its relation to the physical world, including the body, would continue to be a central challenge in the development of a psychological approach to understanding human beings throughout the rest of the pre-modern and modern periods.

Training in law was undertaken to prepare young men for civil and political service. Centering around the organization and systematic interpretation of personal conduct, legal studies dealt with both civil statutes and canon (or Church) law. These two spheres were never fully separated, and developments in each area influenced the other. As with the humanities, pre-modern legal thought dealt heavily in the interpretation and elaboration of rediscovered texts describing Roman law. The need to articulate clear definitions and practical rules to provide a basis of legal decision-making provided a model for both systemizing and applying knowledge of human beings that would be an important legacy not just in jurisprudence and political thought but in all of the human sciences from the eighteenth century on. Specialization was another aspect of professional training in law that developed during the pre-modern period. In many European universities by the late 1500s, legal curricula expanded beyond civil and cannon law to include novel areas such as customary (or common) law, natural law, and an area referred to as "law among nations."[7] This tendency to further refine categories of knowledge with increasingly specific areas of study would become a hallmark of psychology and the other human sciences during the modern era.

The connections between canon and public law during the pre-modern period were many as local governance was conducted under the watchful eye of clergy and bishops. Legal decision-

---

[6] A. Kenny, A, "Body, Soul, and Intellect in Aquinas," in M. J. C. Crabbe (ed.), *From Soul to Self* (New York: Routledge), 33-48.
[7] L. Brockliss, "Curricula," in H. de Ridder-Symoens (ed.), *A History of the University in Europe*, Vol. II (NY: Cambridge Univ. Press, 1996).

making was seen as the shared task of each, and often laws were written and administered through the cooperative efforts of both entities. What constituted "the Church" was not as monolithic or centralized as is often suspected during the Renaissance; as we shall see, the Protestant Reformation and Catholic Counter-Reformations of the sixteenth and seventeenth centuries tended to solidify ecclesial power in places like Rome, Geneva, and Canterbury.

Compared with theological and legal studies, medieval medicine tended to have a more unbroken tradition of training and knowledge that dated back to the second century Roman philosopher and physician Galen Claudius. Known primarily for his articulation of the Hippocratic doctrine of bodily humors or spirits, Galen's ideas provided a foundation for medical intervention and an intuitive language for explaining everyday behavior widely used among medieval and pre-modern Europeans. In this view, explanations of physiological and psychological functioning were based upon the relative balance of four bodily fluids and their basic qualities: blood (hot), phlegm (cold), yellow bile (wet), black bile (dry). Galen expanded these four to a total of nine temperaments that were used to explain both disease and individual differences in what today we would call personality.[8]

Galen's ideas found widespread acceptance because of their perceived utility in explaining individual differences and helped to establish a way of explaining human behavior that shifted away from external intervention (i.e., God and an "enchanted" natural world) towards internal traits and physical substances (i.e., the self and a "disenchanted" natural world). Although it was solidly rooted in Aristotelian metaphysics, the teleological character of his system appealed to the theism of Christian readers. In addition to what could be considered a primitive trait theory of personality grounded in biology, Galen also articulated an early form of natural theology in which the workings and purposes of the gods could be seen in the physical world, especially in anatomical structures.[9] By the end of the early

---

[8] S. Smith, *Ideas of the Great Psychologists* (San Francisco: Harper & Row, 1983).

[9] D. C. Lindberg, D. C., *The Beginnings of Western Science: The European Scientific Tradition in Philosophical, Religious, and Institutional Context, 600 B.C. to A.D. 1450* (Chicago: University of Chicago Press, 1992).

modern period, medical training and practice grounded in empirical science began to replace Galenic medicine in the West and was eventually condemned by Puritans in late sixteenth century England as being unscriptural and occult.

Taken together, these areas of learning suggest that a diffuse yet invigorated conception of what it meant to be human existed in pre-modern Europe. Each also reflects that Christian belief and practice provided an overarching framework from which sustained self-reflection was undertaken. While theological concerns set the parameters of discourse and discovery about human nature, they were also modified by those same ideas as the roots of what would become the modern human sciences that began to take shape. Smith has described this as "a gradual change that tended to emphasize the value of subjective experience and the relation of that experience to responsible agency in civil society . . . perhaps [providing] the basis for psychological and sociological ways of thought" that would appear in the nineteenth century.[10] In fact, individual subjective experience would become a foundational tenet of the Western intellectual and cultural tradition, seen in such diverse movements as the Reformation and Counter-Reformation, the scientific and industrial revolutions, the rise of market capitalism, Romantic poetry and the Victorian novel, psychotherapy, and modern art. But in the pre-modern period of the Renaissance, subjective experience was valued because it was regarded as seamlessly linked to practical issues of social life, especially Christian belief and practice. This connection between self-reflection and its application is one of the clearest legacies of this time to our contemporary understanding of human sciences like psychology.

Two figures appeared towards the end of the pre-modern period reflect well this "psychological" nature of European intellectual life: Michel de Montaigne (1533–1592) in France and Francis Bacon (1561-1621) in England. Montaigne's *Essays* were widely read and immensely influential as a witty and insightful record of one person's thoughts on his own experience and reigning social conventions. Bacon's famous critique of intellectual "idols of the mind" provided a guide for clear thinking that was recognizable within the social and cultural context of a turbulent seventeenth century England. In both we see the influences of four centuries of intellectual change since the late

---

[10] *Norton History*, 40.

Middle Ages (ca. 1200s) as ancient thought was grafted into the theological tradition of Western Christianity and the life of the mind. The value of thoughtful reflection on direct, personal experience as a resource for understanding and solving the problems of daily life formed a "psychology" of sorts that would come to play a central role in the cultural development of Europe for the next four hundred years.

Although a specific, identifiable field of psychology did not exist beyond this broad, sustained self-understanding imbedded among the humanities and professions in the pre-modern period, cultural and intellectual changes appeared in the next few hundred years that would help to create a very successful and specialized "science of man." Widespread religious violence, unprecedented demographic shifts, and the discovery by Europeans of peoples in the New World were among the many challenges that helped to birth the early modern era and its intellectual innovations, including what would become psychological ways of understanding human beings.

*"Psychology" During the Long Eighteenth Century*

Stretching roughly from the mid-1600s to the early 1800s and covering two centuries of European history, "the long eighteenth-century"[11] saw the realization of human science as an identifiable and coherent intellectual and cultural project. Where theology once dominated discourse about the nature and purpose of human existence, philosophies that muted such themes drew the attention of the educated elite as well as of the public. Although these philosophies varied greatly, they tended to share a common commitment to a sort of "methodological certainty," a foundational belief that truth could be attained only through the proper use of rationality. How did this shift influence the eventual development of psychology as a route to truth about human nature and its flourishing? In this section I will survey three key challenges facing the formation of a "science of man" during the long eighteenth century associated with three key figures in the development of psychological thought before modern psychology.

First, in his treatment of the origins of modernity, philosopher and historian of science Stephen Toulmin[12] makes the

---

[11] Ibid.

[12] S. Toulmin, *Cosmopolis: The Hidden Agenda of Modernity* (New York: Free Press, 1990).

case that religious violence associated with the Protestant Reformation and Catholic Counter-Reformation led many Europeans to doubt the moral and intellectual authority of the Church, whatever ecclesiastical form it took. The Thirty Years' War (1618-1648) pitted Christian against Christian, both claiming God's side in the conflict. In its wake, the important intellectual gains of the Renaissance, culminating in a widely accepted humanism grounded on Christian theology and practical wisdom, were rejected for a increasingly narrow rationalism, one it was hoped would provide universal agreement on all human understanding. This commitment to rationality sought such certainty through method rather than authority, a commitment Toulmin refers to as modernity's "hidden agenda." Put another way, in the face of fundamental disagreement, widespread violence, and theological uncertainty, the solution sought by many European intellectuals was the achievement of certainty through individual rationality, especially embodied in science.

Thus the long eighteenth century stands as a critical period in the historical development of the modern human sciences, especially for what would come to be the field of psychology. As we have seen, exploration of the nature of humanity existed prior to the long eighteenth century, but it lacked a specific method of inquiry beyond self-reflection and practical application. Two hundred years of cultural change transformed this loose humanism into a rigorous, objective rationalism that would allow psychology to form as the "science of mental life" by the late nineteenth century.[13] After observing firsthand the horrors of Europe's religious wars, French philosopher and mathematician René Descartes (1596-1650) wrote his *Discourse on Method* in 1637.[14] His famous dictum, "I think, therefore I am," was arrived at through systematic doubt of all knowledge and provided a pure starting point from which to build a new philosophy, one that would be objective, mathematical, and above all, certain. Descartes contemplated a world that reflected God's ordering of nature and our experience, yet one that rested not on the authority of scripture or tradition, but on individual reason.

Secondly, along with a deepening trust in individual experience and the ability of persons to regulate their own affairs, global exploration and colonial expansion brought Europeans into contact with peoples very different from themselves in

---

[13] W. James, *The Principles of Psychology* (2 Vols.) (NY: Holt, 1890).
[14] R. Fancher, *Pioneers of Psychology*, 3rd ed. (NY: Norton, 1996).

appearance, culture, and religious belief. At the beginning of this period, differences among peoples of the world were seen primarily as oddities to be marveled at, or at least documented as curiosities among traveler's tales. By the middle of the 1700s on, however, the need to categorize such differences along a continuum from savage and civilized appeared, with the former (and "lower") seen as a cautionary example of what Europeans would be without the refinements of Christianity, language, and rationality. Missionary activity in the New World combined with economic opportunity led to sustained interactions among Europeans and the people they met, raising the question of what constituted human nature. Toward the end of the long eighteenth century, such differences would be explained in terms of inherent racial differences—in fact the concept of humans being made up of distinct racial categories defined by physical appearance appeared only as late as the 1840s[15]—beliefs that were used to justify both slavery in the United States and genocide in Germany in the following centuries.

Language was one of the primary challenges of human diversity posed by global exploration. Although linguistic variety was the norm for Europeans, the sheer multitude of foreign tongues among the newly discovered people of the New World moved some intellectuals to pursue the creation of a universal language. In Germany, Gottfried Leibnitz (1646-1716) unsuccessfully sought to create a linguistic system that would not only make communication among different peoples possible but would also usher in an age of peaceful coexistence, cooperation, and mutual understanding.[16] Stripped of all cultural references, it was hoped that this universal system would "help heal man from his fallen nature" and "heal a divide Christendom."[17] This attempt to create a timeless, universal solution to what was a persistent theological and social problem would come to be a fixture of the modern human sciences.

The third and final change that occurred during the long eighteenth century occurred in the subject matter of psychological discourse. In England, John Locke (1632-1704) replaced Aquinas'

---

[15] D. N. Livingstone, "Situating Evangelical Responses to Evolution," in D. N. Livingstone, D. G. Hart, & M. A. Noll (eds.), *Evangelicals and Science in Historical Perspective* (New York: Oxford University Press, 1999); Smith, *Norton History.*

[16] Fancher, *Pioneers.*

[17] *Norton History*, 195.

notion of an embodied soul with an active mind as that which gave rise to rationality and therefore human uniqueness. In arguably his most influential work, *An Essay Concerning Human Understanding*, Locke chose for his topic not the nature of man's essence or the physical basis of the mind but the activities of mental life itself:

> I shall not at present meddle with the physical consideration of the mind; or trouble myself to examine wherein its essence consists; . . . it shall suffice to my present purpose, to consider the discerning faculties of a man, as they are employed about the objects which they have to do with.[18]

This shift in subject matter stripped human nature of much of its immediate theological connections, although Locke himself continued to write on topics like the psychological implications of the doctrine of bodily resurrection.[19]

The move towards regarding the mind and its functions as the proper focus of a science of man had profound implications for Locke and his contemporaries. First, the mind was loosened from its theological moorings. While this loosening did not lead to the total abandonment of theology as a resource for psychology (which would happen most fully by the early twentieth century), it did move considerations concerning human nature in a much more secular direction. Second, reason itself in the form of mental activity became a subject for examination and critique. Like its distancing from theology, this trend would continue into the late nineteenth century and reach its peak in the introspectionist methods of what would become the "new psychology." Third, the proper formation of the mind's abilities became the focus of educational efforts. A kind of "mental rationalism" would come to

---

[18] J. Locke, *An Essay Concerning Human Understanding* (retrieved October 21, 2002, from Columbia University Institute for Learning Technologies Website: http://www.ilt.columbia.edu/publications/locke_understanding.html (1995; original work published 1690), Introduction, §2.

[19] F. Vidal, "Brains, Bodies, Selves, and Science: Anthropologies of Identity and the Resurrection of the Body," *Critical Inquiry*, 28 (2002), 930-974.

dominate discourse about pedagogy in which education was seen as the development of cognitive faculties, rather than of individual character. Each of these implications reflected the shifting character of the human sciences in which theological concerns made room for philosophical ones.

In contrast to the pre-modern period, what can more properly be called a "psychological" understanding of human experience began to take shape during the long eighteenth century as Europeans faced several cultural challenges. As theological concerns made room for more secular ones, discussions that would have previously been seen as discourse "on the soul" were undertaken under the banner of moral philosophy, an endeavor focused on exploring human nature and its guidance for the good of society. Theological concerns that once set the agenda for explorations of human nature came to be regarded more as resources among others, such as rationality and subjective experience, which became regarded as the primary way to understand personhood. The goal of human science was no longer just a matter of understanding human beings as part of God's created order but increasingly to find ways of fashioning human life as an ordered and "good" society.

Three key factors in this understanding emerged that allowed Western thinkers to chart a course that would eventually lead to the spread of modern scientific psychologies in the late nineteenth and early twentieth centuries. These included a philosophical commitment (individual reason), an overarching goal (universalism), and a subject matter (the mind)—all of which contributed to a variety of early explorations into a scientific approach to psychology.[20] Of course these factors themselves were historical entities that continued to change over time; however, by the end of the long eighteenth century, they combined with two additional factors that formed the modern, scientific study of psychology.[21]

---

[20] G. Hatfield, "Remaking the Science of the Mind: Psychology as Natural Science," in C. Fox, R. Porter, & R. Wokler (eds.), *Inventing Human Science: Eighteenth Century Domains* (Berkeley: University of California Press, 1995), 184-231.

[21] G. Richards, "Of What is History of Psychology a History?" *British Journal for the History of Science*, 20 (1987), 201-212.

## Trey Buchanan

*The Appearance of Modern Scientific Psychology*

Most textbooks recount that modern psychology fully appeared as an independent discipline in Europe and North America by the beginning of the twentieth century. Such disciplinary markers as the granting of postgraduate degrees, the creation of academic journals, and the chartering of professional organizations specifically for promotion of a new empirical psychology were all well in place by that time. Perhaps just as important would be the initial histories of the new discipline that appeared as shortly after the first decade of the 1900s[22] and culminated in E. G. Boring's vastly influential *A History of Experimental Psychology* published in 1929. As a rule, these writers exemplified the presentist tendency to view the past from the standpoint of the present; the founding of psychology by physiologist Wilhelm Wundt was regarded as occurring in Germany in 1879, and non-laboratory and applied aspects of psychology were entirely ignored in these treatments. However, given what has been said in this chapter about the contributions of the pre-modern periods of the Renaissance and the long eighteenth century, there are connections that allow us to see more continuity between psychology as an empirical science and earlier attempts to articulate what was often referred to as a "science of man."[23]

As suggested above, the last half of the nineteenth century did see the appearance and wide influence of two critical features of what really was a "new psychology." The first was a methodological commitment to empiricism as the sole basis for generating knowledge of the mind. Rooted in a broad commitment to sensory experience that had been part of the Western intellectual tradition since the late Middle Ages through the long eighteenth century (i.e., from Roger Bacon to John Locke), psychological empiricism found new life when grafted into the established laboratory tradition of natural science. Astonishing advances in anatomy, physiology, and medicine were made possible by the use of quantification, experimental control, and an assumption of mechanism that underlay biological

---

[22] C. A. Ruckmich, "The History and Status of Psychology in the United States," *American Journal of Psychology*, 23 (1912), 517-531.
[23] C. Fox, R. Porter, & R. Wokler, R. (eds.), *Inventing Human Science: Eighteenth-Century Domains* (Berkeley, Ca: University of California Press, 1995).

processes. Not surprisingly, many of the most influential persons in the rise of modern psychology had initial training in human physiology—Wilhelm Wundt, William James, Ivan Pavlov, and, of course, Sigmund Freud. The empirical methods of laboratory science laid open the workings of the brain as the organ of mentality and the scientific study of the processes of cognition itself. What once was considered by some to be impossible—an objective science of the mind—now was one of the fastest growing fields of empirical inquiry.

This close association of mental activity with the brain was by no means an uncontroversial issue. Concerns were raised about the theological and philosophical implications of the new physiological approach to psychology in both academic journals and popular periodicals.[24] In addition, as recent historians of psychology have shown, this approach was only one of a multitude of "psychologies" that existed in the Victorian era.[25] As identifying terms, "psychology" and "psychologist" were stretched beyond the new laboratory-based science to include such diverse topics as spiritualism, novel religious movements, and the treatment of mental disorders. Over time the various empirical psychologies found ways to align themselves into an identifiable profession, especially in North American colleges and universities, successfully promoting this profession as *the* new psychology.[26]

The second factor critical in the rise of a specialized science of the mind was a worldview that wedded human science to the physical world. Although the term "human nature" had been part of the lexicon of the human sciences since the pre-modern period, the ambiguity of the term "nature" was exploited in the nineteenth

---

24 R. Smith, "The Physiology of the Will: Mind, Body, and Psychology in the Periodical Literature, 1855-1875," paper presented at the conference "Science in the Nineteenth-Century Periodical," Dibner Institute for the History of Science and Technology, Massachusetts Institute of Technology, Cambridge, MA (2001).

25 D. J. Coon, "Testing the Limits of Sense and Science: American Experimental Psychologists Combat Spiritualism, 1880-1920," *American Psychologist*, 47 (1992), 143-151; E. Taylor, *Shadow Culture: Psychology and Spirituality in America* (Washington, D.C.: Counterpoint, 1999) and "Psychotherapeutics and the Problematic Origins of Clinical Psychology in America," *American Psychologist*, 55 (2000), 1029-1033.

26 D. E. Leary, "Telling Likely Stories: The Rhetoric of the New Psychology, 1880-1920," *Journal of the History of the Behavioral Sciences*, 23 (1987), 315-331.

century to link human *essence* with the natural world. As Smith argues, "the ambiguity of the term *nature* enabled belief to change slowly without too great a sense of personal loss or too great a fear of social disruption."[27] While public discourse surrounding human nature did raise specific theological concerns, such as the physical basis (or not) of the soul and the relation of biology and morality, most nineteenth century authors seemed to assume that study of the natural world would shed light on human nature.

Of course this trend cannot be understood without acknowledging the revolutionary impact of Charles Darwin's theory of evolution that appeared at mid-century. Those interested in exploring human nature quickly absorbed Darwin's ideas—especially those contained in his *Origin of Species*, published in 1858 and *Descent of Man* published in 1871—because they tended to conform with this broad notion of "nature." As its most recognizable example, evolutionary theory helped bring a "unifying naturalism"[28] to the human sciences, one that pushed psychology more deeply in the direction of established scientific practice. Although heated exchanges occurred among scientists, philosophers, and theologians over its implications, there was a rather widespread acceptance of evolutionary thought and social policies associated with it, including eugenics, among Christians.[29]

Thus the nineteenth century saw the appearance of a scientific approach to understanding human beings that both continued the tradition of pre-modern psychology as "sustained self-reflection" and configured its method and worldview to fit the emerging modern world. The valuing of individual experience, seen in the commitment to empiricism, and the naturalizing of human "nature," seen in the acceptance of a physiological foundation for psychological processes, reflected that this new psychology was a different way of thinking about human beings, even though one that was not created in 1879 out of nothing. The precise definition of psychology as a science, which included articulating its proper methods and subject matter, would continue to be a contested one well into the twentieth century.

---

[27] R. Smith, "The Language of Human Nature," in Fox et al., *Inventing Human Science*, 97.

[28] Ibid.

[29] L. Zenderland, "Biblical Biology: American Protestant Social Reformers and the Early Eugenics Movement," *Science in Context*, 11 (1998),511-525.

Similar to the ambiguity of the term "human nature" a century before, "psychology" was broad enough to house experimental psychology, clinical and other applied psychologies, and even for some, aspects of spiritualism and parapsychology.[30]

*Conclusion*

As we consider the historical development of psychology, its diversity serves to remind us that the written and received history often learned in textbooks does not fully represent the variety of the human sciences. For this attempt to convey something of this diversity, much more detail of the relationships among theology, philosophy, and science has been left unexplored. The preference for a specific and localized approach to scholarship over a more general and sweeping one is a current trend among historians of science; however, important insights can be gained from viewing the history of psychology as a human science a bit more broadly, especially when trying to explore its links with religion and philosophy.[31]

What lessons concerning "psychology before psychology" can be gained from the broad approach taken in this chapter? Although summarizing almost 700 years of cultural change is a daunting task, several important conclusions are important to state. The first is that since at least the late Middle Ages, what may have counted as "psychology" had been embedded within an intellectual tradition and set of social practices that included elements of theology, philosophy, and science. In that order historically, each has tended to dominate reflection on what it means to be a human being. Echoing Carol Hoare's description of such a shift quoted toward the beginning of this chapter, the preeminence of religious concerns gave way to more secular ones first in philosophical, then in scientific, ones.

Because our understanding of human beings was the result of continuing negotiation of these interconnected views of personhood, is there any relevance of this prehistory of psychology for making sense of contemporary psychology? It does help to explain, in part, the continuing presence of "big ideas" in

---

[30] Taylor, *Shadow Culture.*

[31] R. Smith, "History of the Human Sciences: What Voice?" *History of the Human Sciences*, 10 (1997), 22-39, and "The Big Picture: Writing Psychology into the History of the Human Sciences," *Journal of the History of the Behavioral Sciences*, 34 (1998), 1-13.

psychology, such as the nature of consciousness, the role of spirituality in defining personhood, and the roots of human morality. It also sheds light on recent attempts to articulate what is often referred to as an "integrated" psychology that takes religious belief and practice seriously, revealing the intimacy with which theological, philosophical, and scientific approaches still exist for many psychologists. Perhaps this continuing breadth should not be surprising, given that psychology has always had such a varied and mixed heritage.

# Self and Other in Kierkegaard's Psychology: God and Human Relations in the Constitution of the Self

## C. Stephen Evans
### Baylor University

Well, of course every human being is something of a subject. But now to become what one is as a matter of course—who would waste his time on that?[1]

What is a self? Kierkegaard's pseudonym Anti-Climacus famously begins *The Sickness Unto Death* with this question. But it is a question contemporary western culture still does not know how to answer. We are torn between two types of answers. One type of answer that can be given to the question could be called a metaphysical answer. A metaphysical answer is one that regards the human self as a type of *entity* and it answers the question about the self by saying what kind of entity the self is.

The philosophical roots of this kind of view go back to Greek philosophy. Aristotle tells us that human beings are rational animals. In the middle ages, philosophers attempted to say what kind of entity the human self is by specifying where humans are in the great chain of being: We rank lower than God and the angels; higher than the other animals. In the early modern period, Descartes employs the concept of "substance" to tell us that he (and presumably other human persons) is a "thinking thing."[2]

Although there continue to be defenders of traditional religious metaphysical views of the person, probably the dominant

---

[1] Søren Kierkegaard, *Concluding Unscientific Postscript*, trans. by Howard V. and Edna H. Hong (Princeton: Princeton University Press, 1992), p. 130. (*Samlede Værker*, 1st ed., VII, 105). First reference will be to an English translation. Second reference will always be to the first edition of the *Samlede Værker* as in this note. Translations will sometimes be modified.

[2] In this paper I shall treat the concepts of "self" and "person" as roughly synonymous, so that if some individual is or has a self, that individual is a person, and if some being is a person, then that being must have or be a self.

contemporary view of the self that is the heir of this metaphysical tradition is *scientific materialism*, which understands the human self simply as an entity in nature that can be explained via the categories of contemporary natural science. Most versions of this scientific materialism are rightly regarded as reductionistic in character. Richard Dawkins provides an excellent example when he assures us that the self can be explained in terms of the evolution of the gene: "We are survival machines—robot vehicles, blindly programmed to preserve the selfish molecules known as genes."[3]

The alternative type of answer to the question "What is a self?" is harder to characterize; it is easier to say what it is not than what it is. I think that the non-metaphysical type of answer to the question is best characterized as providing what could be called a *relational achievement theory* of the self. (We could call it simply an achievement or a relational theory for short.) This type of answer attempts to say what a self is, not by describing a type of entity, or specifying an entity that possesses certain natural properties, but rather by viewing the self in terms of its achievements and relationships. Being a self is not being a special type of entity, but rather it is a matter of having a special status, a status that is linked to social relationships. On such a view, a human being may become a self, or might cease to be a self.

Such theories, like the metaphysical theories, can vary tremendously, depending on how this special status is conceived, and how it is understood to be gained and lost. The simplest relational theory would be one that simply regards "being a self" as a status that is granted by being attributed by others. On such a view, to be a self is simply to be regarded as a self by others. On such a theory, in a racist society, members of the despised minority may not be regarded as truly selves; if artificially intelligent robots ever become a reality, such entities will be selves if the rest of us decide to treat them as selves.

More sophisticated versions of such a relational theory may recognize that the attribution of this special status of "self" to individuals is not an arbitrary decision, but is grounded in certain criteria. On such views, for example, to be a self might require one to be capable of certain activities or to fulfill some particular social role or function. Many of the most plausible accounts of this special status connect being a self to *language*. Such accounts

---

[3] Richard Dawkins, *The Selfish Gene* (New York: Oxford University Press, 1976), p. ix.

move further away from the metaphysical tradition that sees selfhood as a fixed entity by understanding selfhood as linked to the phenomenon of *meaning*.

On this kind of view, which has roots in such thinkers as Dilthey, understanding a human self is not like understanding a physical system. Rather, it is akin to interpreting a text. The human self, like a text, has multiple layers of meaning. There may be no definitive "correct" understanding of a self, but rather, as is the case for the interpretation of a great work of fiction, multiple "readings" are possible, each of which is contestable and may offer greater or lesser degrees of insight.

Charles Taylor, for example, argues that to be a person one must be able to feel emotions such as shame, guilt, and fear. As Taylor understands these emotions, they incorporate "a certain articulation of our situation." To feel such emotions is "to be aware of our situation as humiliating, or shameful, or outrageous, or dismaying, or exhilarating, or wonderful."[4] Such awareness is impossible without a language that can mark out such distinctions by enabling us to construe our situations in particular ways. We could call this type of relational achievement theory an *interpretivist* theory.

As I see it, metaphysical and achievement theories have different characteristic strengths and weaknesses. Metaphysical theories, especially in their contemporary scientific materialistic forms, tend towards reductionism; they tend to lose the uniqueness and significance of human selfhood. Relational achievement theories, especially in their interpretivist versions, do a better job of capturing the unique aspects of human selfhood. However, these accounts have difficulty understanding the place of the human self in the natural order.

What I shall try to do in this paper is give a sketch of the philosophical anthropology of Kierkegaard, in which I show that Kierkegaard's understanding of selfhood points us beyond this argument between metaphysical and interpretivist theories. Kierkegaard's view of the self clearly incorporates the insights of an interpretivist view. As he sees it, selfhood is an achievement, something one must become. Furthermore, there are various ways of becoming a self and these do involve fundamental rival interpretations of the meaning of human existence. However, I shall try to show that there is also a metaphysical dimension to

---

4 Charles Taylor, "Self-Interpreting Animals," in *Human Agency and Language* (Cambridge: Cambridge University Press, 1985), p. 63.

Kierkegaard's philosophical anthropology. One could say that he rethinks and reinterprets the metaphysical tradition in light of existential and interpretivist themes. Even though Kierkegaard is pre-eminently the philosopher of either/or, we shall see that in his philosophical anthropology Kierkegaard's thought is both/and: relational but also metaphysical.

## I. The Self as Achievement

There is no question that the *emphasis* of Kierkegaard's writings is on selfhood as an achievement, something I must strive to become. This is a theme that can be found throughout the pseudonymous writings. In *Either/Or II* Judge Wilhelm advises the young aesthete to "choose despair."[5] What distinguishes the ethical life is precisely that through choice the ethical individual can acquire an identity, can *become* someone who is capable of enduring and having a history. By choosing his despair, the aesthete can take responsibility for his despair; he thereby begins to acquire a self and can begin to live in ethical categories.

In *Concluding Unscientific Postscript* Johannes Climacus pours out sarcasm on those who assume that they have already achieved selfhood and have consequently gone on to higher tasks. For Climacus, becoming a self is equivalent to "becoming subjective," and this turns out not to be such an easy thing after all. Fundamentally, becoming subjective is a matter of developing a capacity for action. Therefore, to get a better grasp of what becoming subjective means and why it is necessary to become a self in truth, we must take a look at a Kierkegaardian understanding of action.

In *Postscript* Climacus argues with vehemence against an intellectualist understanding of human action. Though he agrees with the Aristotelian tradition that human action is preceded and informed by reflection, he argues that reflection alone cannot lead to action. If "knowing" the right thing were sufficient to account for action, then "the intellectual would swallow the ethical."[6]

As Climacus sees it, intellectual reflection is potentially infinite. When considering an action I can always continue to

---

[5] Søren Kierkegaard, *Either/Or* II, trans. by Howard V. and Edna H. Hong (Princeton: Princeton University Press, 1987), p. 211. (*Samlede Værker*, 1st ed., II, 189)

[6] *Postscript*, p. 338. (SV VII, 293) Hong translation here has been modified.

reflect on the reasons for the action, to look for additional reasons or re-evaluate the reasons I have. Eventually, if action is to occur, this process of deliberation must be brought to a close. However, thought itself cannot bring about this closure. This infinite character that reflection possesses can be seen, for example, in doubt. Hegel is criticized harshly for putting forward the "fairy tale" that doubt somehow brings itself to a close.[7]

Deliberation is only brought to a close when we care enough about something to stop thinking and act. Action is not the product of the intellect alone, nor even the intellect combined with some kind of pure abstract "will."[8] Of course many thinkers would recognize that it is not enough intellectually to recognize a good; we must somehow desire or have some kind of motivational push to act. However, many philosophers see such desires as essentially facts about a person. Kant, for example, tends to view "inclinations" as things for which a person cannot be morally responsible and which therefore have no moral worth.

It is true that there are what might be called "original impulses" for which people are not responsible. But merely to have such impulses is to lack a self in the deepest sense. To live solely on the basis of such impulses is the heart of the aesthetic life. We do, however, have the capacity to develop and form these raw materials of selfhood, and that is what the process of "becoming subjective" is all about. Climacus cites with approval the words of Plutarch: "ethical virtue has the passions for its material, reason for its form."[9]

These "formed passions" are I believe similar to the "articulated emotions" that Charles Taylor regards as essential to human selfhood. "Subjectivity" as understood in *Postscript* is far from an emotion that simply overwhelms a person, and it is clearly not a matter of a radical, arbitrary choice of a lifestyle for which no reasons can be given. Rather, becoming subjective is a matter of becoming a subjective *thinker*, not in the sense of someone who knows facts, but in the sense of someone who understands what it means to get married, to face the certainty of death, and to be

---

[7] *Postscript*, p. 336. (SV VII, 290)
[8] Kierkegaard consistently rejects the notion of a *liberum arbitrium* understood as an ahistorical faculty that can choose between options to which it is essentially indifferent. See *Søren Kierkegaard's Journals and Papers*, ed. and trans. by Howard V. and Edna H. Hong (Bloomington: Indiana University Press, 1970), entry 1268, p. 73 in vol. 2.
[9] *Postscript*, pp. 161-162n. (SV VII, 133n)

thankful to God in all the circumstances of life. The person who is truly thankful to God is not merely the person who can parrot certain truths; nor is she simply a person who has a particular momentary feeling of gratitude. She is rather the person who can construe all the particular circumstances of her life as a gift from God and who is therefore disposed to feel thankful not just on occasion but continuously.

The theme of the self as something that one must become is similarly prominent in *Sickness Unto Death*. There Anti-Climacus describes the "purely immediate self" who is in despair but has so little consciousness of self that he is ignorant of his despair. Such a person may acquire "a little understanding of life, he learns to copy others, how they manage their lives."[10] Though in Christendom such a person will be a kind of Christian, "a self he was not, and a self he did not become."[11]

## II. *The Substantial Character of the Self*

We have seen that for Kierkegaard the self is an achievement, something one must become. Many people do not choose to become anything. They are content to drift with the crowd and be like "the others." Kierkegaard accuses such people of failing to become a self.

Nevertheless, on reflection we can see that Kierkegaard's view cannot be a *simple* achievement theory. This is because the self that the individual is charged with failing to become is in some sense the self the individual *is* already. Certainly there is a tremendous difference between what we could call the minimal self, who is a "bit of a subject," and the responsible self who has a formed character. Nevertheless, even this minimal self must in some sense *be*; if it were nothing at all, then there would be nothing to become—or fail to become. If there were no self present at all, there could be no self to become in the richer sense. Thus, even if Kierkegaard rejects the metaphysical concept of the self as a fully formed entity with a fixed identity, he nevertheless still understands the self in ontological terms: the self is rooted in being and cannot be understood solely in ethical terms. It is because selves are beings with certain qualities that they are

---

[10] Søren Kierkegaard, *The Sickness Unto Death*, ed. and trans. by Howard V. and Edna H. Hong (Princeton: Princeton University Press, 1980), p. 52. (Samlede Værker, 1st ed., XI, 165)
[11] *Sickness Unto Death*, p. 52. (SV XI, 165)

beings who can become, whose identity is defined through their becoming. If this be metaphysics, so be it.

The ontological roots of personhood are clearly seen in two important passages in Kierkegaard's literature. In *Philosophical Fragments* Johannes Climacus discusses the nature of specifically historical existence as a "coming into existence within a coming into existence."[12] This means, I think, that human history involves a double contingency. It shares the contingency of all of nature, since it is part of the natural order that has been actualized by a "free effecting cause."[13] The second level of contingency is found in human actions, which also involve the exercise of free causality. Thus, human actions represent a "coming into existence" that mirrors the contingency of nature itself.

I think this passage points clearly to Kierkegaard's conviction that humans are both unique and yet part of the natural order. The whole of the natural order rests on God's free creative power. Within that natural order, God has created human beings with the capacity for free, responsible choice. The capacity of the human self to define itself and be a "self-interpreting animal," in Charles Taylor's phrase, is rooted in God's creative power and intentions. The self I must become is in some sense a substantial self.

The substantial character of the self is then linked logically to God as the ground of the self. This can be seen even more clearly in the second passage I wish to focus upon, the famous passage in *The Sickness Unto Death* where the self is understood as a "relation that relates itself to itself" by "relating itself to another."[14] Here we also see that the self is not simply chosen; certainly it is not chosen in the sense of being created by an autonomous individual out of nothing. Rather, the self must be seen as having a ground, as being rooted in "a power."[15] If we are to understand Kierkegaard's anthropology, we must probe more deeply into this relationship. I shall try to show that the substantial character of the self that Kierkegaard embeds in his achievement theory is grounded in the *relational* character of that self.

---

[12] Søren Kierkegaard, *Philosophical Fragments*, trans. by Howard V. and Edna H. Hong (Princeton: Princeton University Press, 1985), p. 76. (*Samlede Værker*, 1st ed., IV, 240)

[13] *Philosophical Fragments*, p. 75. (SV IV, p. 239).

[14] *Sickness Unto Death*, pp. 13-14. (SV XI, 128)

[15] *Sickness Unto Death*, p. 14. (SV XI, 128)

## III. The Relational Self

That Kierkegaard's concept of the self is fundamentally relational will come as a surprise to many. Kierkegaard has been frequently criticized for being an arch-individualist who failed to appreciate fully the importance of community for selfhood. Martin Buber is probably the best known critic of Kierkegaard on this score, but numerous other writers have sounded this note of correction.[16]

Nevertheless, it is clear that the famous definition of the self in *The Sickness Unto Death* precludes any account of the self as autonomous and self-contained: "The human self is such a derived, established relation, a relation that relates itself to itself and in relating itself to itself relates itself to another."[17] Kierkegaard, in this passage, clearly holds a view of the self structurally similar to that advanced by Hegel in his *Phenomenology of Spirit*, who affirms that "self-consciousness exists in and for itself when, and by the fact that, it exists for another; that is it exists only in being acknowledged."[18] Why is it that Kierkegaard's critics have not been led by this passage to conclude that Kierkegaard has a relational view of the self?

I think it is because the critics hold two other assumptions. One is that the "other" to whom the self is said to relate is thought to be exclusively God. The second is that God somehow does not count as a real "other" or at least does not make the self part of a real community. So, the critics think, even though Anti-Climacus's definition clearly states the self becomes itself only through a relation, that relation is only to God and not other human persons, and the idea of the individual self standing before God is still excessively individualistic.

I shall criticize both of these two assumptions. I shall try to show that God is not the only "other" to which selves can relate to and thereby become selves, though God remains the crucial "other" for selfhood in the highest sense. And I shall try to show that God as Kierkegaard conceives him is genuinely personal, and

---

[16] See Martin Buber, *Between Man and Man*, trans. Ronald Gregor Smith (New York: Macmillan, 1965), p. 50.

[17] *Sickness Unto Death*, pp. 13-14. (SV XI, 128)

[18] G. W. F. Hegel, *Phenomenology of Spirit*, trans. by A. V. Miller (Oxford: Oxford University Press, 1977), p. 111.

that the relationship with God forms both the model and foundation for other types of communal relationships.

Let us consider first the identity of the "other" to whom the self must relate to become itself. It is certainly natural, given our knowledge of Kierkegaard's Christian convictions, to identify this "other" with God. Such identification even seems to be demanded by some of the texts in Part One. For example, in discussing the despair of necessity that lacks possibility, Anti-Climacus argues that the lack of possibility is grounded in a failure to have the right kind of faith in God, the one for whom all things are possible.[19] Throughout Part One God represents the ground of authentic selfhood and the antidote to despair. Nevertheless, there are textual reasons not to be too hasty in concluding that the "other" Anti-Climacus views as essential to selfhood must always be identified with God.

The main such reason is rather obvious, yet it is something to which some commentators have not paid sufficient attention. Anti-Climacus tells us quite explicitly that in Part One of the book, the gradations in the consciousness of selfhood that were considered were all "within the category of the human self, or the self whose criterion is man."[20] Only in Part Two, which discusses despair as sin, is there an account of what Anti-Climacus calls, "hoping not to be misinterpreted," the "theological self, the self directly before God."[21] Even if Anti-Climacus had not given us this direct instruction, the alert reader would surely have perceived that there is a dramatic shift in language between Parts One and Two. Part One consistently uses abstract, formal language to describe the self's "other." The relationship by which the self becomes itself is described simply as a relation to an "other." The ground of the self's identity is described as "the power that established it."[22]

It is not possible that the use of this abstract language should be accidental or inadvertent; Anti-Climacus is careful and exact in his linguistic usage, and certainly not reticent to use religious language. When he means to talk about God, he is quite capable of using the term "God." By using this abstract language, I believe he wishes to talk about the formal structure of the self in a way that allows us to understand that God is the ultimate basis of

---

[19] *Sickness Unto Death*, p. 38. (SV XI, 151)
[20] *Sickness Unto Death*, p. 79. (SV XI, 191)
[21] Ibid.
[22] *Sickness Unto Death*, p. 14. (SV XI, 128)

selfhood without claiming that the actual identity of the concrete self is always grounded solely in God.

The ontological structure of the self is relational, he wishes to claim. It is not possible to be a self apart from a relation to something outside the self from which the self derives its identity.

In arguing that the "other" that defines the self does not consist solely of God, I do not wish to minimize the importance of God for the self in Kierkegaard's thought. God is related to the self in a twofold way. First of all, as Creator, God is the ontological ground of the self, the one who made the self a relational entity that can only be itself by *becoming*. The self is an ethical task, not a fixed entity, but that task is itself part of the self's ontological givenness. It is the form of being granted the self by the Creator. Its *being* essentially requires the self to *become*.

Secondly, as I shall argue below, a conscious relation to God provides the basis for true or genuine selfhood. A relation to God is not merely the foundation of the self ontologically, but the task of the self existentially. The self that I should become is a self that is conscious of itself as standing before God.

Nevertheless, the self that fails to have this kind of relation to God is still a self, at least a self "of sorts." Though a failure to relate to God produces despair, that spiritual suicide in which the self refuses selfhood, despair is impotent and cannot achieve its goal. The self cannot tear itself away from God ontologically: "the eternal in a person can be proved by the fact that despair cannot consume his self." The power that grounds the self ontologically is stronger than the self that wishes to tear itself away and destroy itself and does not allow the self to lose its selfhood.[23]

God is the ontological ground of the self, but in creating the self to be a *self* "God, who constituted man a relation, releases it from his hand, as it were."[24] Ontologically, the self is not released; it finds itself *as if it were released*. However, this "as it were" release means that though human selves cannot cease to be relational—they are always defined by a relation to some "other"—the self can consciously ground its identity in many different kinds of "others." There is no ontological freedom from God, but there is ethical freedom.

This can be clearly seen in the description Anti-Climacus gives in Part Two of the "gradations" of types of self:

---

[23] *Sickness Unto Death*, pp. 20, 21. (SV XI, 134, 135)
[24] *Sickness Unto Death*, p. 16. (SV XI, 130)

aliveness

> And what infinite reality the self gains by being conscious
> of existing before God, by becoming a human self whose
> criterion is God. A cattleman who (if this were possible) is
> a self directly before his cattle is a very low self, and
> similarly, a master who is a self directly before his slaves is
> actually no self—for in both cases a criterion is lacking.
> The child who previously has had only his parents as a
> criterion becomes a self as an adult by getting the state as a
> criterion, but what an infinite accent falls on the self by
> having God as the criterion![25]

In this passage Anti-Climacus brings together the "achievement"
and "relational" character of the self.

What makes the self a self is a "criterion," a goal or end by
which the self measures itself. However, that criterion, that sense
of an "ideal self" is given in and through relations with others.
Someone whose sense of self is provided only by animals (the case
of the cattleman) or only by other people who are not regarded as
persons (the case of the slave master) fails to be a self. Such a
person's identity is still relational, but the quality of the relation is
insufficient to given the individual a criterion that makes for
selfhood. Even the child whose sense of self is completely
dependent on the parents still lacks a self in the deepest sense.
That deeper sense of self is made possible when the child is
differentiated from the parents, and relates to society in the
broader sense, symbolized by the state.

We could easily expand on the rather terse comment of
Anti-Climacus here. What is involved in becoming a self in this
sense? I think that it is fundamentally a matter of coming to
understand for oneself the ideals of selfhood that are embedded in
the language and institutions of a society, so that one can
consciously pursue those ideals for oneself.

Anti-Climacus is therefore very far from claiming that
human selves are isolated from other human selves. Selfhood is a
thoroughly social phenomenon; I cannot become a self all by
myself, and every human self is shaped by relations to other
human selves: initially parents and other early care-givers, and
eventually ideals of selfhood that are embodied in the language
and institutions of a society. Such ideals of selfhood are
embedded in those relations by which humans are socialized and

---

[25] *Sickness Unto Death*, p. 79. (SV XI, 191)

become parts of concrete communities.

## IV.  God as the Foundation of Authentic Selfhood

I have argued that Kierkegaard's anthropology is relational, and that the relations that genetically constitute actual human selves include relations with other human persons.  However, it cannot be denied, and I have already admitted, that God still plays a decisive role in that anthropology.  Not only is God the ontological foundation of the self; God is also the highest ethical task, in the sense that the highest form of selfhood requires a conscious relation to God. Some critics will still find such a view objectionable and overly individualistic. Does not Kierkegaard underemphasize the value of human relations in focusing so strongly on God?  Cannot human persons become authentic selves through relations with other human persons?

Kierkegaard is well aware that a life lived outside the boundaries of Christian faith, and indeed outside of religious faith of any kind, can be rich and meaningful.  Even the polemical Anti-Climacus points that "individual pagans as well as pagan nations *en masse* have accomplished amazing feats that have inspired and will inspire poets."[26]  In *Concluding Unscientific Postscript*, Johannes Climacus, while praising Christianity as "a glorious lifeview in which to die, the only true comfort," maintains stoutly that the non-Christian kind of religious life that he terms religiousness A, which is how he says he lives his own life, "is so strenuous for a human being that there is always a sufficient task in it."[27]  His goal is not therefore to depreciate the meaningfulness of the lives of those who do not share Christian religious convictions.

I think that Kierkegaard stresses the importance of "standing before God," not because he is unaware of the importance of human relationships, but because he is so sensitive to the power of those relations.  It is not because he does not realize the importance of such human institutions as the family and the state, but because he sees how easily these relationships can become confining and even dehumanizing.  It is not that he is unaware of the importance of the finite, but that he is very aware of how easily human beings can create idols from finite goods, even when those goods are relations to other people.

---

[26] *Sickness Unto Death*, p. 45. (SV XI, 158)
[27] *Concluding Unscientific Postscript*, p. 557. (SV VII, 486)

The dangers Kierkegaard perceived are more apparent today than they were in the middle of the nineteenth century. We live in a world in which relations such as those of family, clan, nation-state, religion, class, race, and gender fundamentally shape the identity of human selves. Such relations are a necessary part of our finite human selves; we exist as concrete selves—as men and women, North Americans and Europeans and Africans, Christians and Muslims, Catholics and Protestants, rich and poor. Such relations are not inherently evil, and could not be avoided even if they were. Nevertheless, we live in a world racked by hatred and violence, and much of it is violence directed by "us" at "them," those who are not part of my family, my nation, my sex, my race, my religion, my class. It seems perilously easy for us humans to move from an affirmation of our identity based on those relations that define us to a negation of all those who do not share that identity.

From Kierkegaard's point of view, this amounts to idolatry. When the "criterion" of the self is derived solely from relations to other humans, then that finite human identity becomes invested with ultimate authority. God in the sense of what is of ultimate worth is completely immanent; there is no place left for transcendence. Surely, one of the reasons for Kierkegaard's vigorous rejection of Hegelianism was his conviction that Hegel, by viewing the state as the ultimate ethical authority and human philosophical reason as the ultimate expression of the divine, had eroded the majesty and authority of the divine. The transcendence of the divine for Kierkegaard is not a crushing weight that threatens individual liberty; it also represents the liberation of the individual from every form of human oppression and tyranny.

The God-relation for Kierkegaard must be understood as an ultimate and intrinsic good, since God is a genuine person who loves me, and is capable of a relation in which I am addressed, demands may be made on me, questions may be addressed to me, and so on, just as is the case for other persons. However, though the God-relation is not merely a means to bettering human social arrangements, it ultimately must be seen as functioning so as to humanize those arrangements.

Kierkegaard's argument for this can be seen most clearly in *Works of Love*. The argument of that book begins with a strict contrast between all forms of "natural" human love, such as erotic love and friendship love, and neighbor love, the kind of love that is commanded by Christianity. All natural human loves contain an element of self-love.[28] They are forms of "preferential love" in that such loves always select some people as objects of love rather than others: I love one woman and not another; I choose one person as my closest friend and not another; my patriotic love is for my own country and not another. Such loves are grounded in self-love because the basis of the preference is always some relation to the self; I love my wife because she is my wife, my friend because he is my friend, my country because it is my country. It is this element of self-love that allows these natural loves to become corrupted and which makes it possible for them to generate the strife associated with the "us against them" thinking that is so prevalent throughout the world.

Neighbor love by contrast is unselfish, because the ground of neighbor love is not a relation to myself. When I love my neighbor, I love him or her simply as one of God's creatures like myself. The basis for the love is not myself but God and on that foundation there is perfect equality.[29] In neighbor love, God is always present as the "third" or "middle-term." Hence, neighbor love is not preferential or selfish in character. As soon as I begin to draw boundaries and exclude some people as neighbors, I am no longer loving my neighbor. Though neighbor love is concrete—it is my duty to love the actual individuals I encounter—it does not and cannot exclude anyone.

This contrast between natural human love and neighbor love can be and has been understood as one more instance of Kierkegaard's inhuman individualism, his failure to grasp the positive significance of human relations. However, I believe that this reading is a mistake. Kierkegaard's purpose in contrasting neighbor love and natural human loves is not to argue that the natural human loves must be replaced by neighbor love. Rather, he claims that these natural loves must be transformed by incorporating neighbor love as their foundation. It is not that I must cease to love my wife in a special way, or my friend as a special friend. It is rather that I must, in loving my wife romantically, first love her as my neighbor. My friend is not only my friend, but also my neighbor. "Love the beloved faithfully and tenderly, but let love for the neighbor be the sanctifying element in

---

[28] This critique of natural human love is found most clearly in *Works of Love*, trans. by Howard V. and Edna H. Hong (Princeton: Princeton University Press), Chapter IIB, pp. 44-60. (SV IX, pp. 47-62).

[29] *Works of Love*, p. 60. (SV IX, 62)

union's covenant with God. Love your friend honestly and devotedly, but let love for the neighbor be what you learn from each other in your friendship's confidential relationship with God."[30]

The implications of this run deep. Making neighbor love the foundation of these natural human loves protects them against two types of dangers, the dangers of dehumanization and idolization. First of all, the preferential love can no longer serve as a screen for exploitation or domination. If I love my wife as my neighbor, then I recognize her intrinsic value and dignity that are equal to my own in God's eyes. I cannot therefore treat her as existing solely to satisfy my needs.

Secondly, when I love my wife as my neighbor, then I cannot make her an idol. Of course in loving her as my wife, an element of preference will remain. I can only be married to one person. However, since I also must love her as my neighbor, I dare not allow our special relation to imply that other people are not my neighbor. Nor should she allow me to become an idol for her. Our relation must not become an excuse for ignoring our responsibilities to others. In our love we must not turn solely inward, but in turning towards each other also, in mutual love, we must understand our responsibilities to those others.

What is true of marriage will also be true of the family as a whole, of the nation, and indeed every preferential human relation. Neighbor love is in the end therefore a deeply humanizing love. And this shows that love for God is in turn not a replacement for human love, but the condition of human love becoming truly humane. It is for this reason that Kierkegaard can claim that "the religious is the transfigured expression of that which the politician has thought of in his happiest moment, in so far as he truly loves what it is to be human and loves human beings."[31]

Hence, "standing before God" as an individual is not a rationale for an objectionable individualism. It is in fact a protection against the kind of individualism that permeates and corrupts contemporary western cultures. If society is the highest authority, then there is no way of redeeming a corrupt society. It

---

[30] *Works of Love*, p. 62. (SV IX, 64).

[31] Søren Kierkegaard, *The Individual: Two "Notes" Concerning My Work as an Author*, trans. by Walter Lowrie (New York: Harper and Row, 1962) p. 107. (SV XIII, 589). The reference is given to the English Lowrie edition for convenience, but the translation is my own.

is only if my identity is rooted in a transcendent power that I will have the power to stand up against evil when that evil becomes pervasive and accepted by my culture. This is a message that Socrates and Jesus understood and practiced. They provide us with models of what means to be true individuals, whose individuality is grounded in a relation to the divine that transcends society, and whose individuality is seen not in selfish acquisitiveness, but a life of devotion to the good of others.

# Theodicy, Autonomy, and Community: The Nature of Personhood in *The Brothers Karamazov*

*Ralph C. Wood*
Baylor University

There is not one problem of evil, nor is there a single conception of human personhood: there are many. How one answers the former very largely shapes one's conclusions about the latter. God's goodness can be challenged not only at the philosophical level, but also at the political and the religious and the existential. And in so challenging divine beneficence we also agitate the question of human freedom and selfhood. Whether we can affirm the reality of divine power and love in face of the world's monstrous suffering requires us to ask not only what we must think about this apparent contradiction, but also how we should order our common life (especially if there is no God), how we must believe and worship (if there is indeed God) and, in either case, whether human personhood is constituted primarily by autonomous or communal means. The aim of this essay is to argue that Ivan Karamazov raises the intellectual problem of evil as acutely as it has ever been posed, but that his rejection of all theological answers to it causes him to offer a political and existential cure worse than the disease. Ivan argues that he must become an atheist because the world is rife with undeserved suffering, because it is a godless and meaningless realm that doesn't deserve his vote. Beginning with this rightful intellectual concern about the terrors of injustice, he turns the philosophical problem of evil, I will argue, into his own means of avoiding the political and religious requirements of authentic personhood.

I maintain, moreover, that Dostoevsky construes these questions in a decidedly Orthodox way. Though he was a student of western Christianity and culture, Dostoevsky remained fundamentally Russian in his conception of God and the world, of good and evil, of divine and human nature. We cannot properly understand his treatment of these matters, therefore, until we grasp his Orthodox reading of them. Thus must we examine his parable of the Grand Inquisitor vis-à-vis the Orthodox doctrine of human personhood as being founded not on autonomous choice but in communal dependence on God.

I. Ivan Karamazov is no straw atheist.  On the contrary, he gives voice to the philosophical problem of evil perhaps more clearly and cogently than any other speaker or actor, any other philosopher or theologian, in the whole of world literature.  Yet he is also a very Russian atheist.  He thinks with his *solar plexus* as D. H. Lawrence might have said.  He is *passionately* intellectual.  Ivan does not pose the question of theodicy as a mere philosophical conundrum, as it is often posed in the West.  From Leibniz through Hume, from Alvin Plantinga to J. L. Mackie, the problem of evil has often been cast in bare intellectual terms: how to *think through* the contradiction that stands between the goodness, omniscience and omnipotence of God, on the one hand, and the massive misery and undeserved suffering that characterize God's world, on the other: *si Deus bonum est, unde malum?*  In *J.B.*, his dramatic contemporizing of the Job story, Archibald MacLeish puts the intellectual problem of evil tersely but accurately: "If God is good He is not God.  If God is God He is not good."  If, in other words, God is imbued with the charity which He himself enjoins his creatures to live by, then He must lack the divine power to create and sustain a world in which such charity obtains: He is not God.  If, by contrast, God possesses the sovereignty and strength to perform what He wills, then this misery-riddled world must be proof that he is deficient in love itself: He is not good.  Ivan does *not* make his case against God's goodness in this intellectualized fashion.  He is not a philosophical thinker who abstracts ideas from experience in order to test their logical clarity and coherence.  As Albert Camus observed, "Ivan really lives his problems."[1]  They are matters, quite literally, of life and death, of eternal life and eternal death, of ultimate bliss or final misery.  Ivan is willing to face the anguish and terror inherent not only in thinking but also in living without God.

As one who knows the truths of the heart, Ivan also knows that reason alone cannot fathom the deepest things.  On the contrary, reason can be put to nefarious purposes: "Reason is a scoundrel," he confesses.  Ivan is willing, therefore, to live "even

---

[1] Albert Camus, "Ivan and Rebellion against God," in *The Brothers Karamazov and the Critics*, ed. Edward Wasiolek (Belmont CA: Wadsworth, 1967), p. 75.

. . . against logic" (236).[2] Yet he is unwilling to live as a mindless vitalist, embracing life without much regard for its meaning and, even less, with a blithe disregard for its injustice. So huge are the world's moral horrors, Ivan argues, that they undermine any notion of divine order and purpose. Hence Ivan's truly wrenching quandary: Can he love life without believing that it has ultimate meaning—believing, instead, that it is godless and absurd? Ivan is young and strong. He brims with intellectual curiosity no less than bodily energy. He wants to travel to Europe and to learn its science and its history. As a good romantic, Ivan cites Schiller's celebrated line about the "sticky little leaves" whose gummy unfolding in spring seems to signal the whole world's rebirth. They remind Ivan of all that is precious in life, the glories of human love and natural splendor, the inward movement of all things toward life's energizing center.

> There is still an awful lot of centripetal force on our planet, Alyosha. I want to live, and I do live, even if it be against logic. Though I do not believe in the order of things, still the sticky little leaves that come out in the spring are dear to me, the blue sky is dear to me, some people are dear to me, whom one loves sometimes, would you believe it, without even knowing why; some human deeds are dear to me, which one has perhaps long ceased believing in, but still honors with one's heart, out of old habit. (230)

It is noteworthy that Ivan makes this confession to his young brother, Alyosha, just after he has broken off relations with Katerina Ivanovna. Ivan feels as free and light as the air. Living in this detached and uncommitted—indeed, this almost angelic—state, Ivan makes qualifications that are altogether as important as his affirmations. Though he wants to drink life to the lees, he confesses that only "some people" and only "some human deeds" are dear to him, and that he loves them only "sometimes." Ivan deliberately denies the teaching of Father Zosima, the head of an Orthodox monastery who also stands at the religious center of the novel. Father Zosima insists that love cannot be selective, that it must be at once universal and concrete, that we must not love those who are conveniently remote so much as those who are

---

[2] All quotations from *The Brothers Karamazov* are taken from the Richard Pevyear-Larissa Volonkhonsky translation (New York NY: Vintage, 1991) and will be paginated within the essay.

inconveniently near. Already, it is evident, the philosophical and the religious arguments are linked. Ivan not only thinks but also lives in autonomous and anti-communal terms. It is precisely the neighbor whom we *cannot* love, he insists. The neighbor's objective and objectionable otherness—his bad breath, his foolish face, his ill manners—threaten Ivan's sovereign selfhood. Of such a neighbor, Ivan complains like an early Jean-Paul Sartre that "He is another and not me" (237). Despite his eager embrace of the world, therefore, Ivan wants to remain a solitary and transcendent judge over it, a godlike withholder no less than a gracious giver of praise. Others must satisfy his own criteria before he will embrace them. And because God does not satisfy the requirements of Ivan's logic, he will not believe in God.

Yet Ivan's logic is not sophomoric. He makes a strenuous case against God's goodness. He refuses, for example, to cite the many natural calamities—typhoons and tornadoes, floods and droughts, fires and earthquakes and disease—that seem to disclose a ham-fisted Creator. Ivan knows that such cosmic evils might be attributed to a natural process which is divinely ordered. Like Job, he might discover that, while the natural order seems inimical to human happiness, its operations might have their own purposes, not revealing any divine hostility toward human well-being. Ivan wrestles not with natural, therefore, but with moral evils, with the crimes that we human creatures commit. The standard explanation of such moral evils is that they are the unfortunate consequence of human freedom. God's uncoerced creatures, so the argument runs, are capable of grossly misusing their liberty. If God were to prevent such evil misuses of human freedom, his world would be no longer free.

Ivan subjects the standard free-will defense of the divine goodness to devastating critique. At best, he says, the free perversion of human will explains only the suffering of adults, the grown-ups who are accountable for the evils that they both cause and suffer. They have eaten the apple of knowledge, says Ivan. Because they have followed the demonic temptation to become "as gods," they deserve their self-wrought misery. What the Augustinian theodicy cannot account for, Ivan maintains, is the agony of children whose wills are still innocent. That their suffering results from human cruelty more than natural mishap makes it all the more horrible. As Ivan notices, animals rarely torment their prey. Only our human kind derives erotic pleasure from its savagery, becoming virtual voluptuaries of cruelty. In a passage that must have made even the Marquis de Sade tremble,

Ivan declares the awful allurement of unprotected innocence. "It is precisely the defenselessness of these creatures that tempts the torturers, the angelic trustfulness of the child, who has nowhere to turn and no one to turn to—that is what enflames the vile blood of the torturer" (241).

Ivan offers searing examples of such wanton and motiveless malignity. Indeed, he creates a virtual phantasmagoria of suffering from actual instances of human barbarity that he has read about in Russian newspapers: Turkish soldiers cutting babies from their mother's wombs and throwing them in the air in order to impale them on their bayonets; enlightened parents stuffing their five-year old daughter's mouth with excrement and locking her in a freezing privy all night for having wet the bed, while they themselves sleep soundly; Genevan Christians teaching a naïve peasant to bless the good God even as the poor dolt is beheaded for thefts and murders which his ostensibly Christian society caused him to commit; a Russian general, offended at an eight-year old boy for accidentally hurting the paw of the officer's dog, inciting his wolfhounds to tear the child to pieces; a lady and gentleman flogging their eight-year old daughter with a birch-rod until she collapses while crying for mercy, "Papa, papa, dear papa."

Such evils cannot be justified, Ivan argues, either by religious arguments based on history's beginning or by secular arguments that look to its end. The Edenic exercise of free will is not worth the tears of even one little girl shivering all night in a privy and crying out from her excrement-filled mouth to "dear, kind God" for protection. Yet neither will Ivan accept the Hegelian-Marxist thesis that the harmonious final outcome of history sublates its present evils. The notion that such savagery reveals the necessary consequences of human freedom or that it contributes to history's ultimate result is, to Ivan, a moral and religious outrage. Neither is he any more satisfied with the conventional doctrine of hell, which holds that the monsters of torment will themselves be eternally tormented. Hellish punishment for heinous malefactors would not restore their victims, Ivan reminds us. The impaled babies would not be brought back to life nor would their mothers be consoled, the dismembered boy would not live out his years, the weeping girls would not dry their tears. Ivan rejects *all* such theodicies because he believes that they commit unforgivable sacrilege against innocent sufferers. Indeed, theodicy itself is a heinous evil. With a dramatic metaphor drawn again from Schiller, he refuses to offer his hosanna for such a world: he returns his ticket to such a life.

Ivan's brief against belief seems philosophically unanswerable. Dostoevsky makes no attempt to provide one anywhere in the course of the novel, thus conceding that there is no *logical* justification for the suffering of innocents. Yet this is hardly to say that there are no *religious* answers to Ivan's protests. It is rather to say that they will be found, if at all, elsewhere than in abstract argument; they will be located in the realm of religion and politics and the everyday requirements of true personhood. In seeking to embody such answers in living form, Dostoevsky offers the figures of Zosima and Alyosha as his religious counters to Ivan's atheist revolt. The most notable fact about the monastic elder and his young disciple is that, unlike Ivan, they are not Euclidean men. They believe that, in the most important matters, parallel lines do indeed meet. Things counter can converge because the deepest truths are not univocal but analogical and paradoxical. Theirs is not a three-dimensional block universe but rather a layered cosmos containing multiple orders of being. For Zosima and Alyosha, the material and immaterial worlds are never distant and remote from each other, as in much of western thought. The created and uncreated realms are deeply intertwined, each participating in the life of the other.

Ivan remains opaque to this interstitial cosmos that demands interstitial discernment. Dostoevsky calls it *proniknovenie*, an "intuitive seeing through" or a "spiritual penetration."[3] Such theological sight is the product not of any special intelligence but of the iconic imagination. The icons of Eastern Orthodoxy are formed out of a theology of presence rather than one of representation. God's own splendor is said to radiate through the icon, confronting worshippers with the experience of Uncreated Light. It is not an image that one looks *at* in order to discern an earthly image of something holy, in an attempt to portray the invisible in visible terms. Nor is it an expression of the artist's own subjective experience of the sacred. Rather does the icon look *out* at the beholder. It seeks to open up the eternal realm so that its light might shine forth. Icons do not seek to embody a discarnate world, therefore, but rather to reveal an earthly world that has been rendered transparent by a spiritualization that embraces the entire cosmos. Worshippers are

---

3 Vyacheslav Ivanov, *Freedom and the Tragic Life: A Study in Dostoevsky*, ed. S. Konovalov (New York NY: Noonday, 1960), p. 30.

themselves transformed by the invisible light that emanates from the icon, penetrating to the depths of their being and forming their true personhood.[4]   At Zosima's funeral, Alyosha has such a transfiguring experience of the mystical touching of the visible and invisible worlds.   It prompts him to repeat the example of his dead master in an iconic gesture of prostration:

> Filled with rapture, his soul yearned for freedom, space, vastness.   Over him the heavenly dome, full of quiet, shining stars, hung boundlessly.   From the zenith to the horizon the still-dim Milky Way stretched its double strand.   Night, fresh and quiet, almost unstirring, enveloped the earth.   The white towers and golden domes of the church gleamed in the sapphire sky.   The luxuriant autumn flowers in the flowerbeds near the house had fallen asleep until morning.   The silence of the earth seemed to merge with the silence of the heavens, the mystery of the earth to be touched by the mystery of the stars .... Alyosha stood gazing and suddenly, as if he had been cut down, he threw himself to the earth.
>      . . . It was as if threads from all those innumerable worlds of God all came together in his soul, and it was trembling all over, "touching other worlds."   He wanted to forgive everyone for everything, and to ask forgiveness, oh, not for himself!   but for all and for everything, "as others are asking for me," rang in his soul. (362)

Ivan is blind to this iconic joining of the earthly and heavenly realms, perhaps because he is also blind to the Orthodox understanding of human personhood.   After all, he is man obsessed with Western ideas.   Yet Ivan is not a rationalist, as is often said, but rather a thinker who wants to disjoin his thought from its rightful engagement with God and the world.   He lives a dichotomous life.   Ivan's mind is even more severely perverted than his will.   He fails to discern, for example, that the doctrine of immortality concerns not only the life that is transfigured in the world to come, but also the life that is meant to be transformed within this world.   To use the language of St. Paul found in I Corinthians 15 and of the Fourth Gospel contained in the novel's epigraph, mortality is meant to put on immortality, the dying seed

---

[4] Michel Quenot, *The Icon: Window on the Kingdom* (Crestwood NY: St. Vladimir's Seminary, 1991), p. 155.

to bring forth much fruit.  To become immortal is to become a unique and unrepeatable person who has been perfected in both loving and being loved.

Ivan's contention that no one can truly love others as he loves himself is linked, therefore, to his denial of immortality. Ivan holds, as we have seen, that other persons stand like dense Euclidean clumps to block the path of his own autonomy.  So long as we are confined within the realm of mere human possibility, Dostoevsky agrees with Ivan.  He despised the soupy benevolence that pervaded much of 19th century Euro-American culture. "Those who love men in general," he often said, "hate men in particular."5  Yet he also insisted that Christ's divine *kenosis*—the divine self-emptying hymn in Philippians 2—enables what is humanly impossible: the emptying of human egoism for the sake of true charity.  Through this kenotic love that Zosima and his disciple Alyosha embody, one actually becomes a person by becoming another self, not an Ego but a Thou, a person who exists only in self-giving solidarity with Christ and thereby with others.6

When personhood is measured in this kenotic manner, Alyosha can be seen as a credible character, rather than the ghostly and gossamer creature he is often accused of being.  Unlike Ivan, Alyosha does not clip newspaper accounts of suffering children and then offer anti-theological arguments *about* them; instead, he actually seeks out the insulted and injured, identifying himself *with* them.  He joins faith with practice, thinking with doing, thus answering the problem of evil with deeds rather than reasons—with his whole personhood, not with his mind alone. Through his patient and long-suffering friendships, Alyosha helps redeem the pathetic Ilyusha Snegirov, even as he also helps to set the nihilistic Kolya Krassotkin on the path to new life.  Alyosha is able to pull these boys out of their misery only at great cost to himself.  Dostoevsky makes clear in the novel's final scene, when the boys gather to cheer Alyosha as if he were their savior, that he is a true icon of Christ, a man through whom the invisible light of eternity brightly shines.  Yet Alyosha deflects all praise away from himself and toward Christ.  As the only Man who has suffered absolutely everything, says Alyosha, Christ alone has the right to

---

5 Quoted in Ellis Sandoz, *Political Apocalypse: A Study in Dostoevsky's Grand Inquisitor* (Baton Rouge LA: Louisiana State UP, 1971), p. 127.
6 Steven Cassedy, "P. A. Florensky and the Celebration of Matter," in *Russian Religious Thought*, ed. Judith Deutsch Kornblatt and Richard F. Gustafson (Madison WI: U of Wisconsin, 1966), p. 96

forgive absolutely everything—even the tormentors of children. Yet Alyosha's mere mention of the "only sinless One" so enrages Ivan that he comes forth with his "Legend of the Grand Inquisitor."

II. Ivan's parable appears to be an assault on the character of Jesus, when its real target is humanity itself. Though he professes to love "some men," Ivan can give himself to other persons no more than he can grant the goodness of God. For Dostoevsky, the one follows from the other: one cannot scorn the love of God and still love human beings. Ivan ends as a misanthrope, I will argue, because he has a modern secular conception of freedom that is incapable of fulfillment except by monstrous supermen.

    The plot of Ivan's parable is familiar enough, even if its meaning remains quite unfamiliar. The risen Christ returns to earth in 15th century Seville, where he immediately begins to perform miracles. The people hail him as their liberator from the awful *autos da fé* that the Spanish Inquisition is carrying out. Jesus is quickly arrested by the church authorities and imprisoned in a dimly lit dungeon. There the ninety-year old Cardinal Grand Inquisitor relentlessly grills the silent Christ. This ancient church-ogre accuses Jesus of having required men to live by the strength of their strong wills, cruelly ignoring the fact that they are impotent creatures who can live only for the sake of a swinish happiness. The Inquisitor thus upbraids Christ for having rejected the Tempter's wilderness offerings of bread and power and fame. These, he says, are the satisfying substitutes which human beings crave. They do not want the awful autonomy that Christ allegedly commanded:

> Instead of taking over men's freedom, you increased it still more for them! Did you forget that peace and even death are dearer to man than free choice in the knowledge of good and evil? There is nothing more seductive for man than the freedom of his conscience, but there is nothing more tormenting either. And so, instead of a firm foundation for appeasing human conscience once and for all, you chose everything that was unusual, enigmatic, and indefinite, you chose everything that was beyond men's strength, and thereby acted as if you did not love them at all . . . . You desired the free love of man, that he should follow you freely, seduced and captivated by you. Instead of the firm and ancient law, man had henceforth to decide

for himself, with a free heart, what is good and what is evil, having only your image before him as a guide . . . . (254-55)

It is astonishing that so many readers have taken the Grand Inquisitor's conception of freedom as if it were Dostoevsky's own—and also as if it were true. Camus regarded it as an unprecedented statement of the human cry for liberty against all religious restraints. Camus can make such a claim only because, together with Ivan, he embraces the thoroughly secular conception of freedom that has largely prevailed in the modern West, from John Mill to John Dewey to John Rawls. Ivan's Inquisitor belongs to their lineage. Liberty, he declares, entails a brave and lonely autonomy, as each individual determines for himself the difference between good and evil. Jesus serves not as savior who redeems corporate humanity from sin, therefore, but as moral example to guide solitary and heroic individuals—having himself trod the same lonely path of self-determination.

Michael Sandel has shown what is problematic about this notion of freedom and personhood as consisting entirely of unfettered choices. Such choices are prompted by nothing other than the individual subject and his private conscience acting either on persuasive evidence or the arbitrary assertion of will. Just as this modern secular self is not determined by any larger aims or attachments that it has not chosen for itself, neither does it have obligations to any larger communities, except those it autonomously chooses to join. The one moral norm, it follows, is the injunction to respect the dignity of others by not denying them the freedom to exercise their own moral autonomy. Such an understanding of human liberty, says Sandel, opposes

> any view that regards us as obligated to ends that we have not chosen—ends given by nature or God, for example, or by our identities as members of families, peoples, cultures, or traditions. Encumbered identities such as these are at odds with the liberal conception of the person as free and independent selves, unbound by prior moral ties, capable of choosing our ends for ourselves. This is the conception that finds expression in the ideal of the state as a neutral . . . framework of rights that refuses to choose among competing values and ends. For the liberal self, what matters above all, what is most essential to our

personhood, is not the ends we choose but or capacity to choose them.[7]

Dostoevsky repeatedly attacked this modern secular notion of freedom and personhood, dismissing it scornfully as "socialism." Astounded by the Inquisitor's similar idea of personal liberty as absolute autonomy, Alyosha cries out to Ivan: "And who will believe you about freedom?" "Is that the way to understand it? It's a far cry from the Orthodox idea . . . ." (260). It should be added that it is also a far cry from the Jewish and Catholic and classical Protestant ideas of freedom. In all four traditions, we are not made into free persons by becoming autonomous selves who have been immunized from all obligations that we have not independently chosen. Rather does our personhood reside in our becoming communal selves who freely embrace our moral and religious and political obligations. These responsibilities come to us less by our own choosing than through a thickly webbed network of shared friendships and familial ties, through political practices and religious promises. In a very real sense, such "encumbrances" choose us before we choose them. There is no mythical free and autonomous self that exists apart from these ties. There are only gladly or else miserably bound persons—namely, persons who find their duties and encumbrances to be either gracious or onerous.

Alyosha's idea of freedom is communal because it is first of all religious. Athanasius of Alexandria articulated it most clearly in the 4th century: "God became man so that man may become God." The central Orthodox doctrine is called *theosis* or *theopoesis*—the divinizing or deifying of humanity. The Eastern Church does not call for believers to imitate Jesus through the exercise of moral choice, as in the familiar western and liberal Protestant pattern. It summons them rather to participate in the life of Christ through the transformative power of the liturgy and sacraments of the church. To become persons in the true sense is to become what the New Testament calls "partakers of the divine nature" (2 Pet 1:4). The modern secular notion of freedom articulated by the Grand Inquisitor is, for the Orthodox, the very definition of slavery. John Meyendorff is deeply Dostoevskyan in his counter-description of true liberty: "Man can be authentically free only 'in God,' when, through the Holy Spirit, he has been

---

[7] Michael J. Sandel, *Democracy's Discontent: America in Search of a Public Philosophy* (Cambridge MA: Harvard UP, 1996), p. 12.

liberated from the determinism of created and fallen existence and has received the power to share God's lordship over creation."[8]

Orthodox theologian Vladimir Lossky observes, in a similar way, that the Eastern Church regards choice as the mark not of freedom but of fallenness, as a debasement of true liberty, as a loss of the divine likeness: "Our nature being overclouded with sin no longer knows its true good . . . ; and so the human person is always faced with the necessity of choice; it goes forward gropingly."[9] To deliberate autonomously in the face of alternatives, it follows, is not liberty but servitude. True freedom, says Lossky, is revealed in the Christ who freely renounces his own will in order to accomplish the will of his Father. Alyosha is free in precisely this way. Jesus has not abandoned him to his lonely conscience in order to let him solitarily determine good and evil for himself. The self-emptying Christ has freed Alyosha to empty his own ego, to live and act in joyful obedience to God, and thus to be bound in unbreakable solidarity with his father and brothers, with his friends and enemies, and (not least of all) with the miserable children of his neighborhood.

Given the Grand Inquisitor's anti-Orthodox conception of freedom as unencumbered self-determining choice, it is not surprising that he should have contempt for the average run of men. He despises their dependence, their animal desire for security and comfort. The Inquisitor thus informs Jesus that the Catholic Church has been forced to correct his impossible summons to autonomy. Rome understands, says the Inquisitor, what Christ did not—that men must first be fed before they can be made virtuous. "Better that you enslave us," the Inquisitor's masses cry out, "but feed us" (253). Thus has the cynical church of the Grand Inquisitor replaced Christ's purported call for unfettered autonomy with its own sheepish substitutes: "miracle, mystery, and authority." Yet even these pitiful placebos will not finally suffice, the Inquisitor insists, for the modern world will confront men with such scientific wonders and terrors that the vast human horde will not be content even with comfort and security. They will finally demand the ant-heap of personal

---

[8] John Meyendorff, *Byzantine Theology: Historical Trends and Doctrinal Themes* (New York NY: Fordham UP, 1983), p. 76.
[9] Vladimir Lossky, *The Mystical Theology of the Eastern Church* (Crestwood NY: St. Vladimir's Seminary, 1976), pp. 125, 144.

oblivion, in order that they might be relieved of their freedom. They want only to live in childish self-indulgence:

> Freedom, free reason, and science will lead them into such a maze, and confront them with such . . . insoluble mysteries, that some of them, unruly and ferocious, will exterminate themselves; others, unruly but feeble, will exterminate each other; and the remaining third, feeble and wretched, will crawl to our feet and cry out to us: "Yes, you were right, you alone possess his mystery, and we are coming back to you—save us from ourselves" . . . . Yes, we will make them work, but in the hours free from labor we will arrange their lives like a children's game, with children's songs, choruses, and innocent dancing. (258-59)

Inverting the Gospel entirely, the Grand Inquisitor declares that only the Master Managers like himself will suffer.[10] Yet these new secular christs of the omnicompetent state shall bear their torment heroically. Knowing their totalitarian paternalism to be a gargantuan lie, they nonetheless retain the courage to feed it to the gullible millions: "For only we, we who keep the mystery, only we shall be unhappy. There will be thousands of millions of happy babes, and a hundred thousand sufferers who have taken upon themselves the curse of the knowledge of good and evil. Peacefully [these multiplied millions] will die; peacefully will they expire in [Christ's] name, and beyond the grave they will find only death. But we will keep the secret, and for their own happiness we will entice them with a heavenly and eternal reward" (259).

This final prophecy of the Grand Inquisitor is perhaps the most frightening augury in the entirety of Dostoevsky's work. With amazing prescience, he foresaw the rise of the totalitarian state that has dominated much of late-modern life, killing more people by violent means than in all of the previous ages combined. This is the era of blood and ours is the culture of death. That Dostoevsky mistakenly linked our late-modern calamity with the Catholic Church, and that he did not foresee its first triumph in his own beloved Russia, hardly invalidates his vision. On the contrary, Dostoevsky was right to prophesy that, if we begin (as Ivan does) with absolute anti-communal freedom, we will end

---

10 The Conditioners is the name that, in *The Abolition of Man*, C. S. Lewis gives to these *Übermenschen* who, having mastered the natural world, now manage the human realm as well.

(again as Ivan does) with absolutely anti-communal slavery, whether in its individualist or its totalitarian form. Were Dostoevsky living at this hour, he might well ask whether the American reduction of nearly every aspect of human existence, including religion itself, to either entertainment or commodification constitutes a yet worse herd-existence than the one Ivan describes—a subtler and therefore deadlier attempt to relieve humanity of its suffering and sin, and thus of its real character and interest.

Given Ivan's horrifying vision of this grim and Christless future, it is not surprising that Alyosha regards Ivan's "poem" as praising Jesus rather than reviling him. Yet Alyosha does not commend the Christ of the parable because he commands autonomous self-determination as the answer to a totalizing politics of oppression. Rather is the Jesus of Ivan's parable to be praised because his silence indicates his patient confidence that evil will eventually undo itself, and that Ivan is to be embraced rather than condemned in his concern for the suffering of innocents. In fact, Ivan ended his parable by having the silent Savior gently kiss the Inquisitor on "his bloodless, ninety-year-old lips" (345). Alyosha confirms the rightness of Christ's act by repeating it: he kisses his tormented brother. It's another Russian iconic gesture of humility and submission, and it calls for an iconic response—namely, a recompensing kiss wherein Ivan would offer his own act of humble recognition and identification. Ivan will not grant it, of course, for thus would he have embraced the same kenotic suffering and joy that imbue Alyosha's entire life. Instead, Ivan dismisses Alyosha's act as mere plagiarism. Ivan must rid himself of this Christ-like gesture that is the real answer to suffering. It is appropriate, therefore, that the Inquisitor's final command to the truth-gesturing Christ who would have kissed him is not *Maranatha*, but "Go and do not come again . . . do not come at all . . . never, never!" (262).

Alyosha, as Christ's earthly embodiment, will not depart. Instead, he confronts Ivan with the moral and religious consequence of his atheism. If God is dead, Alyosha declares, "everything is permitted" (263). We must not misread Alyosha here. He does not deny that men can be moral without believing in God. He insists, instead, that such morality has no ultimate basis, that merely human freedom is finally self-destructive, that it hovers over an abyss of nihilism, and thus that all godless peoples and cultures await their inexorable plunge into the barbaric void. I John 3:4 defines sin precisely as lawlessness: *hé hamartia estin hé anomia.* Ellis Sandoz observes that John of Damascus, the 8th century Greek theologian, linked this definition of sin to the larger claim that barbarism is the primal heresy: "every man as independent and a law unto himself after the dictates of his own will."[11]

Dostoevsky regards individualist autonomy not only as barbaric but also as satanic. Perhaps the chief of Ivan's demonic deceptions is the widespread acceptance of the Inquisitor's argument that "miracle, mystery, and authority" are pathetic necessities for weak-willed men. Yet just as Ivan misreads freedom to mean unencumbered autonomy, so does the Inquisitor pervert the meaning of miracle, mystery, and authority. Nowhere in the novel does God perform miracles by jumping in and out of his creation like a divine factotum who accedes to human petition if it is sufficiently pious. It is exactly such a sentimental and superstitious understanding of miracles—namely, as God's arbitrary violation of the natural order to heed clamant human request—which Alyosha is required to *surrender*. Hoping that Zosima's corpse would be wondrously preserved, giving off the sweet odor of sanctity, Alyosha is horrified when it putrefies prematurely. The saint's rapidly rotting body demonstrates to Alyosha that God is not a sacred Santa Claus who brings him whatever he wants. In the "Cana in Galilee" chapter, Alyosha learns that miracles do not *precede* and thus produce faith; rather do they *follow* faith as the by-product of the transformed life. That Alyosha can kiss the earth and bless the creation despite its rampant suffering, that he can live as a monk in an sex-sodden world, that he can increase men's joy amidst human misery as Christ increased it by turning water into wedding wine—this, he learns, is the true miracle: the divine possibility that overcomes human impossibility.

Like a brittle Enlightenment *philosophe*, perhaps a Diderot or a Comte, the Inquisitor also slanders mystery. He reduces it to a cynical mystification, to a new secular priestcraft, a political anesthetizing of the masses with the morphine of heaven. "For only we, we . . . keep the mystery," he boasts. For him, mystery can be hoarded as a weapon in his arsenal of deceit, as a spiritual poison-gas meant to blind true vision and stifle true thought. For Alyosha and all other believers, by contrast, the *mysterion*

---

[11] Sandoz, 215. Sandoz also notes that, in ancient Russian folk legend, Christ kisses Judas in response to the betrayer's own kiss.

enlivens such vision and thought. It is a word that can also be translated *sacrament*. The mystery of God is not therefore a riddle or a conundrum, not a brain-straining puzzle; it is the one reality that prompts an endless delectation of mind no less than heart and soul. "In the proper religious sense of the term," writes Orthodox bishop Kallistos Ware, "'mystery' signifies not only hiddenness but disclosure . . . . A mystery is . . . something *revealed* for our understanding, but which we never understand *exhaustively* because it leads into the depth or the darkness of God."[12]

Perversely if also consistently, Ivan has the Inquisitor voice a skewed understanding of authority. He regards it as the tyrannical power of the state or the church to suppresses individual autonomy. For him, authority can have only the negative meaning of raw coercive force. For Alyosha, again in notable contrast to the Inquisitor, rightful authority (both human and divine) invites free submission of the will for the sake of the good—submission to the rightly constituted state, to his elder Zosima, to the incarnate Christ, to the merciful God. Free subjection of the will begins in penitence, as when Zosima confesses that all men are sinners and that he is the worst. It ends in the acceptance, even the embrace, of suffering.

Perhaps the novel's chief irony is that Ivan has turned rightful religious concern for injured innocents into wrongful personal justification of his own hatred and scorn. Claiming to care about the world's innocent sufferers, Ivan cannot care for the creature who is his own closest kin, his father. In a nightmare interview with the Devil, Ivan is made to recognize his own moral culpability for his father's death. He had poisoned Smerdyakov's mind with the demonic gospel that God is dead and that all things are permitted. Acting out what Ivan had intellectually advocated, Smerdyakov has killed old Fyodor in a dreadful demonstration that, in a godless world, absolutely nothing is forbidden. Since Satan is the primal Deceiver, it is no wonder that Ivan has been made into his agent. Far from being harmless intellectual exercises, Dostoevsky maintains that demonic perversions of mind issue in demonic perversions of will. Philosophical deicide results in existential parricide. The mental killing of God breaks the deepest of human bonds. It is thus fitting that Ivan the perverted

---

[12] Kallistos Ware, *The Orthodox Way*, rev. ed. (Crestwood NY: St. Vladimir's Seminary, 1995), p. 5.

intellectual should end in madness.

Yet Ivan's final insanity is not to be explained as psychosis alone. In the Orthodox tradition, to deny the presence and reality of God is to be subject to a psychopathic condition. Not sharing the western doctrine of original sin, the Orthodox hold that every person retains efficacious awareness of God, even after the Fall. "Just because it is light," writes Vladimir Lossky, "grace, the source of revelation, cannot remain within us unperceived. We are incapable of not being aware of God, if our nature is in proper spiritual health. Insensibility [to God] in the inner life is an abnormal condition." Lossky adds, far more darkly, that total unawareness of God "would be nothing other than hell, the final destruction of the person."[13] It follows that Zosima is not a golden-hearted humanist when he defines Hell as "the suffering of being unable to love." He is describing Ivan's spiritual condition exactly. Ivan suffers the hellish laceration of the soul that occurs when freedom is exercised negatively—not to engender life but to bring death. "Death for a person," declares Orthodox theologian John Zizioulas, "means ceasing to love and to be loved, ceasing to be unique and unrepeatable, whereas life for the person means the survival of the uniqueness of its hypostasis [personification], which is affirmed and maintained by love."[14]

To possess true personhood through love is, in Dostoevsky's view, to suffer rightly. It is to accept responsibility, not only for one's own sin, but also for the sins of others. All theodicies fail if they do not recognize that only the embrace of innocent suffering can answer the infliction of innocent suffering. One who is willing to suffer must be willing, moreover, to suffer fools. Father Zosima exhibits such foolish suffering when, early in the novel, he makes a low bow of humility before the cruel buffoon who is old Fyodor Karamazov. It's an act utterly unlike the abstentions practiced by Nietzsche's *Übermensch*. The Overman is akin to a lion that has claws but refrains from using them. He doesn't show mercy, therefore, so much as he seeks to humiliate the weaklings of the world with his contemptuous self-restraint. Though having the rightful authority to condemn the despicable old lecher, Zosima gestures forth his solidarity with Fyodor in bowing down before him. Unlike Nietzsche's Overman, Zosima identifies himself with the wretched creature. He knows that old

---

[13] Lossky, pp. 225, 217.
[14] John Zizioulas, *Being as Communion: Studies in Personhood and the Church* (Crestwood NY: St. Vladimir's Seminary, 1985), p. 49.

Fyodor has become a buffoon, in large part, because everyone regards him as a fool. In secret pride and contempt for them, he fulfills their scornful judgment. Zosima refuses such judgment. He humbles himself before the despicable Fyodor, discerning in him the divine image and likeness: a person who is meant for agapeistic community rather than buffoonish autonomy. For Dostoevsky, the gospel of suffering in communal love is the only lasting answer to the perennial problem of evil and thus to the perennial question of human personhood. It is a gospel peculiar neither to east nor west because it centered in the common Christian ground of the Incarnation and Cross and Resurrection.

# The Influence of John Macmurray: A Philosophical Foundation of Object Relations Psychology

*Trevor M. Dobbs*
Pacific Oaks College

> In the work of psychoanalysis links are formed with numbers of other mental sciences, the investigation of which promises results of the greatest value: links with mythology and philology, with folklore, with social psychology and the theory of religion.
>
> Sigmund Freud, *Introductory Lectures on Psychoanalysis.*

## The Place of the Personal in Psychoanalysis

The stereotype of psychoanalysis in America is probably best represented by the images courtesy of Woody Allen: the detached doctor who silently listened to Allen pontificate about his childhood as he lay on the couch. Perhaps most unfortunate is that this picture of psychoanalysis *has* been characteristic of the American tradition.

A significant development within the Independent Tradition of British Object Relations theory in psychoanalysis has been a derivative of the "personal object relations" between Harry S. Guntrip and his mentors.[1] Guntrip's elaboration of this tradition in psychology reflects his respective relationships with his psychoanalytic mentors, Ronald Fairbairn and Donald Winnicott, along with the "Persons in Relation" theological philosophy of John Macmurray as his unifying point of reference.

Guntrip was a champion of the *Personal* in psychoanalysis. His legacy is seen in the naming of his collected papers by his

---

[1] Trevor M. Dobbs, *The Psychoanalytic Psychology and Philosophical Theology of Harry S. Guntrip* (unpublished dissertation: Newport Psychoanalytic Institute, 1998).

protégé, Hazell, as *Personal Relations Therapy*,[2] a more humanized version of the traditional "object relations" language. Guntrip himself was a protégé of John Macmurray, professor of Moral Philosophy at London University and later at Edinburgh University. Volume II of Macmurray's Gifford lectures of 1954, *Persons in Relation*, is the capstone of three decades of writing that I will show is the principal influence in molding Guntrip's theological-philosophical thinking. Guntrip traces his own development in stating,

> I found my earlier studies in religion and philosophy were by no means irrelevant. I had been thoroughly trained in a "personal relations" school of thought, not only in theology but in the philosophy of Professor J. Macmurray. Such books as J. Oman's *Grace and Personality*, Martin Buber's *I and Thou* and J. Macmurray's *Interpreting the Universe, The Boundaries of Science* and *Reason and Emotion* had left too deep a mark for me to be able to approach the study of man in any other way than as a "Person."[3]

Guntrip did not approach integration of these influences in his life as a harmonizing of disciplines, which he would have called "an artificial attempt to 'fit them together.'" His *personal* journey led him to his consulting room with patients, where for many years he was in the process of working out this blending of his theology, philosophy, and psychology of the person. Within the intimacy of the encounters with his patients, and in the form of "the natural emergence of a fully psychodynamic theory of personality within psychoanalysis," he digested and metabolized these various aspects of the human person.[4]

*Macmurrary's Influence on Guntrip's Thinking*

Guntrip, in his doctoral dissertation (later published as *Personality Structure and Human Interaction*), traces the development of psychoanalytical theory as "an unconscious

---

[2] Jeremy Hazel, ed., *Personal Relations Therapy: The Collected Papers of H. S. Guntrip* (Northvale, NJ: Aronson, 1994).
[3] Harry S. Guntrip, *Personality Structure And Human Interaction* (New York: International Universities Press, 1961), 19.
[4] Ibid.

pattern of development of a dialectical type."[5]   "The original *European psychobiology* of Freud" is presented as this Hegelian *Thesis*: the classic psychoanalytical teaching. He then presents the *psychosociology* in America, including Horney, Fromm, and H. S. Sullivan as the *Antithesis* to the classical stance. Guntrip's *Synthesis* is his British object relational orientation that "comes to correlate the internal and the external object-relationships in which the personality is involved" (*emphasis* in the original).[6] This approach is a way to interrelate the internal, intrapsychic Freudian emphasis with the external, interpersonal one of the American schools.

Guntrip's first mentor in his journey down the path of his theoretical development was John Macmurray, Professor of Moral Philosophy during Guntrip's days at University College at London University. The object relational themes within Macmurray's philosophical teaching were to have a profound influence on Guntrip.

Harry Guntrip cited John Macmurray as the philosopher who had "thoroughly" trained him in the "personal relations" school of thought. Professor of Moral Philosophy at University College in London in the 1930s, and eventually at the University of Edinburgh in Scotland by the 1950s, Macmurray's teaching and writings in the 1930s came to provide Guntrip with a transitional space between what he referred to as his traditional, conservative Salvation Army heritage, and the liberal modern theology of the twentieth century, both of which Guntrip found wanting. Macmurray was addressing the philosophical development of the twentieth century western mind, with a particular focus on the respective characters of science and religion, and the relationship between the two. This he set out in a rather technical way in his *Interpreting the Universe* (1933)[7] and in a much more compelling fashion in his book published in 1935, *Reason and Emotion*.[8]   A summary of his basic arguments from this latter work will lay out his principal philosophical viewpoint that shaped Guntrip's own thought and worldview.

---

[5] Ibid. 50.
[6] Ibid. 51.
[7] John Macmurray, *Interpreting the Universe* (New York: Humanities Press, 1933).
[8] John Macmurray, *Reason and Emotion* (London: Faber and Faber, 1935).

In a series of what were originally lectures, Macmurray lays out his philosophical metapsychology under the rubric of "Reason in the Emotional Life, I, II, and III," followed by what would be considered his theory of technique, "Education of the Emotions." In the latter part of the book he takes up directly the topic of what we might call "religion and its vicissitudes," as he develops his theological philosophy that would so strongly influenced Guntrip. He explores the nature and meaning of religion through its various comparisons with science, reason, reality, and his view of its maturity in contrast to the religious "superstition" so commonly practiced.

*Reason in the Emotional Life*

Macmurray begins with a critique of the individualism and egocentrism of the dominant intellectualized culture, positing that "we are all enmeshed in that network of relation that binds us together to make up human society," like it or not.[9] He goes on to develop this theme that Winnicott would echo in his musing that "there is no such thing as a baby without a mother." Macmurray's version is that "we have no existence and no significance merely in ourselves."[10]

"What is emotional reason?" Macmurray asks. It is that which has been dissociated from the popular notion of reason as "thinking and planning, scheming and calculating," losing its connection to "music and laughter and love."[11]

> We associate reason with *a state of mind which is cold, detached and unemotional.* When our emotions are stirred we feel that reason is left behind and we enter another world—more colourful, more full of warmth and delight, but also more *dangerous.* If we become *ego-centric,* if we forget that we are parts of one small part of the development of human life, *we shall be apt to imagine* that this has always been so and always must be so; that reason is just thinking; that emotion is just feeling; and that these two aspects of our life are in the eternal nature of things distinct and opposite; *very apt to come into conflict and requiring to be kept sternly apart.* We shall be in danger of

---

[9] Ibid. 14.
[10] Ibid. 15.
[11] Ibid.

slipping back into a way of thinking from which we had begun to emerge; of thinking that emotion belongs to the animal nature in us, and reason to the divine; that our emotions are unruly and fleshly, the source of evil and disaster, while reason belongs to the divine essence of the thinking mind which raises us above the level of the brutes into communion with the eternal (emphasis added).[12]

What was it that captured Guntrip's interest that he would identify Macmurray as playing such a central role in the development of his own thinking? Macmurray's style of writing is one which Guntrip himself would eventually emulate: a colorful and engaging prose that artfully communicates concepts that are normally discussed with abstract and mind-numbing technical language in their respective fields, philosophy and psychoanalysis. Yet I would offer that the stronger appeal was very personal as Macmurray essentially describes the schizoid landscape of western culture that Guntrip wrestled with as his own psychological self-experience. Guntrip, I believe, found in Macmurray the hope of transcending the qualities of *the cold, detached and unemotional* schizoid adaptation: the *egocentrism* of the withdrawn ego that engages in the use of the splitting of the ego to manage the internal conflict between good and bad objects by *keeping them sternly apart*. What Guntrip would later jointly pursue with Fairbairn in the remaking of Freudian metapsychology was the redemption of the emotional "id" experience as *unruly* and portending *disaster* to that of a hungering after attachment to the object that was the experience of meaningful aliveness.

Macmurray continues his own treatise that would foreshadow Guntrip. He describes reason "in general" (both the intellectual and emotional dynamics), as that which differentiates humans from the rest of organic life, as reflected in the common notions of speech, the invention and use of tools, and the organization of social life. "Behind all these there lies the capacity to make a choice of purposes and to discover and apply the means of realizing our chosen ends."[13] Here he foreshadows his volume I of the Gifford Lectures in *The Self as Agent*,[14] which challenges the Cartesian "thinking 'I'" as intellectualized and narcissistic.

---

[12] Ibid. 16.
[13] Ibid. 18.
[14] John Macmurrary, *The Self as Agent* (New York: Harper & Brothers, 1953).

"Against the assumption that the Self is an isolated individual, I have set the view that the Self is a *person,* and that personal existence is *constituted* by the relation of persons."[15] The "capacity to make a choice" has the ring of existentialism to it, yet Macmurray will hold out for the language of the "practical." He sums up this enterprise of the 1950s, read by Guntrip, in his introduction: "All meaningful knowledge is for the sake of action, and all meaningful action for the sake of friendship."[16] This line, penned two decades after *Reason and Emotion,* is a distillation of his earlier writings. Yet, let us continue with our exposition of the latter as it coincides with Guntrip's seminal development.

In his complementary fashion, Macmurray cites science, art, and religion as the central expressions of reason in man, with science reflecting its intellectual nature and art and religion that of the emotional. Here he develops what is essentially his philosophical basis for object relations. "Reason is the capacity to behave in terms of the nature of the object, that is to say, objectively. Reason is thus our capacity for objectivity."[17] Macmurray critiques the one-person psychology that looks for "something in the inner constitution of the human being to explain the peculiar nature of his behavior."[18] He defines reason as the capacity to behave in terms of knowledge of the outside world, rather than merely as a reflex of one's own. Science, as that which gathers data about the object, reflects the intellectual side of the coin of reason. Yet science itself has its own form of countertransference, the "desire to retain beliefs to which we are emotionally attached to for some reason or other. It is the tendency to make the wish father to the thought. Science itself, therefore, is emotionally conditioned."[19] Macmurray essentially describes the projective process "where we colour the world with our own illusions," to which the intellectual enterprise is as susceptible as the emotional.[20] Thinking is as subjective as feeling. In gaining knowledge of the outside world, of the nature of the object, the painful process of *disillusionment* applies to thinking as well as feeling. The central problem is that of the tendency toward

---

[15] Ibid. 12.
[16] Ibid. 15.
[17] John Macmurray, *Reason and Emotion* (London: Faber and Faber, 1935), 19.
[18] Ibid. 20.
[19] Ibid. 21.
[20] Ibid. 22.

egocentrism, which prefers the illusion of self-sufficiency over the painful awareness of one's need for connectedness to the outside world. Again, this echoes the schizoid dilemma of a desire for connection and the fear of engaging in it. Fairbairn would later take the dependency of the infantile state, and rather than make it something to be outgrown, dependency becomes that which one matures into, an echo of Macmurray's basic premise.

Macmurray goes on to develop this parallelism between thought and feeling as both striving toward an objectivity that allows one to behave in light of the nature of the object. It is interesting that during this same decade Heinz Hartmann was developing his own version of this theme of *adaptation to the environment* yet in the rationalistic manner to which Guntrip would take such exception for many years. What would be the difference? Macmurray makes the process of observation of the outside world, the external object, one based on action, whose motives are ultimately emotional. He cites that he follows Plato in his *Republic* and *Philebus*, that not only thoughts but also feelings could be true or false. It is a false dichotomy that thoughts are *rational* and that feelings are *irrational*, secondary and subordinate to cognitions. Macmurray ultimately takes a stance of embodiment toward the nature of reason. "For if reason is the capacity to *act* in terms of the nature of the object, it is emotion which stands directly behind activity determining its substance and direction, while thought is related to action indirectly and through emotion, determining only its form, and that only partially."[21] Thought ultimately becomes a form of reflection on the existential act that arises from one's (e)motives.

Macmurray turns to the issue of psychoanalysis directly, citing its contribution in revealing the extent to which our emotional life is unconscious. He takes a rather Winnicottian tack at this point, noting that "psychoanalysis has only extended and developed a knowledge which we all possess."[22] In the same way that Winnicott saw that all mothers knew intuitively what it meant to hold and care for their child,[23] Macmurray presents this same sort of intuitive approach toward the functioning of the emotional life. Bringing this intuitive, emotional world into awareness is the daunting task undertaken by psychoanalysis, but common to all

---

[21] Ibid. 26.
[22] Ibid. 27.
[23] D. Winnicott, *Babies and Their Mothers* (Reading, PA: Addison-Wesley, 1987).

for emotional development to occur. He draws out his thread of *egocentrism* as the confounding variable to development, which affects both thinking and feeling. This essentially is the narcissism of the *paranoid-schizoid* position of British Object Relations, where one *assimilates* one's experience of the outside world and reshapes it to fit one's internal world. Here the nature of the outside object is distorted to spare one the pain of the *disillusionment* of realizing where it is different from one's internal object representation. "The real problem of the development of emotional reason is to shift the center of feeling from the self to the world outside. We can only begin to grow up into rationality when we begin to see our own emotional life not as the center of things but as part of the development of humanity."[24] The process of emotional development is that of *accommodating* our current model of the world to the nature of the outside object in order to act toward it based upon its actual nature, rather than our projection upon it. Macmurray is essentially describing the development of the capacity for empathy, which he illustrates as learning to "appreciate" art as expressions of the artist's essential being, rather than evoking some form of aesthetic "pleasure" that narcissistically leaves us in an isolated state. He concludes with making a differentiation between notions of "love" that are essentially experiencing a pleasurable emotion that is stimulated by the other person, and that of "appreciating" the person for who he or she is in their own right. "Is he an instrument for keeping me pleased with myself, or do I feel his existence and his reality to be important in themselves? The difference between these two kinds of love is the ultimate difference between organic and personal life. It is the difference between rational and irrational emotion. The capacity to love objectively is the capacity which makes us persons."[25]

*Education of the Emotional Life*

Macmurray addresses what is essentially the clinical application of his thesis in the context of education. He seems to take a page from what Bion would later call in his book *Learning*

---

[24] John Macmurray, *Reason and Emotion* (London: Faber and Faber, 1935), 30.
[25] Ibid. 32.

*from Experience,*[26] as he uses the organic senses as his schoolhouse for the education of the emotional life. He takes pains to develop the idea of *sensuality* as the perceptual gathering of data from the outside world, much in the same way that Carl Jung described it in his *Psychological Types.*[27] Jung's category of *perception* entails the dominant use of one or other side of a psychological polarity, apprehending the (external) object world with either *Intuition* or *Sensing*. Intuition is the perceptual process of apprehending the "bigger picture" through mental mapping, while Sensing is the perceptual process of ascertaining "facts" through sensory input.[28] Ironically, Macmurray earlier described a rather intuitive process of apprehending the emotional life in general, yet his methodology is patently empirical. On the one hand he substitutes the word *sensibility* for *sensuality* in order specifically to avoid the popular shameful connotations of the latter, but his choice of *sensibility* seems to me to reflect his integrative style of thinking where *sensing* takes on a rather *intuitive* character. Here again I see the appeal to a Guntrip whose interest in integration of polarities would resonate with Macmurray.

Macmurray notes that the normal sensibility of Europeans is "under-developed and irrational because of the way we have treated it," that is, the egocentric focus on satisfaction of the senses, rather than using the senses as "the avenues along which we move into contact with the world around us."[29] He champions sense-life as the fundamental source to fullness and richness in life, providing "the material out of which the inner life is built."[30] Here the object relations theme of Guntrip's use of both Fairbairn and Winnicott stand out in bold relief. Guntrip's basic stance that all psychological roads lead to schizoid phenomena and the earliest oral experiences of "swallowing" up life can be seen in Macmurray's version of the introjection process. That the human is primarily object-seeking rather than pleasure-seeking is central

---

[26] Wilfred Bion, *Learning From Experience* (London: Heinemann, 1962; Karnac, 1984).

[27] C. G. Jung, *Psychological Types* (*The Collected Works of C.G. Jung,* Vol. 6), trans. R. F. C. Hull (Princeton: Princeton University Press, 1971). (Original work published 1921).

[28] Kiersey & Bates, *Please Understand Me* (Corona Del Mar: Prometheus, 1978).

[29] Macmurray, *Reason and Emotion,* 39.

[30] Ibid. 40.

to Macmurray's whole enterprise. The sensual experience of the infant with the mother was even better illustrated through Winnicott's descriptions as his development of the idea of "body ego" echoes Macmurray's sensibilities. Indeed, Macmurray waxes very "Winnicottian" in his own language as he develops this theme. Rather than employing utilitarian motives of applying "awareness" of the world for purposeful striving, Macmurray argues for sense awareness "for the sake of awareness itself," in order to "use them in a different and fuller way."

> We look at things not because we want to use them but because we want to see them. We touch things because we want to feel them. Sensitive awareness becomes then a life in itself with an intrinsic value of its own which we maintain and develop for its own sake, because it is a way of living, perhaps the essence of all living. When we use our senses in this way, we come alive in them, as it were, and this opens up a whole new world of possibility. We see and hear and feel things that we never noticed before, and find ourselves taking delight in their existence. We find ourselves living in our senses for love's sake, because the essence of love lies in this . . . You don't want merely to know about the object; often you don't want to know about it at all. What you do want is to know *it*. Intellectual knowledge tells us about the world. It gives us knowledge *about* things, not knowledge *of* them. It does not reveal the world as it is. Only emotional knowledge can do that.[31]

The complement to the immediacy of sensuous perception is that of spontaneous expression, "activities which are spontaneities of emotion, activities which are performed for their own sake, and not for any end beyond them."[32] These are words that Winnicott could have written himself. In his own turn of phrase, Winnicott coins the term "spontaneous gesture" of the infant and essentially of the person as that which expressed one's "true self." This seems very reminiscent of Macmurray's view of emotional life and the sensual apparatus through which such aliveness emanates.

Macmurray also offers a theological illustration of his treatise on the "sense-life" in a New Testament quotation. "'I am

---

[31] Ibid. 42-43.
[32] Ibid. 73.

come,' said Jesus, 'that they might have life, and that they might have it more abundantly.' The abundance of our life depends primarily on the abundance of our sensuous experience of the world around us. If we are to be full of life and fully alive, it is the increase in our capacity to be aware of the world through our senses which has first to be achieved."[33] This sounds rather similar to the words that Fairbairn wrote in his diary entry during his college days, his own lobbying for a "full blooded Christianity." We shall now turn to Macmurray's specific description of "religion" and how it reflects the emotional rationality of humans.

*Science and Religion*

"For centuries, until relatively recent time, the pride and prejudice of religion tyrannized over the minds and consciences and even the bodies of men." So begins Macmurray's treatment of religion. He goes on to chronicle essentially the development of what he calls "religious imperialism, under the pseudonym of Christianity."[34] He describes the tradition of Jesus as having flowed into the vast organization of the Roman empire, mixed with Stoicism, and ultimately adopting the Roman tradition of empire in pursuing "universal domination over the spirit of civilized humanity."[35] The medieval spirit was the culmination of suppression of personal freedom, whose limits were reached in the Renaissance and Reformation. "The rediscovery of the art of Greece awakened the medieval spirit to the artistic spontaneity of the Renaissance, which in turn led to the rediscovery of the religious spontaneity of Jesus in the Reformation."[36] The "vast tissue of prejudice" that was Christianity was set on a course of disintegration, with the "continuous disruption of Protestantism into sectarian fragments" burning up like a meteor on reentry to the atmosphere of the earth. Macmurray cites science as the one creative achievement of the Reformation, "the one proper, positive expression of Christianity that the world has yet seen. The rest of modern culture—its art, morality, and religion—is simply the disrupted remnants of the pseudo-Christianity of the Medieval world. That is why the newly awakened pagan world clutches at

---

33 Ibid. 40.
34 Ibid. 171.
35 Ibid.
36 Ibid. 172.

our science while scorning our culture."[37] He describes an ongoing competition between the Roman and Protestant camps as the aftermath of the disruptive force of the Reformation, each competing for the re-establishment of the old autocracy. Control over the "inner springs of human life" was the "nut" over which the two sides have battled, with science, as the Reformation's child, being neglected by both. " . . . [W]hen science, come of age, entered upon the stage as arbiter of the dispute, it was only to crack the nut, give either party half of the shell and keep the kernel for himself."[38] Macmurray further illustrates his disgust for authoritarian structures in describing the religious system's attempt at rigid control over philosophy and science, and describes its ultimate demise and arrival at a form of impotence, the turning point being the loss of the battle over evolution, religion's "Waterloo" as it were. By the end of the nineteenth century, science was supreme, triumphing over the jealousy, fear, and superstition bred by medieval religion. "But it is difficult to fight an enemy who uses such underground methods without learning to use them oneself."[39] In the same way that Anna Freud was to describe the child who is abused as one who will "identify with the aggressor" as part of its survival, the same is said to have happened to this child of the Reformation.

> In the hour of its triumph science has become as full of pride and prejudice as ever religion was . . . There is nothing like pride for blinding us to our own limitations, driving us to assert as truth what is only our own speculative opinion . . . Modern science is very liable to superstition, and tends to breed superstition in its devotees. The visionary dream of the medieval church of a universal empire over the hearts of mankind, purified by obedience and submission, was not so madly irrational as the modern dream of a world made peaceful and happy by obedience to the dictates of scientific thought."[40]

Macmurray gives a number of examples of this parallelism between science and religion, citing "pride and prejudice" as the ultimate culprits and the "parents of superstition." Macmurray's

---

[37] Ibid.
[38] Ibid. 173.
[39] Ibid. 174.
[40] Ibid. 174-175.

theme of *narcissism* seems to be the unifying one here, differentiating both science and religion in essence from their popular manifestations as authoritarian institutions. Macmurray fits so very well with the spirit of the *Independent* tradition in England.

His discussion echoes the one between Sigmund Freud and his friend the pastor, Oscar Pfister, where Freud critiqued "religion" as simple obsessional neurosis in *The Future of An Illusion*.[41] Pfister's friendly rejoinder in *The Illusion of the Future* presented essentially the same counterpoint as Macmurray, that faith in technology and science, even psychoanalytic science, as promising a brighter future was a neurotic illusion about the nature of being human. Macmurray's ultimate goal is to root out the superstition that he has already defined as irrational egocentrism. "Superstition is not religion because it masquerades in the cloak of religion; neither is it science because it masks itself in scientific terminology."[42]

Macmurray rejects a harmonization between science and religion by assigning them to separate spheres. "Science and religion are not logical definitions. They are forces in the world of men, and in the minds of men. The struggle between science and religion goes on in us, and it is a real struggle, a dramatic struggle, often a tragic struggle. . . . It is a deep seated *schism* in the personal life of every intelligent modern man who wishes to be honest and sincere with himself."[43] He goes on at length in describing the tension between the two, where choosing one over the other is another example of "pride and prejudice," and to want to look at problems from both sides merely restates the problem and does not solve it. "It is as difficult a problem as the combination of the Wave theory of light with the Quantum theory of energy."[44] Here Macmurray cites the classic paradox of the twentieth century where two "truths" of a common phenomenon cannot be reduced down to a common denominator or synthesis, an irreconcilable polarity of the modern world. Ironically as one who has philosophically championed Plato to a degree, Macmurray opposes the common neo-Platonist dualism so characteristic of western culture that separates the "spiritual" and

---

[41] In W. W. Meissner, *Psychoanalysis and Religious Experience* (New Haven: Yale University Press, 1984).
[42] Macmurray, *Reason and Emotion*, 176.
[43] Ibid. 177-178.
[44] Ibid. 179.

the "material." "Both meet in the mind of man, and demand to be related. . . . Science and religion are not concerned with two different worlds but with one and the same world—the only world there is."[45] His ultimate common denominator for the two is to see them both as truth-seekers. "All honest religion necessarily involves a strenuous effort to know the supreme reality, and the knowledge of God must involve all knowledge in its scope."[46]

Macmurray applies a form of analysis, breaking down condensations into elemental parts, a form of theological form criticism: finding the "nut" within the "shell." His goal is to compare "essential religion" with "essential science." On the one hand, he sees science ultimately as "fragmentary," a collection of specializations whose methodology is to "analyze and classify" in abstract terms in order to identify general laws. On the other hand, religion is unitary or one (like philosophy), seeking an at-one-ment with one God, through a methodology of the "concrete" that examines the wholeness of the individual, and is meant to be "always personal."[47]   Of particular note is the relationship to reality itself.

> Science, though it may know everything in general, can know nothing in particular, and reality is always something in particular. It follows that science is not knowledge of reality. Is that startling? It is a commonplace of much philosophy, from Plato to the present day. . . . Science is descriptive, not explanatory. . . .   Knowledge is by definition the apprehension of the real—not the description of it. . . . I do not say that it is not cognition, but simply that it is not knowledge in the full sense. For example, you cannot know anybody, your father or your friend, by science.[48]

For Macmurray, knowledge is ultimately *personal* and must apprehend far more than the data of organic existence, but must embrace all that goes into making up a *person*, which ultimately involves that which is *unseen,* that which technically speaking is *spiritual* (the Greek word for spirit, *pneuma,* literally means "wind" or "air"). The classic theological illustration of this

45 Ibid. 180.
46 Ibid. 183.
47 Ibid. 185-186.
48 Ibid. 187-188.

personal knowledge is the Hebrew rendering from Genesis that "Adam *knew* (*yada*) his wife," and she conceived. Macmurray's concept of *knowing* is intimate and personal, and therefore requires the *religious viewpoint* as he defines it.

## Reason and Religion

Macmurray continues his development of his object relations philosophy. Religion is one of the three general expressions of rationality, along with art and science, where rationality is defined as "objective consciousness" through the perceptive methodology of sensory apprehension as delineated above. This is only possible, he writes, "in beings who stand in conscious relationship to objects which they know and which are not themselves."[49] Macmurray essentially presupposes a developmental level that reflects at least a basic self-other differentiation, what Winnicott would later call "the first Not-Me possession" of the external object. He describes three general fields or types of external objects: "material objects, living creatures, or persons like ourselves."[50] These correspond to his threefold expression of rationality. "Science grows out of our rationality in relation to material things. Art grows out of our relation to living beings. Religion grows out of our relation to persons."[51] Religious institutions and beliefs in themselves may be required to be swept away in the interest of religion itself that is inherent in the human situation. He sees religion as the fuller expression of rationality as it subsumes all three of the fields. The relation of a person to a person also includes the relation of a body to a body and of living creature to living creature. This position would follow in light of Macmurray's use of the sensual (body) as the apprehension of the object, and his focus on wholeness requiring a living creature rather than a dissected one. He is careful to point out that he does not mean "more rational," just more inclusive or a "fuller" expression of rationality.

He describes the appropriate use of science: to relate ourselves "properly to matter, and use it as our material and our instrument. Science is the sign that we have learned not to pretend that matter is what we would like it to be, . . . that we have learned that a patient effort to discover its real nature and to deal

---

[49] Ibid. 195.
[50] Ibid.
[51] Ibid. 196.

with it in terms of its real nature will give us power to use it as our instrument. Through science we relate ourselves *really*, as material bodies, to the material world."[52] Art is the medium through which we would relate ourselves to the organic world with "a pressure toward balance and rhythm and harmony, toward functional relationship," a rationality of the instinctual and emotional life.[53]

The religious field of personal relationships has the drive "to achieve equality and fellowship in the relations of persons."[54] Macmurray purposely defines religion without any reference to God. "The idea of God can have no fixed meaning of its own which is not related to our experience of human relationships; and it is the significance of the term to the persons who use it that matters."[55] Macmurray essentially goes on to critique the "God-talk" of society who "has crystallized a conception of God which is false, [where] the professed atheist may be more truly religious than the theist."[56] He invokes Kant as an ally in this endeavor to differentiate "false self" representations of religion from its essential enactment in genuine human interaction. "Kant is a milestone in the development of rational thought, and a giant among the intellectuals; yet he announced his great work as *'destroying reason to make room for faith'*, and dubbed the process of reason *'a dialectic of illusion.'*"[57] Macmurray here summons support for his own attack on "the arid speculations of the rationalists" in favor of the "experimental empiricism" of science, which he touts as "the secret of its own superb rationality."[58] In short, Macmurray ends up with a form of natural religion, where one finds God on the planet rather than looking to the heavens, yet he does not appear to don the apparel of the more popular natural religion of the Enlightenment, which saw God's fingerprints on the structure, and design of the natural order. He seems to relegate that to the scientific and aesthetic realms without disputing their forms of rationality. Macmurray ultimately comes down on the side of a form of *incarnational* thinking, where it is within the particularly human sphere of interactions

---

[52] Ibid. 202-203.
[53] Ibid. 204.
[54] Ibid. 205.
[55] Ibid. 207.
[56] Ibid.
[57] Ibid. 208.
[58] Ibid.

between persons that God shows his face. "In particular the really religious man will define the nature of God, not in terms of analysis of ideas or of transcendental beliefs, but in terms of his empirical knowledge of human relationships. So Jesus is reported to have said: 'He that hath seen me hath seen the Father, and how sayest thou, then, show us the Father.'"[59]

## The Maturity of Religion

The "Maturity of Religion" was a theme of Macmurray's that was to make a significant impact on another member of the British school of psychoanalysis: Neville Symington. In his *Emotion and Spirit: Questioning the Claims of Psychoanalysis and Religion,* Symington gives his own account of the movement of religion from *primitive* to *mature,* taking a rather eastern slant in championing the detachment model of the *Upanishads* as his organizing principle. He describes Macmurray's "natural religion" as a "Socratic religion in the context of our contemporary world."[60] He essentially is referring to the Socrates "we meet in the dialogues of Plato."[61] He sees Socrates as a co-confronter along with the Buddha and Jesus as challengers of primitive religion, which Symington describes as the "projection of the self as agent—the representational self—into the natural world or the imagined natural world."[62] Driven by the Darwinian survival instinct, and paralleled by the Kleinian vision of the *paranoid position* as defined by the same process, he contrasts this with *mature religion,* the anthropological change which is marked by "burying ones dead," characterizing "the birth of the *representational self* . . . [where] a being in its own right has died, not just a fragment of the tribe."[63] Symington reflects the Kleinian-Winnicottian developmental shift from the *paranoid position* to the *depressive position,* or in Winnicott's turn of phrase, developing the *capacity for concern,* where one becomes aware of one's own agency, the power to make an impact on the world, and the capacity to mourn loss rather than fear attack as coming always from the outside. Symington joins Macmurray in

---

[59] Ibid. 210.
[60] Neville Symington, *Emotion and Spirit: Questioning the Claims of Psychoanalysis and Religion* (New York: Harper, 1994), 43.
[61] Ibid. 37.
[62] Ibid. 7.
[63] Ibid. 10.

criticizing "rites, sacrifices and votive offerings," whether Buddhist or Christian, as essentially a primitive religion of placating the gods "out there" from a paranoid developmental stance.[64] Symington's version of mature religion parts company to a degree with Macmurray, however, as his emphasis is on a much more mystical detachment from narcissism, citing that the Christian mystics were "more spiritual men than Jesus," in contrast to Macmurray's patently interpersonal view.[65] Symington sees Macmurray as Socratic in that the "religion of Socrates differs from that of the Buddha and Jesus in that it resulted from a process of reasoning."[66] This would reflect Macmurray's organizing principle of rationality. Symington makes the greatest use of Macmurray in the movement from use of the object for self-gratification, to that of valuing the other to the point of recognizing that the human world has a claim upon us because each of us has a value that demands recognition. Macmurray says,

> The primary fact is that part of the world of common experience for each of us is the rest of us. We are forced to value one another, and the valuation is reciprocal. The recognition that the 'other' has a claim on me is the religious attitude of mind, and the inner signal of this claim is conscience.[67]

"Socrates said this claim is exerted upon me by the good. Macmurray puts this into a modern perspective by stating that the good is in the other, or that the good is immanent in other human beings, and that this has a claim upon my actions," with God symbolizing this claim. Symington prefers the notion of "Ultimate Reality as comprehended in the Upanishads, which is in me as well as the other."[68] This would appear to fit better with the dual intrapsychic *and* interpersonal view of object relations. He then makes his application to psychoanalysis as the field of concern with "that emotional activity of which we are unaware," that which occurs between people as well as "within the frontiers of the self."

---

[64] Ibid. 12.
[65] Ibid. 14.
[66] Ibid. 37.
[67] Quoted in ibid. 43.
[68] Ibid. 44.

Psychoanalysis' aim is to "transform activity which is invisible and destructive into that which is constructive."[69]

In sum, Macmurray facilitated in Guntrip the articulation of a new direction in his pursuit of freedom from the imprisonment within his intellectualized-schizoid, personal world, one that was given theological structure and reinforcement during his days in the Salvation Army. The promise of "aliveness" spoken of by Macmurray was one that he also did not find within the modernist theology of his Congregational ministry training per se, as it also suffered from a different form of Hegelian "imprisonment in the 'I.'" Macmurray's passionate philosophy of personal relations freed up Guntrip "intellectually" to continue his quest of apprehending this aliveness in his own person, which he pursued in his personal therapy with Ronald Fairbairn, and later with Donald Winnicott. This has been a significant aspect of the contribution of the object relations school to psychoanalytic psychology: bringing the personal back into what had become an overly intellectualized tradition.

---

[69] Ibid.

# Discovering a Dynamic Concept of the Person in Object Relations Psychology and Karl Barth's Theology

*Daniel J. Price*
First Presbyterian Church of Eureka, CA

That the continued application of scientific methods breeds a temper of mind unfavourable to the miraculous, may well be the case, but even here there would seem to be some difference among the sciences. Certainly, if we think, not of the miraculous in particular, but of religion in general there is such a difference. Mathematicians, astronomers and physicists are often religious, even mystical; biologists much less often; economists and psychologists very seldom indeed. It is as their subject matter comes nearer to man himself that their anti-religious bias hardens.[1]

The above quotation by C.S. Lewis illustrates the extent to which he possessed powers of observation which were every bit as keen as his power of expression. But allow me to use his quotation to raise a crucial question. Why should it be the case that the closer the sciences get to 'man himself,' the farther they stand from religion? Some seem to not be troubled by the anti-religious bias, for example, of modern psychology. Yet, I find it puzzling. If anyone cares to read the Scriptures carefully, they would not have to read far to see that the God to Whom the Scriptures attest is often described in highly personal categories and metaphors. So personal is the God of the Old and the New Testaments that one might innocently expect to find that just the opposite should be the case. In other words, the nearer science gets to the study of human persons the nearer it approaches God. There is little evidence for such a relation if we go back to Freud and study his instinctual theory of human personality, but could this relation begin to appear if we look at some of the theorists who departed from Freud? I believe so.

---

[1] C.S. Lewis, *God in the Dock* (Grand Rapids: Eerdmans, 1970), p. 135.

## Barth and Object Relations Psychology

The anti-religious bias among the human sciences poses a problem for those who believe both in Christian revelation and the efficacy of the scientific enterprise. Unfortunately, all too little has taken place to change the unhappy impasse which Lewis describes. The tendency for science and religion to differ sharply over what it means to be human continues right to the present day. The problem comes to a head where we discuss the relation between psychology and theology. If we can find between them no common grounds for what it means to be human, then the world of human sciences would remain severely cut off from the discipline of theological anthropology and vice versa. This would perpetuate an unhappy dualism which separates spiritual from physical realities in a manner thoroughly unacceptable to Biblical anthropology. For those who believe in the unitary nature of reality as provided by the Christian doctrine of the incarnation, it is only natural to expect that there would be certain analogies disclosed as the theologian reflects upon revealed truth and the scientist seeks further understanding about the nature of human psychology.[2]

How have we arrived at the place where the scientists who study human beings are more commonly anti-religious than those who study the sun, moon, stars and atom? Could it be that certain philosophical assumptions about the nature of reality clouded the scientific investigations of the human person from the outset? Could it be that certain concepts were aggressively borrowed from physical sciences and applied to human studies without appropriate consideration given to the uniqueness of persons? Could it be that Freud and other early psychoanalytical theorists borrowed concepts from the physical sciences which were themselves being challenged within the physical sciences at the very time Freud and other reductionists were borrowing them? I believe so. In fact, I will argue that it was precisely the bias toward a biologically reductionist understanding of the person which kept Freud and some subsequent psychoanalytical theorists from seeing the essentially relational nature of psychological development. However, Freud's theories were not only adopted; in many cases his successors significantly revised them. In Britain, psychoanalytic theories underwent a profound change as they became Anglicized through the Tavistock Clinic in London,

---

[2] W. Jim Neidhart, "Relational Disclosure: Analogies in Judeo-Christian Theology and Natural Science," 1991, p. 3f. (as yet unpublished to this author's knowledge).

and further north in Edinburgh, Scotland, in the theories of Ronald Fairbairn. On British soil the post-Freudian psychoanalytic theories of 'object relations' were born. In certain strains of post-Freudian object relations psychology the reductionist blinders were removed. No longer could the instinct of sexual attraction be said to explain everything about human behavior.

In this paper I propose that there are some very intriguing analogies which can be found between Karl Barth's theological anthropology and the anthropology of the post-Freudian psychoanalytical school known as 'object relations' psychology. I develop my argument by beginning with the development of Freud's concept of the person.

*I. The Evolution of the Concept of the Person in Psychoanalytic Theory*

*A. Freud's Three Basic Stages*

Freud began his inquiry about the nature of the human person as a scientist with a particularly strong anti-religious bent.[3] He studied in Vienna under Hermann von Helmholtz and Ernst Brücke and was largely positivist and reductionist—greatly influenced by the laws of thermodynamics and exchanges of energy. Helmholtz had provided the mathematical formulation for the law of conservation of energy. Energy equilibrium would thus play an enormous role in all stages of Freud's theories.

So reductionist was Freud's early scientific training that he attempted in 1895, in his "Project for a Scientific Psychology," to reduce all emotional states of human beings to their neurological origins. Freud himself never published the essay. At first Freud was elated with his "Project," but within a few weeks his elation turned sour as he described the Project as "rubbish." Subsequent reflection had taught Freud that the workings of the human mind could not be directly correlated even to so complex and intricate a system as the human nervous system.

Second, if not synapses and neurons, Freud believed that human mental functioning could be explained in terms of instincts. If not biochemistry, then try biology. Here is where

---

[3] Freud was a gifted neurologist who entered the medical profession mostly because there were no research positions open in neurology when he graduated.

Freud found a much more fitting key with which to unlock the human soul. Id, libido, sexual instincts: these were the reality of the human person and would soon reveal their patterns. Sexuality (*eros*), according to Freud, evolved through three distinct phases: oral, anal and genital. He later added the aggressive instinct, or death wish (*thanatos*). But Freud continued to push against the limitations of instinctual psychology—even though instinct provided the very bedrock of his psychological theory. Essentially, Freud asked why we don't act like "a gland" without inhibitions. Rape and murder were rampant in Freud's time as always. Nevertheless, pure and unbridled, the instincts in and of themselves could not explain 'everything.' Ubiquitous as instincts may be, something restrains them. Freud understood much better than the many who followed him (especially his 'pop' audience) that if the instincts were not reined in, civilization could not exist.

Freud gradually came to realize that another reality must be present within the psychology of each individual. Instincts could hardly be expected to monitor themselves, so something must monitor the instincts. Hence, he theorized that the 'self' or ego (*Ich*) provides some sense of control over the instincts. So, 'ego' psychology began to develop. And yet the self was pitted against itself in a powerful manner: wanting to act out impulses which were nevertheless socially unacceptable. Hence Freud named the 'super-ego' as the primary restraining agent, with the ego mediating between the super-ego and the instinctual impulses. Especially important to Freud was the Oedipus complex, with the development of attraction to opposite sex parent and rivalry with the same sex parent.

Condensing Freud's many volumes into a few strokes (a hazardous task at best), one could say that in the first stage of Freud's theoretical reflections neurology was the measuring stick of human behavior (c. 1900), in the second stage biology (c. 1900-1920), and in the third stage psychology (1920-1939). Freud arrived at the third stage by paying an increasing amount of attention to patient's dreams, guilt complexes, sexual-neurotic problems and feelings toward their parents, developing his famous endopsychic structural triad: id, ego and super-Ego.

It is important to note that in this third stage Freud began to stretch his theoretical framework in order to incorporate the importance of interpersonal human relations. Not isolated instincts seeking equilibrium, but real people interacting with others were indispensable to Freud's most developed theory of the person. Childhood relationship to the father was especially important for Freud (esp. c. 4-5 years of age).

## B. Post-Freudian Developments in the Concept of the Person

With Post-Freudian psychoanalytical theorists like Ronald Fairbairn (and later carried on by others such as Heinz Kohut and Donald Winnicott), the idea of attraction being purely instinctual and sexual began to be questioned. Ronald Fairbairn asked: Could it be that interpersonal attraction is really the most compelling force in the human being, and that sexuality is merely one way in which attraction can be expressed?

Fairbairn, while acknowledging the seminal importance of libido theory, proposes that

> it would appear as if the point had now been reached at which, in the interest of progress, the classic libido theory would have to be transformed into a *theory of development based essentially upon object-relationships*. The great limitation of the present libido theory as an explanatory system resides in the fact that it confers the status of libidinal attitudes upon various manifestations which turn out to be merely *techniques for regulating the object-relationships of the ego*.[4]

While the distinction which Fairbairn is making sounds merely technical, it is an important one for psychoanalytic theory. Instead of libido, Fairbairn proposes to explain the human person on the basis of the interactions between human persons. Fairbairn argues: "My point of view may, however, be stated in a word. In my opinion it is high time that psychopathological inquiry, which in the past has been successively focused, first upon impulse, and later upon the ego, should now be focused upon *the object* towards which impulse is directed."[5]

The important thing about object relations theory for this study is that it incorporates a dynamic understanding of the person into its anthropology. It does not attempt to explain the person merely in terms of an impulse which resides within, but incorporates the insight that personality is always shaped within a social matrix.

---

[4] *Psychoanalytic Studies of the Personality* (London: Tavistock Publications) 1952. p. 31.
[5] *Psychoanalytic Studies*, p. 60. Italics Fairbairn's.

In Fairbairn's view, none of the erotogenic levels is automatically or satisfactorily explained by itself, because even in Freud's theory raw libido could not explain itself; it only made sense as it bore the mark of an interpersonal relation (which as we have seen, was mostly focused upon the Oedipus complex and its resolution). *This is why Freud was forced to posit the theoretical existence of such non-instinctual entities as the ego and super-ego: they represented a repository of the interpersonal conflicts that were impressed upon the individual during the resolution of the Oedipus conflict.* Fairbairn's theory of sexuality, however, depends upon successful object relations; it not only recognizes but also transcends the stages of erotogenic development defined by the instincts. Fairbairn infers: "Libidinal pleasure is not the end in itself, but the 'sign-post to the object.'"[6] Fairbairn concludes that Freud's libido theory was built upon the false assumption of auto-eroticism, not object-eroticism.[7]

The differences here between Fairbairn and Freud signify something about the human person which is highly significant. Their respective theories lead to two very different conclusions with regard to the nature of the human person. For Freud, the *sine qua non* of human existence was found in the instincts: component instincts which succeeded one another during the stages of psychological development. Everything that is constitutive of human ontology is derived from the pleasure principle. In other words, human beings, for all their apparent complexities, are ultimately driven by their glands. In holding fast to the instinctual theory, Freud thought to plant the young field of modern psychology in a place as close to the physical sciences as possible. But later theorists such as Fairbairn were less beholden to a reductionist model, and hence could conclude that the instincts were never an end in themselves, but always a means of either expressing or repressing an object relationship. In other words, glandular realities must be taken seriously, but there is something deeper than a mere sexual attraction when one human being encounters another. Sexuality is one channel for the

---

[6] *Psychoanalytic Studies*, p. 33. Cf. Rom Harré, *Social Being: A Theory for Social Psychology* (Totowa, N.J.: Rowman and Littlefield, 1980), who says: "The deepest human motive is to seek the respect of others."

[7] *Psychoanalytic Studies*, p. 34. The primary emphasis placed upon auto-eroticism is found first in Freud, however, it also can be found in some of Freud's less critical followers, such as Karl Abraham, *Selected Papers of Karl Abraham* (London: Hogarth Press, 1927) p. 496.

expression of human attraction, but there is an even more fundamental force at work when human beings interact on meaningful levels.

Let us take for example the presenting problem of a six-year-old child who continues to suck his thumb. The thumb-sucking continues in public and starts to become an embarrassment both to the child and to his parents. According to Freudian theory the child has arrested his sexual development at the oral stage. But an object relations approach assumes that there is from the start more than a misdirected drive. There is something amiss here with the *interpersonal dynamics* which caused the child to seek oral gratification long beyond the time when such a type of practice is usually needed.

Object relations theory therefore attempts to shift modern psychology from an organic to a dynamic interpersonal model: from picturing the person as an organism seeking satisfaction to seeing the person as a human being in search of meaningful relationships and who uses various organs as means of seeking pleasure and also establishing such relationships. In normal human development the instincts are thus subservient to the forming of meaningful relationships. On the other hand, in Freud's psychoanalytic theory, relationships are nearly impossible because all object relations are primarily the direct effect of the libidinal instinct.

Object relations theory therefore reopens the door for human beings to love and be loved, reintegrating the psychological factors into the somatic realities.

Now let us take the most influential theologian of the 20th century, Karl Barth, and look carefully at his theological anthropology.

## II. The Person in Karl Barth's Anthropology

Like object relations, Barth's doctrine of the person is 'dynamic.' This of course needs further explanation because the term 'dynamic' refers to much more than the mere fact of physical motion. It applies rather to the uniqueness of an interpersonal encounter. The reality that comes into being in interpersonal dynamics is something that German-speaking cultures refer to as *Begegnung*, "encounter."

# Barth and Object Relations Psychology

## A. Interpersonal relationship as 'history'

In order to further clarify what I mean when I describe Barth's anthropology as 'dynamic,' consider Barth's usage of the important theological term 'history.' Barth's gives the word 'history' (*Geschichte*) a technical meaning. A 'history' involves encounter: a relationship of one with another. Barth explains:

> In contrast to the concept of history (*Geschichte*) is that of a state (*Zustands*). There are states that are very much in movement, developing through many changes and varied modes of behaviour. The conception of a stiff and motionless uniformity need not be linked with that of a state. But the idea of a state does involve the idea of something completely insulated within the state in question, the idea of a limitation of its possibilities and therefore of its possible changes and modes of behaviour. It is never capable of more than these particular movements. Even the concept of the most mobile state is not therefore equivalent to that of history.[8]

Barth explains that a plant can have no 'history' as such. It may grow, it may move and take in nourishment, and it will eventually die. But a plant has no history because it always functions within the fixed circles of change that are characteristic of its own state of existence. On the other hand, a history is introduced when something happens to humans at the deepest level that enables them to transcend their biologically determined orientation. Therefore, a history does not describe what happens when an entity makes changes intrinsic to its own nature, but only when another being impinges upon an individual, eliciting a response. Barth reasons: "The history of a being begins, continues and is completed when something other than itself and transcending its own nature encounters it, approaches it and determines its being in the nature proper to it, so that it is compelled and enabled to transcend itself in response and in relation to this new factor."[9]

This is a highly complex and difficult topic to grasp. Perhaps it is so difficult because we rarely think in terms of interpersonal relations, even when we study human persons. Our

---

[8] *Church Dogmatics* (hereafter CD), III/2, p. 157f.
[9] CD, III/2, p. 158.

thinking about persons tends to be based on a somewhat crudely constructed Newtonian concept of ourselves. We tend to view ourselves as more or less autonomous billiard balls, bouncing into one another and exchanging momentum. But Barth's concept here goes much deeper: he argues that we actually influence one another on a deep ontological level when we encounter another human being. In other words, when one human being encounters another, something is called into existence which formerly did not exist.

Barth's anthropology, like the many anthropologies developing within the various strains of object relations psychology is therefore 'dynamic.'

And from what resources does Barth develop this 'dynamic' theological anthropology? He derives in anthropology from Scripture—especially from his Christology.

## B. The Human Person as a Being in Relation to Others

### 1. Jesus, the man for others[10]

Evangelicals have tended to focus mostly upon the divinity of Jesus. This is understandable, since the modern attacks upon the divinity of Jesus would dissolve the Christian message into nothing more than a sentimental distortion written by grief-stricken disciples of a deluded Galilean rabbi.

Nevertheless, the humanity of Jesus remains an equally important aspect of orthodox Christology. If we have tended to overlook the humanity of Jesus, it is probably because we have tended to overlook our own humanity. Barth explores the facets of Jesus' humanity with unparalleled vigor.

In the humanity of Jesus, Barth finds the basis of all human encounters. Jesus was not first for himself, nor for a cause or ideal; Jesus was first and foremost a "man for others." Barth says, "What interests Him and does so exclusively, is man, other men as such, who need Him and are referred to Him for help and deliverance."[11] Therefore, in the life of Jesus we see the living embodiment of a man who is for others. Jesus is not properly understood in isolation. He is, rather, one who encounters his

---

[10] A more contemporary and accurate translation of the German word, *Mensch*, would be 'human person'; however, the translators have used the term 'man,' and so for the sake of clarity shall this author.

[11] CD, III/2, p. 208.

brothers and sisters. He lives "to them and with them and for them. He is sent and ordained by God to be their Deliverer. Nothing else? No, really nothing else."[12] Jesus is ontologically related to the human race. By this Barth means that Jesus could be no other than a man for others. He could not be indifferent and still be Jesus. His relation to others is not accidental, but essential and primary because it flows from the eternal love of the Son for the Father.[13] Jesus is not able to look upon human suffering and sin with stoical indifference; the afflictions of others affect him in his innermost being.[14] Jesus helps others not from without, or even beside, but from within, taking their place, and creating something new from nothing. Jesus' being is both from and to His fellow humans. Barth says:

> If we see Him alone, we do not see Him at all. If we see Him, we see with and around Him in ever-widening circles His disciples, the people, His enemies and the countless millions who have not yet heard His name. We see Him as theirs, determined by them and for them, belonging to each and every one of them. It is thus that He is Master, Messiah, King and Lord.[15]

---

[12] CD, III/2, p. 209. Barth cites Luke 2: 11, Daniel 7, Philippians 2:6f, II Corinthians 8:9, Hebrews 12:2; 2:14, 17f; 4:15, as evidence that Jesus is a deliverer who helps us recover our lost humanity.

[13] CD, III/2, p. 210.

[14] See Barth's word study in CD, III/2, p. 211.

[15] CD, III/2, p. 216. An interesting objection to Barth's emphasis upon the dynamic and interpersonal character of human personhood is that he overlooked the need for an individual to remain distinct from the group—as well as to be connected to it. On the level of every day life, Barth was quite strongly individual, but in his theology might there be a tendency to overemphasize human interconnectedness at the expense of individuality—especially in light of Jesus' frequent withdrawal from the masses? See Mt. 8: 18, Mk. 1:35-45. This objection is worth considering—and yet, it could be argued, especially from the passages in the Gospel of Mark which refer to the supposed 'Messianic secret,' that when Jesus withdrew from the masses he was actually seeking a deeper communion with and guidance from the Father. He was not necessarily seeking isolation for its own sake. The one moment of real isolation was the hell of the cross: "My God, My God, why hast Thou forsaken me?" Matthew 27: 46, Mk. 15:34. But, conceptually, neither should the individual be pitted against the group, as though they were exclusive. A genuine encounter is primarily defined by its capacity to enhance

Therefore, Jesus in his divinity is from and for God, and Jesus in his humanity is from and to his fellow 'man' (*der Mensch*). [16] These are not at odds with one another but closely correspond. There is similarity between the divine and human in Jesus: hence the I of Jesus is determined by the Thou of God the Father, but also the Thou of his fellow humans. Jesus' being for God and for his 'fellow man' are treated by Barth in light of the Chalcedonian formula regarding the two natures of Christ.[17]

*2. The heart of trinitarian anthropology: analogia relationis*

Here we come to the innermost core of Barth's anthropology. Barth's development of yet another technical term, *analogia relationis* ('analogy of relations') may one day prove to be his most lasting contribution to modern theology. We must, however, undergo a major paradigm shift with regard to classical conceptions of being in order to appreciate the significance of the analogy of relations.

Just as there is correspondence between the humanity and deity of Christ, there is also a correspondence between human love and divine love that Barth describes as the *analogia relationis*. Barth offers his *analogia relationis* as an alternative to the Thomistic, *analogia entis* ('analogy of being') which supports so much of Catholic theology. In other words, Barth insists that if we are to talk about the human person in Biblical terms, we must use the language of relations, not simply that of 'being.'

The need to shift theological thinking from 'being' to 'relations' may have some parallels in the scientific shift from classical physics to relativity and quantum theory. The concept of complementarity in microphysics presents an analogous problem to the question about being and becoming: How can a physical

---

individual identity while at the same moment leading to communion, one with the other.
[16] Rather than the term man (*der Mensch*), Barth sometimes uses the more inclusive term "cosmos" (*der Kosmos*) to refer to man and his historical setting. Jesus does not redeem man, understood abstractly, but man in the cosmos. See CD, III/2, p. 216.
[17] Barth's affirmation that man is "soul of his body—wholly and simultaneously both, in ineffaceable difference, inseparable unity, and indestructible order," has *mutatis mutandis*, an unmistakable Chalcedonian ring to it.

phenomenon like light have qualities of both a wave and particle?

The paradigm shift in Barth's thought is perhaps analogous to the shift in the new physics. Once the shift is made, the possibility that there could be an individual being who exists apart from interpersonal relations is nonsense, as is the notion that light must be either wave or particle but cannot be both. Being and relations are simultaneous to one another. Being is inseparable from the important relations which constitute any human person's existence: all of which relations are simultaneous, multileveled and complex.

Another analogy can be found in the discovery by microphysics that matter is inseparable from motion. When it comes to thinking about what makes human beings tick, our minds tended to run toward a kind of Newtonian understanding in which external forces act upon distinct particles in absolute time and space. In other words, theologians tended to look at human beings as isolated, thinking individuals, each set apart from one another by the encasement which we call the human body. Yet the Newtonian paradigm holds true only within certain limited parameters of physical reality based on the classical physics. On the other hand, the more modern theories on the nature of light and subatomic particles are influenced by the dynamic thought of relativity and quantum mechanics—and have a wider application. The Newtonian framework is not false but incomplete. Might it be worth our time to probe for some analogies here? I think so.

Just as the basic building blocks of the universe have turned out to be best described as pulsating fields of energy, so the human reality may turn out to be best described as an encounter—or rather, a history of many encounters. There are thousands of encounters going on within the composite history of each individual human. There are the first encounters with parents, and then with others or wider family members, society, and the world (including the natural environment). For Barth, our most important encounter is with God; then follows the encounter with others, self and time. All of this is Barth's way of interpreting what it means for human beings to be created in God's image and likeness.[18] In other words, we mirror or reflect God's dynamic character. Just as He is the triune God who encounters himself as Father and Son in the Spirit, performing mighty acts in the salvation of Israel, and ultimately encountering us through his

---

[18] See Genesis 1:26-27.

Son, so each human individual is a being-in-becoming, a relation who by definition exists only as she or he acts in relations to God, self and others.

Of course, the term, 'encounter' applies not to mere motion but to interpersonal relations (there *is* an undeniable difference between personal and impersonal realities). The point I wish to emphasize here is simply that we can no longer attempt to find out what something is by analyzing it in isolation from the things to which it normally relates. In physics, the further the physicist probes in trying to find "the thing in itself," the more the basic qualities of the thing tend to be absorbed into a whole series of relations to other things. In similar fashion, but on an altogether different level, Barth has argued that the isolated self cannot be fathomed *in and of him or herself.* The true self can only be understood by apprehending the vital spheres of relations to which one belongs. We can see, therefore, why Barth would consider the solitary self to be living an unnatural existence, on conceptual as well as on Biblical grounds. In launching a new conceptual framework by which to see ourselves as creatures made in God's image and likeness, Barth is attacking the radical individualism of Western societies with a crusader's zeal.[19]

This dynamic anthropology is further explained by Barth's discussion about I and Thou.

### 3. *'I am as Thou art'*

Barth expresses the problem of self-conscious individual identity with the question: "What is meant by 'I'?" In speaking of 'I' the individual does not only make a distinction but also a connection. 'I' does not make sense in isolation but only in relation to 'Thou.' Here Barth adopts the technical term 'encounter' which was developed by the Jewish philosopher and theologian Martin Buber. Barth however, makes some important modifications of Buber's I and Thou.

In the logic of interpersonal encounter, human dialogue must take place between an I and Thou. What does Barth mean by 'I'? 'I' does not make sense in isolation but only in relation to 'Thou': "The declaration 'I' in what I say is the declaration of my

---

[19] See especially CD, III/2, pp. 319ff. Cf. also, Barth, Fragments Grave and Gay, tr. E. Mosbacher (London and Glasgow: Collins, 1971) p. 99. And who in the modern Western world today can fail to be instructed by such a crusade?

expectation that the other being to which I declare myself in this way will respond and treat and describe and distinguish me as something like himself . . . Thus the word 'Thou,' although it is a very different word, is immanent to 'I.'"[20]   For Barth, the I is relationally understood in the sense that I always stands over and against the Thou.  I is in relation to Thou, and I cannot say 'I' without also saying 'Thou.' The self-sufficient I is an illusion, because, as Barth points out, even the concept or thought of I implies relation to another: to a Thou, who necessarily stands over against myself as I.  The I and Thou are related because I stand over and against Thou—and only in distinction to Thou do I have an identity.  In developing this interpersonal ontology, Barth takes issue with the isolated *cogito*[21] of Descartes:

> A pure, absolute and self-sufficient I is an illusion, for as an I, even as I think and express this I, I am not alone or self-sufficient, but am distinguished from and connected with a Thou in which I find a being like my own, so that there is no place for an interpretation of the "I am" which means isolation and necessarily consists in a description of the sovereign self-positing of an empty subject by eruptions of its pure, absolute and self-sufficient abyss.[22]

Therefore, the I is not absolute but is defined both by distinction and connection with the Thou.  The necessary relation between I and Thou is one of the chief descriptions of a dynamic anthropology.  It is 'dynamic' because it always entails the active relation of one person to another.

We can now begin to see more clearly in what sense Barth's anthropology is 'dynamic': it is so in the sense that it refers to a necessary relation between persons.  It is important to see that Barth does not derive such an anthropology from anywhere else than from a theological foundation.  Specifically, Barth derives his doctrine of the person from his understanding of the doctrine of the Trinity.  Concerning God's Being, Barth states :

> Entering into this relationship, He makes a copy of Himself.  Even in His inner divine being there is relationship.  To be sure, God is One in Himself.  But He is

---

[20] CD, III/2, p. 245.
[21] "I think"—with the logical implication that therefore, "I am."
[22] CD, III/2, p. 245f.

not alone. There is in Him a co-existence, co-inherence and reciprocity. God in Himself is not just simple, but in the simplicity of His essence He is threefold—the Father, The Son and the Holy Ghost . . . He is in Himself the One who loves eternally, the One who is eternally loved, and eternal love; and in this triunity He is the original and source of every I and Thou, of the I which is eternally from and to the Thou and therefore supremely I. And it is this relationship in the inner divine being which is repeated and reflected in God's eternal covenant with man as revealed and operative in time in the humanity of Jesus.[23]

Because the relational nature of God is reflected in the humanity of Jesus,[24] and thus is the determination or destiny of every human person, it follows that the person who corresponds to, and reflects, the being of God (*analogia relationis*) bears the stamp of God's own dynamic character. Each human person then is destined to be in relation: to be I and Thou. I implies Thou, and Thou refers back to I. I and Thou are not coincidental or incidental but "essentially proper to the concept of man."[25] This I and Thou, asserts Barth, is illustrated most succinctly in sexual polarity.

*III. Some Similarities Between Barth and Object Relations Psychology in Their Concept of the Person*

*A. Being is Doing and Doing is Being*

The first, and most important parallel between Barth and object relations is the emphasis each has placed upon interpersonal relations in constituting the person. Both Barth and object relations show how the person is shaped by a social context: by relation to an 'Other.' In each case the person is defined not only by what mental faculties or instinctual energies an individual might *have* but also by what the individual *does*—especially in relation to another (or others). Both show, on their respective level of inquiry, how interpersonal relations are the fundamental

---

[23] CD, III/2, p. 218.
[24] Barth cites John 17: 5-21. He concludes that here "the divine original creates for itself a copy in the creaturely world." III/2, p. 221.
[25] CD, III/2, p. 248.

building block of an individual's personhood; each individual person is shaped by their peculiar history of interpersonal relations.

In Barth's anthropology, relation to God is the primary relation. We might say that God is the primary external object. This relation has some important implications for the development of individual consciousness. It is only in the relation to God as an 'Object' (*Gegenstand*) that consciousness begins to develop: that cognition, volition and affection take on a valid existence.

In object relations self-identity develops only within the history of complex social interaction. The child is born within a social matrix, and the self develops likewise. For Barth, of course, the social coefficient of knowing and being has a theological foundation. From Barth's theological perspective, the social matrix of human personhood reflects the relational character of the triune God. God is a being who is in relation to Himself: not just within the economic Trinity but also within the immanent Trinity. In other words: God does not pretend to be triune, nor become triune, merely to save us—he actually is a triune community eternally. This is one of the basic tenets of Nicene orthodoxy.

Therefore, the human person who reflects God's nature cannot be actualized as fully human apart from a right relation to the Creator, other creatures, self and time. Modern psychology, of course, cares nothing for the Christian doctrine of the Trinity. Since knowledge of the Trinity is knowledge which comes about only as a result of revealed truth, it falls outside the proper bounds of psychology. Nevertheless, we should not be surprised to discover that there exist some curious analogies between Barth's theological anthropology and the psychologist's reflections upon the data presented in early childhood relations to parents.

## B. The Psycho-Somatic Unity of the Whole Person

The social development of human consciousness highlights another similarity between Barth and object relations: both insist upon the unity and integrity of the person as a whole, rejecting any dichotomies between body and soul, mind and matter, or psychological self (ego) and instinctual self (libido). The explicit holism of both Barth and object relations shows the extent to which both attempt to discover the unity of the theoretical and the practical person, the biological and the psychological. There is little that smacks of idealism in either anthropology. Their respective anthropologies are not merely derived *a priori* but give a good deal of respect to the empirical observation of the person's physical existence. On the other hand, neither fall into materialism in their reflections upon the nature of the person. Rather than idealism or materialism, a deep-seated realism runs through both the thought of Barth and object relations psychology. For Barth his realism leads him to respect both the revealed nature of the person as it is interpreted in the person of Christ, and the physical existence of the person—which the Scriptures clearly indicate has an equal importance with the spiritual and psychological realities. Once again, the Trinity plays a major role in Barth's understanding of the person. This means that the incarnation of the Son must shatter the traditional categories which separated soul and body, instincts and reason: replacing them with a hearty affirmation of the dynamic interdependence of each with the other.

The psycho-somatic unity of the person has some very important implications for the relation between science and theology. It profoundly influences the ways in which we see ourselves both through the lens of modern science and that of faith. Listed below are some of the issues in need of further reflection.

*1. A dynamic anthropology breaks out of the deterministic mold*

Barth and object relations psychology's concept of the person are dynamic in the sense that the person is not construed as a closed system determined by antecedent causes and tending toward a state of equilibrium. They are dynamic in the sense that neither allows the reductionist criteria to stand. They are dynamic because the person in each case is open to an almost infinite variety of creative options in respect to their possible interactions with other persons. While certain patterns of human behavior can be observed within the field of interpersonal relations, there is nevertheless an overriding openness to the almost infinite variety of possibilities which obtain between human persons who engage in relations one to another.

*2. Getting beyond the old dualisms: the hierarchical structure of reality*

At the heart of biblical anthropology the Scripture is always concerned about the whole person in relation to God. Also, at the foundation of the modern human sciences and medicine a similar view is beginning to prevail. The endless and mostly fruitless speculations as to whether the biological or the psychological components are primary, have begun to give way to newer paradigms which accept biological priority, and psychological supremacy. These paradigms are usually constructed upon models which reject both dualism and reductionism—arguing instead that reality is structured as a bi-directional hierarchy in which things are ordered according to their complexity—beginning with physical, and graduating upward to the chemical, biological, social, and psychological components. At the highest level, all the lower levels are not excluded but included.[26] What makes the hierarchy bi-directional is that the components at the lower level have priority, while the higher level components exert a certain amount of control over functions at the lower levels.

These hierarchical paradigms have gained increasing acceptance in the human sciences. Yet they are mostly belated theoretical attempts to explain the practical death of anthropological dualism: a death which has been a self-evident fact of modern medicine for many years. For examples: Do we not live in a world today in which increasing numbers of psychological illnesses are susceptible to treatment with chemical drugs? Can we ignore the fact that highly sensitive instruments can register amazingly slight electrical impulses in the human central nervous system which correlate to certain emotions? And, do we not also live in a time when the *psychosomatic* origins of many physical illnesses are being discovered? There is, therefore, no going back to the naive but attractive notion that the psychical and somatic run down parallel tracks—as if they were simultaneously at a similar milestone but never intersecting one another and exerting a mutual influence. *If Christian anthropology continues to endorse anthropological dualism, to which it has traditionally adhered, it will find itself defending a position which is both scientifically untenable and Biblically indefensible. Such a*

---

[26] See, e.g., Hector C. Sabelli and Linnea Carlson-Sabelli, "Biological Priority and Psychological Supremacy: A New Integrative Paradigm Derived From Process Theory," *American Journal of Psychiatry*, Vol. 146:12, (December 1989). In order to push beyond the old stalemate of "either biology or psychology," the authors look back to the philosophy of Heraclitus for more dynamic and integrative paradigms. I see no reason not to include at the highest level of the hierarchy, the 'spiritual.'

*position which will continue to push many of the thoughtful people of our age headlong into either materialist or spiritualist monism: both of which have enormous shortcomings.*

In my view, Barth's anthropology presents a viable alternative to the prevailing dualistic anthropologies of most Christian theologians. These dualisms surfaced not so much from the Biblical data themselves as from the Hellenistic perspectives which theology had up until the 20th century largely adopted.

*3. Dynamic anthropology: could it be analogous to a field theory?*

The employment of field theory in describing the relational nature of the person is advocated by T.F. Torrance, who comments on Clerk Maxwell's field theory:

> We must now take up Clerk Maxwell's concept of the field . . . and not least the concept of relational thinking which he found, for example in the teaching of Sir William Hamilton. Evidence for this is apparent in Clerk Maxwell's 1856 essay on analogy where he showed that analogical resemblances and differences are embedded in the structural patterns of nature throughout the universe. Analogies are sets of relations which bear upon each other and point beyond themselves and thus supply us with fundamental clues for heuristic inquiry beyond the limits of empirical and observational knowledge. Hence, he claimed, 'in a scientific point of view the relation is the most important thing to know.' Clerk Maxwell insisted, however, that the relations he referred to were not just imaginary or putative but real relations, relations that belong to reality as much as things do, for the inter-relations of things are, in part at least, constitutive of what they are. Being-constituting relations of this kind we may well speak of as 'onto-relations.'[27]

By inference, then, Torrance is saying the same thing which Barth said above: a relation is not peripheral or incidental to human ontology but is constitutive of the human essence. This is what Barth has said on a theological level and what object

---

[27] *Transformation and Convergence in the Frame of Knowledge* (Grand Rapids: Eerdmans, 1984) p. 229f.

relations confirms by its empirical studies of human psychological development.

Barth clearly stands within the stream of theological reflection which views the individual in terms of relations rather than isolation. Torrance continues:

> In the Reformed theological tradition the notion of the person is held to be controlled by the person-constituting and person-intensifying activity of God in the Incarnation, such that union with Christ becomes the ground for interpersonal relations in the Church. Relations between persons have ontological force and are part of what persons are as persons—they are real, person-constituting relations.[28]

The relational structure of both Barth's and object relations' anthropology allows them to understand the person as a reality which is analogous to the modern field concept developed by Faraday and Maxwell.[29] The 'field' is, according to Torrance, a better model for a dynamic anthropology than the more mechanistic terms which, for example, describe human persons as if they could be explained exclusively in terms of instincts or other biophysical causes.

## IV. Conclusion

I have argued that both on a theological and psychological level human persons are best described by their interpersonal relations. All of this has been in order to create a dialogue between the theological understanding of the person and the studies of modern science applied to human psychology. It is increasingly the case that when we study human persons in a modern conceptual framework we study not only individuals in isolation, but we also take into consideration the various relations which constitute their normal environment. Human persons are necessarily connected to the other living things in the world. In

---

[28] *Transformation and Convergence*, p. 230.
[29] In addition to Torrance, see also W. J. Neidhardt, "Thomas F. Torrance's Integration of Judeo-Christian Theology and Natural Science: Some Key Themes," *Journal of the American Scientific Affiliation* (June 1989) pp. 87-98, esp. 93f.

other words, each person lives by virtue of certain biological, genetic, and social endowments. Almost as a form of confession, the theologian should admit that he or she had for too long neglected the physio-biological realities of human existence, thus isolating theology needlessly from the various disciplines which have a healthy respect for our physical realities. One strength of Barth's theological anthropology is that he considers the Biblical data seriously and breaks away from the exaggerated asceticism which maintained a firm grip on theologians from Augustine right up to the late 20th century. What makes us peculiarly human, according to Barth's interpretation of the Bible, is not the mere fact that we possess intelligent souls. Rather, we are chemical, neurological, biological and sexual creatures who are called into a unique relation to our Creator via the Redeemer. If, as the older theologians have insisted, we are distinguished from the other creatures by our superior intelligence, it is only because intelligence itself is a dynamic event—teased out in relation to our Creator, our parents, society and the world.

Theology has nothing to fear in admitting that we humans are indeed biological creatures who are connected to our foreparents and the world in which we live. However, we must insist on Biblical and theological grounds, that we are connected to our ancestors and others by interpersonal relations not *only* by impersonal causes. It is precisely where interpersonal relations enter, that we begin to reflect upon what it is that makes us peculiarly human.

In this author's view, Christian anthropology can make its way forward in the 21st century if we will explore dynamic paradigms which attempt to integrate both the biological and the psychological-spiritual elements of what it means to be human. Such dynamic anthropologies can more closely represent the Biblical pictures of what it means to be human—and perhaps hold the promise of increasing the dialogue between theological anthropology and the human sciences.

# The Social Ecology of Human Personhood: Implications of Dietrich Bonhoeffer's Theology for Psychology

*Ray S. Anderson*
Fuller Theological Seminary

For twenty-five years I have team-taught courses with psychologists in the integration curriculum at our graduate school of psychology. At the very outset, a colleague challenged me with regard to my use of the terms 'person' and 'personhood' in referring to the self as a proper subject for psychological study. "In our discipline," he suggested, "we can only speak of what we observe as human behavior. To speak of such a thing as 'personhood' lying behind personality is only a metaphysical theory and not an empirical reality."

Because we both were committed to the integration of theological as well as psychological constructs, I argued that personality as applied to God, for instance, is not a proper construct. To say that God is 'one who loves' is a statement about the very being of God, not merely about his personality.[1] In the same way, I suggested, if we are to find a common denominator in our discussion about the human self we must agree that whatever we mean by the term 'personhood,' it must refer to a substance of being lying behind behavior rather than merely a cluster of behavioral attitudes and actions. After all, what is empirical is not just behavior, but that which causes behavior. As I recall, we agreed to disagree. But it was a beginning.

My own approach toward integration begins with the question, "What is the nature of the human person as an objective reality which makes a claim upon both theological and psychological concepts and theories as to their validity?" Regardless of the specific discipline from which we seek to understand the nature of human persons, it is not a theory of personhood that constitutes the objective reality of the study, but

---

[1] For a discussion of the problem of positing 'personality' in God, see Karl Barth, *Church Dogmatics*, II/1, 287-297.

the nature of that which is to be studied. In his insistence that theological method follow that of scientific inquiry, theologian Thomas F. Torrance argued that the nature of the object to be known determines the method of knowing.[2]

For example, those who view their task as primarily one of promoting spiritual edification as a component of authentic humanity must be able to answer the question in such a way that it does not rule out emotional, physical and mental health as of equal concern to spiritual health. In the same way, those who view their task as primarily one of promoting mental health as psychologists and therapists must be able to answer the question in such a way that it does not rule out the spiritual dimension of the human self as of equal concern.

In this chapter I will present a schematic profile of what may be called a pre-theoretical model of human personhood as a basis for testing the adequacy of both psychological and theological theories relating to emotional/mental health and spiritual growth and development. I will then follow with a discussion of the ecology of social and spiritual personhood. The unique contribution of Dietrich Bonhoeffer will then be considered as a basis for the integration of psychological and theological approaches to the recovery of authentic personhood in light of what psychologists call pathology and theologians call sin.

*The Self as a Systemic Relationship: A Pre-Theoretical Model*

The lack of a coherent and viable vision of the human person as spiritual as well as emotional/mental being plagues the traditional discipline of psychiatric and psychological mental health care. Mental health practitioners and psychologists have tended to rely on models which are inclined more toward analytic and individual concepts of the self rather than social and relational constructs. Theoretical models of therapeutic approaches toward healing often lack a pre-theoretical understanding of the nature of

---

[2] "In ever positive science it is the subject-matter that determines form, content that affects method—and so it is in theology. It is the object of our theological statements that determines the logic of their reference, in accordance with its nature and activity. . . . To be truthful theological statements must correspond in form and content to that divine Object, and they must be enunciated in a material mode appropriate to that correspondence." Thomas F. Torrance, *Theology in Reconstruction* (Grand Rapids: Eerdmans, 1965), 61.

human personhood. As a result, effectiveness of a given strategy of providing care can only be measured by judging therapeutic outcomes in accordance with the built-in limitations of the theoretical model being used.

Freud, for example, as a representative of classic psychoanalytic theory, considered religious ideation as illusions, "fulfillments of the oldest, strongest, and most urgent wishes of mankind."[3] By ruling out spiritual reality as a component of the self, Freud measured the effectiveness of his therapeutic strategy by assisting his clients in the task of eliminating such illusions as a means of reaching ego maturity. Post-Freudian psychology, it should be noted, has become more open to the reality of religious projection of the self as an authentic expression of the struggle within the ego for a transcendent 'object' with which to identify. Some go further and emphasize the importance of one's belief in God and that God relates to humans in a meaningful way, especially through prayer.[4]

*A Pre-Theoretical Approach to Defining Human Personhood*

I use the term 'pre-theoretical' in a very specialized sense. In developing theories about why persons behave in certain ways, therapeutic strategies are devised in accordance with these theories. For example, behavior modification therapy is grounded in the theory of a cause and effect relation in human actions. Therefore, if one can modify the cause, one can condition the effect and produce change in behavior. When anecdotal evidence can be found which supports such a theory, it is assumed to be appropriate. By 'pre-theoretical,' I point beyond an explanation of why persons behave in certain ways toward what we may understand as the fundamental nature of human persons.

For example, theoretical physics attempts to explain the behavior of nature as it is observed, assuming some cause and

---

[3] Sigmund Freud, *The Future of an Illusion* (New York: Norton & Company, 1961), 39.

[4] For example, see A. Ulanov and B. Ulanov, *Primary Speech: A Psychology of Prayer* (Atlanta: John Knox Press, 1982): " . . . we suggest that fantasy becomes an enlarging means of exposure to being. The task is not to get rid of fantasy, which usually results in just making ourselves unconscious of the fantasies that continue anyway below the threshold of awareness. The task is to know our fantasies and disidentify ourselves from them" (36).

effect relation which accounts for what is observed. Newtonian physics operated on this principle holding certain assumptions about the fixed relation of time and space. Einstein, along with others, sought to understand the underlying structure of physical particles and came up with what may be called a pre-theoretical assertion as to the fundamental nature of reality. It was the objective nature of reality in its subatomic structure that concerned the new physics, not merely theories which explained the behavior from the perspective of the observer.

It is in this sense that I use the term 'pre-theoretical' to denote the objective nature of human persons lying behind human behavior. All attempts at describing the pre-theoretical are just that—attempts. The point is that each attempt, as with modern physics, must assume that there is an objective reality called human personhood which controls and finally determines the validity of such attempts. The validity of any pre-theoretical model of human nature is to be judged by how useful and viable the pre-theoretical model is in explaining how the various theoretical models work in dealing with human behavior. The pre-theoretical model cannot be viewed as just another 'theory.' Nor is the pre-theoretical model free to claim theoretical independence. In the end, theories will be judged not by their relation to other theories, but by their correspondence to the pre-theoretical model itself—assuming it to be a valid one. Not every physicist agrees with Einstein, but no physicist dares to develop a theory which ignores a pre-theoretical view of reality.

Human persons may be viewed as a set of sub-systems, systemically related. That is, each sub-system, with its relative autonomy, which makes up the human person, is part of a whole—which is more than the sum of the parts. We enter into life as infants held in a social relation to a parenting person or persons. We are not yet differentiated as 'persons' with a self-identity which exists over and against others. Further development entails sexual differentiation with gender identity assimilated into the core self-identity, again with respect to the sexual and personal identity of other persons. The development of psychical experience and capacity comes later, with a deeper capacity to feel and express feelings and emotions.

*A Pre-Theoretical Diagram*

A pre-theoretical schematic diagram can be constructed which shows the way in which components of the self as an individual and in relationship can be viewed. A schematic diagram is somewhat like a wiring diagram for a television or computer. It is not intended to show 'which buttons to push' in order to operate the thing. Rather, it reveals how each 'system' is connected so that if a malfunction occurs a trained technician knows where to locate the problem. Figure 1, below, is just such a 'wiring diagram' for the human person and is meant to be read accordingly.

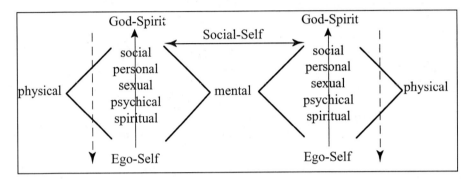

**Figure 1**

Reading from top to bottom (dotted line) we see that the progression is from social to personal, to sexual, then psychical and finally spiritual. As spiritual beings, we then have an orientation to God as Spirit which runs right back through each of the other sub-sets or sub-systems of the self. The dotted line represents the growth of the self through each of the spheres, beginning with the social and moving toward the spiritual. The solid line moves from the center of the self through each sphere toward God. This depicts the integration of the self as the self that it is and, at the same time, in relation to the other. The physical and mental aspects of personal life impinge upon each of the spheres and the physical and mental health of each have an effect upon the spheres.

This serves to preserve a balance and positive tension between the physical and mental aspects of personality for each of the components. If the spiritual dimension should be moved to the side and related primarily through the mental side of the self, the religious self will become either rationalistic or mystical—both essentially movements away from the concreteness and embodiedness of the self. In the same way, there are both physical and mental aspects to a healthy psychical and sexual life. And should these become primarily either physical or mental, this will represent a distortion and dysfunction for the self in its process of growth and development.

The developmental model depicted in Figure 1 has a two-fold dimension. There is a vertical integration of the self as personal being through each of the spheres, with an ego-self identity which includes appropriate mental and physical self-reference. This developmental process requires constant adjustment to the ego-self as changes occur both inwardly and with reference to the embodied life of the self. At the same time, there is a developmental process where integration of the ego-self with the social-self must take place through the changes which are occurring in this dimension of personal experience. From the standpoint of the self, this integrative project and process is a single one provided that it takes place in a relatively healthy and holistic way. The depiction of the ego-self and the social-self is schematic and not intended to suggest that the self actually has two centers.

These system components are not 'stages' through which one passes developmentally in a strict linear fashion. Rather, the model should be viewed more like a spiral staircase, where one continues to make progress developmentally but with each 'rotation' through the process enters into and experiences each 'system' from a more mature (hopefully!) perspective. The psychical life of the infant, for example, is present from birth, and no doubt before. At the same time, the full range of the psychical range of feelings and experiences is quite limited. Children cry when they experience pain, both physically and mentally, but they do not weep out of the depth of sadness of which an adult is capable. Children experience joy and feelings of happiness but have not yet developed a depth of joy that is able to integrate pain and loss into that joy.

*The Concept of Subsystems*

The concept of persons as functioning subsystems, independent and yet essential to the integrity and health of persons, has been suggested by Anthony G. Greenwald:

> The usefulness of the concept of self in psychology has been limited by psychologists' attempting to deal simultaneously with the self both as an empirical object of study and as the assumed vehicle of conscious experience. This seems an impossible task. . . . In the multisystem

analysis of the person (here labeled personalysis), the self is a subsystem of the person and is partially independent of body, verbal, and social subsystems.[5]

The term, 'personalysis' was created by Greenwald and intended to serve parallel to psychoanalysis to indicate indebtedness to Freud's approach. The elements which comprise the set of subsystems of the self are meant to describe a pre-theoretical or meta-theoretical model rather than having well-defined referents. Personalysis thus characterizes the person as a set of subsystems, which Greenwald identifies as body, self, verbal, and social. This differs from Freud's theory of the id, ego, and superego, which provided an analysis of the *psyche* (mind) by proposing an analysis of the *person* into subsystems.[6]

Greenwald acknowledges that criticism can be leveled against this personalytic account as unfalsifiable and merely a theory. Indeed, admits, Greenwald,

> personalysis has been described here in a fashion that renders it (like psychoanalysis) difficult to disprove . . . Psychoanalysis orients researchers to look for antecedents and indicators of motivational conflict, and to seek evidence for an active barrier (the agency of repression) that restricts access to knowledge. Personalysis, on the other hand, suggests a search for evidence of independent operation of person subsystems and suggests that important general research tasks for psychologists are to seek and to decipher the codes that define subsystems with the person. [7]

Greenwald's four subsystems are not identical with the elements of the subsystem of the self as I have proposed above but share some interesting similarities. First, both models are built on a more holistic concept of person, including the physical and mental aspect as well as social dimension. What Greenwald terms 'self' I would call 'spirit' as the essential core of the person with its

---

[5] "Is Anyone in Charge? Personalysis Versus the Principle of Personal Unity," Anthony G. Greenwald, Ohio State University; in *Psychological Perspectives on the Self*, Volume 1, Jerry Suls, editor (Hillside, NJ; London: Lawrence Erlbaum Associates, Publishers, 1982), 152.
[6] Ibid., 157.
[7] Ibid., 169-170.

own 'limited access' and 'language code,' to use his concepts. More significantly, Greenwald supports the methodology of developing a 'pre-theoretical' model of the function of persons in order to aid psychology in developing therapeutic theories and methods. 'Personalysis' comes close to describing an integrative model such as I have presented.

## The Concept of Soul

My task as a theologian is to speak to the deeper yearnings and struggles of human existence as much as to bring to those existential human concerns some insights from the Word of God. At the same time, because the concept of a 'soul' as an entity residing in the body leads often to a dualistic view of the human self, I view the concept of 'self' as denoting the inner core of the whole person, including the body. By 'soul' I mean the personal and spiritual dimension of the self. Thus, the phrase 'body and soul' is not intended to suggest that the soul is something which is merely 'in' the body, or separate from the body, but the whole person with both an interior and an exterior life in the world.[8]

Charles Gerkin suggests that the core of the self can be termed the 'soul' in a theological sense, incorporating the various psychological terms.

> To use the designation self is to emphasize the line of experienced continuity and interpretive capacity which emerges from the self's object relations. To use the term ego is to emphasize the coming together of a nexus of forces demanding mediation and compromise . . . . The term *soul* is here used as a theological term that points to the self's central core subject to the ego's conflicting forces and to the ultimate origins of the self in God. The soul is the gift of God bestowed upon the individual with the breath of life. It is thus the self, including its ego conflicts, as seen from an ultimate perspective—the perspective of

---

[8] For a discussion of the concept of 'soul,' see my essay, "On Being Human: The Spiritual Saga of a Creaturely Soul," in Warren S. Brown, Nancy Murphy and H. Newton Malony, editors, *Whatever Happened to the Soul? Scientific and Theological Portraits of Human Nature* (Minneapolis: Fortress Press, 1998), 175-194.

the self as nurtured and sustained in the life of God.[9]

My own use of the term 'self' accords with Gerkin's attempt to speak of a central core of the self as grounded in social differentiation and also including the ego-dynamics subject to psychological assessment and therapeutic attention.

Inadequate integration through the developmental process, however, can lead to a splitting of the ego-self from the social-self to some degree resulting in some level of dysfunction. In extreme cases, the ego-self may also suffer splitting, which may account for the phenomenon of multiple personality disorder.

From the perspective of a theology of the self as grounded in the image of God, this depiction of the self is intended to show both a developmental process as well as an integrative process as a foundation for further consideration of the healing process which needs to take place where disorder and dysfunction has occurred.

What can be called therapeutic gains in a clinical sense are corrections made in the various subsystems of the self which facilitate a positive and creative relation of each system to the other and to an orientation to God and other persons. This opens up a variety of therapeutic strategies to be used, depending upon the specific therapeutic gain to be achieved within each subset. For example, behavior modification works well where there are cause and effect mechanisms which contribute to the functioning of a sub-system. Biofeedback techniques recognize the systemic connection between the physical and psychical subsystem. Psychoanalytically-oriented therapy can uncover factors in identity formation that are repressed. Object relations psychology can provide new therapeutic strategies for persons who lack positive identity formation and continuity.

My teaching colleague, a psychologist, was critical of my presentation of the pre-theoretical model. "Typical of a theologian, your model is abstract and analytical with no reference to behavior. As a psychologist and therapist, I begin by observing people in the context of their existence in real time. After all, it was you who said that there is a person there behind the behavior. Where is the person?"

His point was valid, though he offered no critical response to the model itself. By that I mean, he had no pre-theoretical

---

[9] Charles V. Gerkin, *The Living Human Document—Revisioning Pastoral Counseling in a Hermeneutical Mode* (Nashville: Abingdon Press, 1984), 98.

model to suggest as an alternative. My purpose in offering the pre-theoretical model is not to shift the focus away from concrete, embodied existence in real time. Rather, in somewhat the same way as a physicist seeks to construct a model which represents the invisible but fully empirical inner structure of an atom, practical theology does the same with regard to the inner dynamics of the phenomenon which we call human life. This is what the pre-theoretical model is meant to do by showing how the spiritual core of the ego-self is part of a dynamic gestalt where the physical and mental aspects of personal being interface and interact with the social, personal, sexual and psychical components of the self as an integrative whole.

The term 'gestalt' can be understood as the total configuration or pattern of the lived life. A person's gestalt emerges in the historical process by which a person forms his or her own life pattern in relation to the environment. In this context I am using the term in the broadest sense, not in the technical sense as used by some psychological theorists. Theologian Jürgen Moltmann describes the gestalt of a person as:

> the whole human organism—that historical Gestalt which people, body and soul, develop in their environment . . . In acquiring Gestalt, the person acquires both individuality and sociality; for the Gestalt binds him and his environment into a living unity, and at the same time distinguishes him from that environment as this particular living thing. Gestalt is the form of exchange with the various environments in which a person is identifiable, and with which he can identify himself. . . . Consequently, in the lived Gestalt of a human being, body and soul, the conscious and the unconscious, what is voluntary and what is involuntary, interpenetrate."[10]

In response to my colleague I went on to present an extension of the pre-theoretical model into real time. As with a

---

[10] *God in Creation—A New Theology of Creation and the Spirit of God* (San Francisco: Harper and Row, 1985), 159-161. Gestalt psychology, pioneered by Frederick (Fritz) and Laura Perls, is based on the German word *gestalt*, which is difficult to translate into English. It has the connotation of configuration, structure, theme, or organized whole. See *The Gestalt Approach and Eye Witness to Therapy* (Bantam Books, 1976).

television set, one does not need to see the wiring diagram in order to operate the machine. But there is a screen to observe and buttons to push. So it is with the human self. There is a face to observe, motion to watch, and yes, buttons to push!

*The Social Ecology of Human Personhood*

The concept of ecology in the most general sense simply means the relationship of an organism to its environment, or to a structure of interactive forces which mutually determine both the organism and its environment. In psychology, the term was introduced by Allan Wicker in *Introduction to Ecological Psychology*.[11] I use the term here in a non-technical sense to describe the interaction of the three spheres of the self in its embodied existence, its existence as spiritual being related to God, and its existence with and for the other person(s). The fundamental ecology of human persons is constituted by fellow humanity, or co-humanity.

In Figure 2 below, the spiritual sphere is placed at the center as a reminder that in the pre-theoretical model the spiritual dimension of the self emerges at the core and is the integrative dynamic for the self in its existence as a duality of physical and nonphysical (mental) experience. In its historical existence, that is, in the self's existence in 'real time,' the ego-self is to be understood as the integrative center which is fully present in each of the three spheres and is also dependent upon the three spheres for its existence and well-being.

---

[11] Allen Wicker, *Introduction to Ecological Psychology* (Monterey, CA: Brooks-Cole Publishing Company, 1979). Charles Gerkin also sees the context of self-development as an ecological relationship. "The quality of the self's interpretation is not simply a product of its own individual effort. The infant and mother (and/or other figures who share the mothering role) together make up a social milieu, an ecology, which shapes a certain cast to the 'I am and you are' situation. The later development of partial independence begins to shift more of the interpretive task onto the developing self. But even into adulthood, the basis for interpretation of the meaning of existence remains fundamentally social" (*Living Human Document*, 84-85).

Ray S. Anderson

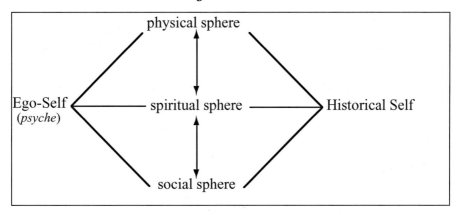

**Figure 2**

In the pre-theoretical model I used the term *psyche* to represent the capacity for feelings as distinguished from the personal, social, sexual, and spiritual aspects of the self. Here I am using *psyche* in a broader sense as equivalent to the ego-self, or soul as the center and source of the life of the person. Thus there is a psychical dimension to the physical, social, and spiritual life of the self as depicted in Figure 2. This is done to show the ecological relationship between the three spheres of the self as the experienced self in the world and with others.

*The Epigenetic Nature of an Ecological System*

There is something of an epigenetic factor in the relationship between social, personal, and spiritual being. It was Erik Erikson, along with Lyman Wynne, who took the concept of epigenesis from biology and introduced it into family therapy.[12] In his model, the early experiences of bonding and nurture were the foundation on which communication, conflict resolution, and commitment developed. A breakdown in the capacity to make and keep commitments, for example, could result from inadequate tools of conflict resolution and communication, along with a lack of core bonding experiences. Therapy thus involved rebuilding from the core foundation.

Placed in an epigenetic and schematic diagram it would look like this:

---

[12] Erik Erikson. *Childhood and Society* (New York: W. W. Norton, 1950).

157

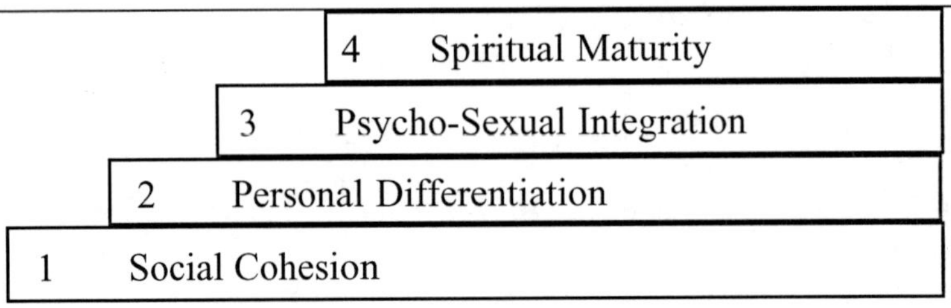

| | 4 Spiritual Maturity |
|---|---|
| 3 Psycho-Sexual Integration | |
| 2 Personal Differentiation | |
| 1 Social Cohesion | |

1. Social Cohesion: A Sense of Belonging

2. Personal Differentiation: A Sense of Self-Identity

3. Psycho-Sexual Integration: A Sense of Affective Wholeness

4. Spiritual Maturity: A Sense of Self-Worth

**Figure 3**

The social structure of human spirituality appears to be grounded in a sense of belonging which is experienced in early bonding relationships. A sense of self-identity emerges out of this foundational social reality leading to a sense of affective wholeness, or a feeling of well-being with regard to one's physical, sexual and psychical self. The movement toward wholeness and spiritual health leads to a positive sense of self-worth.

The epigenetic relation in this model means that spiritual immaturity may reflect inadequate development of psychosexual integration, personal differentiation, or even foundational social cohesion. Spiritual fitness, thus, begins with a sense of belonging issuing out of social cohesion.

It follows from this that spiritual fitness (mental health) must necessarily include the development of human personhood as social being. The core social paradigm of human existence includes spiritual formation as much as it does physical and personal existence.

*The Social Core of Human Personhood*

In a work that is extraordinary in light of his youth (at the age of twenty-one) and precocious insight, Dietrich Bonhoeffer wrote his doctoral dissertation, *The Communion of Saints*, at the University of Berlin. In my estimation this dissertation accomplished what no other work since has achieved in the integration of spirituality, sociality, and human personhood.[13] While his dissertation was ostensibly an attempt to define the nature of the church, he began with a creative and profound examination of the social nature of human personhood as the basis for stating his thesis that Jesus Christ exists in the spiritual structure of human sociality as community (*Gemeinde*) rather than in the institutional form of the church.

Central to Bonhoeffer's concept of the person is his assertion that "the individual exists only in relation to an 'other'; individual does not mean solitary. *On the contrary, for the individual to exist, 'others' must necessarily be there.*"[14] Written in 1925, before Martin Buber wrote his classic treatise on the 'I-thou' relation, Bonhoeffer wrote: "the other can be experienced by the I only as You, but never directly as I, that is, in the sense of the I that has become I only through the claim of a You . . . But since the You, too, stands before me as a person, as a thinking and acting mind, we must understand the You as an I in the general sense, i.e., in the sense of self-consciousness . . . The You as a reality-form [*Wirklichkeitsform*] is by definition independent in encountering the I in this sphere."[15]

Despite the formal and somewhat abstract language that he uses, Bonhoeffer clearly intends to say that the concrete social reality of human existence is also the structure of personal being. "*Social relations must be understood, then, as purely interpersonal and building on the uniqueness and separateness of persons.*"[16]

Bonhoeffer viewed the self as personal being, structurally open to others as well as structurally closed. By this he meant that individuality is derived out of community. Being open to the spirit of other persons awakens and intensifies one's own spirit. Personal being is structurally open and closed. There is no self consciousness without consciousness of the other, that is, of community.[17]

God created man and woman directed to one another. God does not desire a history of individual human beings, but

---

[13] Dietrich Bonhoeffer, *Sanctorum Communio: A Theological Study of the Sociology of the Church* (Minneapolis: Fortress Press, 1998).
[14] Ibid., 51 (italics in the original).
[15] Ibid.
[16] Ibid., 55 (italics in the original).
[17] Ibid., 65ff.; 73ff.

the history of the human *community*. However, God does not want a community that absorbs the individual into itself, but a community of *human beings*. In God's eyes, community and individual exist in the same moment and rest in one another. The collective unit and the individual unit have the same structure in God's eyes.[18]

"Spirit," Bonhoeffer wrote, "is necessarily created in community, and the general spirituality of persons is woven into the net of sociality. We will find that all Christian-ethical content as well as all aspects of the human spirit are only real and possible at all through sociality . . . . It will be shown that the whole nature of human spirit [*Geistigkeit*], which necessarily is presupposed by the Christian concept of person and has its unifying point in self-consciousness (of which we will also be speaking in this context), is such that it is only conceivable in sociality."[19]

*The Third Dimension of Personhood*

The social construct of human personhood is not conceived as existing as mere mutuality of persons, but as a 'structure' in which a third dimension of personhood is created. Bonhoeffer puts it this way:

Two wills encountering one another form a structure. A third person joining them sees not just one person connected to the other; rather, the will of the structure, as a third factor, resists the newcomer with a resistance not identical with the wills of the two individuals. Sometimes this is even more powerful than that of either individual—or than the sum of all the individuals, if this is at all conceivable. Precisely this structure is objective spirit.[20]

This 'objective spirit, or sometimes called 'objective person,' is a social construct of human personhood which, says Bonhoeffer, "fraught with so much contingency, imperfection, and sin, nevertheless . . . becomes the *bearer of the social activity of*

---

[18] Ibid., 80.
[19] Ibid., 62, 66.
[20] Ibid., 98.

*the Holy Spirit.*"[21] The practical implication of this emerges later for Bonhoeffer in his discussion of confession of sin and the grace of forgiveness.

> In confession there occurs a *breakthrough to assurance*. Why is it often easier for us to acknowledge our sins before God than before another believer? God is holy and without sin, a just judge of evil, and an enemy of all disobedience. But another Christian is sinful, as are we, knowing from personal experience the night of secret sin. Should we not find it easier to go to one another than to the holy God? But if that is not the case, we must ask ourselves whether we often have not been deluding ourselves about our confession of sin to God—whether we have not instead been confessing our sins to ourselves and also forgiving ourselves. And is not the reason for our innumerable relapses and for the feebleness of our Christian obedience to be found precisely in the fact that we are living from self-forgiveness and not from the real forgiveness of our sins?[22]

Not only does Bonhoeffer locate the spiritual reality of forgiveness in the social relation, but he points to the reason for our "innumerable relapses" as due to the attempt to relate to God as individuals and not through our relation to others. What psychologists and therapists know to be true about the need for encounter with a significant other in order to experience growth and change, Bonhoeffer acknowledges as a truth of the core social relation. The social construct of human personhood is also the source of our spiritual life and growth.

Because the reality of spirit is first of all a social reality rooted in the nature of human personhood, Bonhoeffer can argue that the social structure of human personhood is intrinsically spiritual. The Spirit of God does not constitute something alongside, or merely inside, an individual person. Rather, the Spirit of God joins the human spirit at the core of its social reality. Human spirituality is the core of the self as it becomes a self through social relation with others. Jürgen Moltmann argues in a similar way when he says, "The Holy Spirit does not supersede the Spirit of creation but transforms it. The Holy Spirit therefore lays

---

[21] Ibid., 233 (italics in the original).
[22] *Life Together: Prayerbook of the Bible*, Dietrich Bonhoeffer Works, Volume 5 (Minneapolis: Fortress Press, 1996), 112-113.

hold of the whole human being, embracing his feelings and his body as well as his soul and reason. He forms the whole Gestalt of the person anew by making believers 'con-form' to Christ, the first born among many brethren (Ro. 8:29)."[23]

The growth of the person into a self-identity takes place in a context of social and spiritual interaction, with intentionality of love as the motive force. The integration of the various components of the self into an I-Self reality is part of the construct of an I-Thou experience. The mental and physical dimensions of the self are correlated through the openness of the self toward a transcending subject (self).

Martin Buber, the Jewish philosopher most remembered for his classic treatise on the nature of the self as personal and relational, wrote:

> The You encounters me by grace—it cannot be found by seeking. But that I speak the basic word to it is a deed of my whole being, is my essential deed . . . . The basic word I-You can be spoken only with one's whole being. The concentration and fusion into a whole being can never be accomplished by me, can never be accomplished without me. I require a You to become: being I, I say you.[24]

The priority of the social relation in the differentiation of the self is a direct implication of the image of God as grounded in co-humanity rather than in individuality. The awakening of the infant to selfhood and the beginning of the development of the image of God as a possibility and personal history of fulfillment is linked to the encounter with others. This begins at the earliest point of the infant's life, and the 'face' that shines upon the infant in love reflects and mediates the love of God, a point articulated eloquently by Hans Urs von Balthasar:

> Through the interdependence of the generations, the social element embraces the individual and influences him . . . . God, who inclined toward his newborn creature with infinite personal love, in order to inspire him with it and to awaken the response to it in him, does in the divine supernatural order something similar to a mother. Out of

---

[23] Moltmann, *God in Creation*, 263.
[24] *I and Thou*, tr. by Walter Kaufman (Edinburgh: T. & T. Clark, 1979), 62.

the strength of her own heart she awakens love in her child in true creative activity . . . The essential thing is that the child, awakened thus to love, and already endowed by another's power of love, awakens also to himself and to his true freedom, which is in fact the freedom of loving transcendence of his narrow individuality. No man reaches the core and ground of his own being, becoming free to himself and to all beings, unless love shines on him.[25]

## Issues of Self-Identity

While the image of God as the total self must be acknowledged as fully present from the beginning of the human person, the *content* of this image is only realized through a developmental process. Self-identity, then, is acquired as the particular form of the image of God resulting from the growth and development of the self. The psychological literature on the stages of self and identity development is an expanding and varied field of study. Along with Erik Erikson's well-known stages of self-development are Kohlberg's stages of moral development, Fowler's stages of faith development, Piaget's stages of cognitive development, Kohut's stages of identity formation, and Gilligan's theory of women's developmental stages.[26]

It is not my intention to add to or interact with these developmental theories but to suggest that from a theological perspective, the image of God is developmentally related to the growth of the self as embodied, personal, and social being. It is my thesis that the integration of psychological and spiritual aspects of the self can best be seen as part of this developmental trajectory of growth. My focus is on the growth of self-identity based upon the nature of the self as described above.

Romney Moseley suggests that there are two factors that enter into self-development. "First, the self is formed as it

---

[25] Hans Urs von Balthasar, *A Theological Anthropology* (New York: Sheed and Ward, 1967), 87.

[26] Erik Erickson, *The Life Cycle Completed: A Review* (New York: W.W. Norton and Company, 1982); E. Erickson, *Identity, Youth and Crisis* (New York: W.W. Norton and Company, 1968); James Fowler, *Stages of Faith* (San Francisco: Harper and Row, 1981); Jean Piaget, *Six Psychological Studies* (New York: Random House, Vintage Books, 1967); Carol Gilligan, *In a Different Voice: Psychological Theory and Women's Development* (Cambridge: Harvard University Press, 1982).

interacts with the world. Second, there are stages of relative stability as the self progresses from egocentrism to higher levels of social perspective taking. In the course of development, the self is liberated from its captivity in the egocentric perceptions of early childhood."[27]

My own formulation of the developmental process is slightly different. Rather than contrasting an egocentric stage with a social stage of self-identity, I see the development of the ego-self as continuous with the development of the social-self.

The newborn infant certainly possesses an ego-self, though largely undeveloped. This ego-self is the seat of feelings (emotions) and the core of what will become self-identity. The infant first of all experiences at a subconscious level a social relation with the primary caregivers through which differentiation at the personal and sexual level gradually emerges. Through this process the full range of psychical feelings and responses are developed from their original limited capacity. The core of the self as spiritual being, which from the beginning has been in place, now is opened up to response to God and to the other. The egocentrism of the self, present from the beginning, is thus developed simultaneously with the self's development of social identity. The process of development is not from egocentric to social consciousness as much as it is from immature self to mature self-identity, both as egocentric and social relating.

The bi-directional nature of human spirituality is represented by the two great commandments first stated in the Old Testament and then reiterated by Jesus: "'You shall love the Lord your God with all your heart, and with all your soul, and with all your mind.' This is the greatest and first commandment. And the second is like it: 'You shall love your neighbor as yourself'" (Matthew 22:38-39; Deut 6:5; Lev. 19:18).

As originally created by God, social spirituality reflects the divine image and likeness constitutive of human personhood. The second creation account (Genesis 2) recasts the creation of the human as though only a solitary individual is present. Despite an obvious relation between Adam and God, the divine verdict is that it is not good for the man to be alone. With the creation of the woman, humans are differentiated and yet bound together as male and female, as social beings. The implication is that the divine image spoken of in Genesis 1:26-27 can only be complete as a

---

[27] Romney Moseley, *Becoming a Self—Critical Transformations Before God* (Nashville: Abingdon Press, 1991), 60.

social construct of personal relation.

Even as the individual self exists as structurally open to the spirit of another person, it is structurally open to the Spirit of God. When we speak of spirituality as a relation with God, we are speaking of the social spirituality which is constitutive of the human person, not a religious instinct, feeling, or practice. Social spirituality is what makes religion possible. Social spirituality is not only the source of authentic relation with God, but it is also the first casualty of sin and in need of redemption.

## The Spiritual Destiny of Human Creaturely Life

All creatures bear a common threat to their existence by virtue of being creaturely by nature, created out of the dust of the ground. Creaturely life is suspended in time by the fragile mystery that binds breath to flesh and connects nerve to muscle. But no other creature experiences the double jeopardy of being human. Human existence is never assured by the sustaining of creaturely life by itself. What is a threat to all creatures is also a threat to humans. The non-human creatures have nothing to lose in being no more than their creaturely nature allows them to be. Their nature determines their destiny. But humans have a divinely and spirit-endowed destiny that, while dependent upon survival at the creaturely level, reaches for more than creaturely nature can give. Humans can live out their natural creaturely life and still fail spiritually to become what they are destined to be.

In the biblical account of creation, there is a 'solidarity of the sixth day' that binds humans to all creatures through a shared creaturely nature. Both are of the dust of the ground. Humans, however, are destined to share God's life and to enter into the 'seventh day' and experience God's 'rest.' Failure to reach this 'rest' is a failure to reach the essential orientation of human life itself (Hebrew 4:1-13). This is what is meant by saying that humans experience a kind of double jeopardy. They are vulnerable as human creatures to the mortal destiny of all that is creaturely. They are also vulnerable as spiritual beings to the tragic loss of spiritual life and a final destiny to share in the life of God as Spirit.

The spirit of life which determines the creaturely experience of human life is a special orientation of the unity of body and soul. The spirit of life for all other creatures is closed and self-contained. That is, their spirit existence is contained and turned in upon their natural creaturely existence.

Human creaturely life, on the other hand, is oriented to a life and Spirit beyond that of sheer creaturely existence. It is the body/soul unity of human existence that is spiritual in its orientation and destiny. Humans are not simply beings which also have spirit; they are spiritual beings in the whole of their body/soul existence. This is what distinguishes them from all other creatures. As Pierre Teilhard de Chardin has said, "We are not human beings having a spiritual experience, but spiritual beings having a human experience."[28]

To be human is to exist as a body/soul unity that has a spiritual openness and orientation toward the source of life itself—the Creator Spirit. To be spiritual, therefore, is to exist as a body/soul unity in which knowledge of and relation to the Creator Spirit is experienced in the dual relation of one human to another. In saying this, I am excluding all concepts of spirituality that either deny one's own humanity as a body/soul unity or, on the other hand, a spirituality that opposes one's creaturely nature to one's human nature as though these are separate entities. The human person does not have a 'higher' spiritual self and a 'lower' fleshly self; there is no antagonism or dualism which sets spirit over and against the flesh. When the Apostle Paul introduces a distinction between fruit of the spirit and works of the flesh in his ethical admonition, he speaks of non-physical attitudes and actions as pride, jealousy, and idolatry as 'works of the flesh' (Galatians 5:19-20). Clearly what Paul means by 'flesh' is an introversion of spirit by which one's spirituality becomes a negative rather than positive aspect of one's being.

*Spiritual Formation and the Social Self*

Since the nature of human life is determined by a spiritual orientation, it follows that the development and maturation of personal life is at the same time a process of spiritual formation. The two cannot be separated as isolated functions and tasks. For this reason, spiritual formation as a task belonging to the process of being human is not the implementation of an alien imperative upon otherwise complete human beings. Spiritual formation is not an extracurricular task that attempts to bring persons under some form of religious tutelage. Spiritual formation properly understood is intrinsic to the development of the self into the gestalt of human

---

[28] Cited by Gordon McDonald, *The Life God Blesses* (Nashville: Thomas Nelson Publishers, 1994), 76.

wholeness. What is more, it precedes and is the essential possibility for the development of healthy religious spiritual life. "We should misunderstand the formation of man," says Dietrich Bonhoeffer, "if we were to regard it as instruction in the way in which a pious and good life is to be attained."[29]

Spiritual formation should no more be understand merely as 'religious education' than as ideological indoctrination. The 'form' that determines spiritual formation as human development as both structure and goal is neither idealistic nor utilitarian. It is personal, historical, and communal.

Spirituality, then, is not only bound up in the communal life which cares for and upholds our personal being, but also in the same community which holds us accountable to our intentions with regard to the spiritual life and being of others. This seems to be why Scripture is so clear in pointing out that faith in God is measured not by religious actions but by human actions as works of love (James 2:15-17). If people claim to love God but hate their brothers and sisters, they are liars, "for those who do not love a brother or sister whom they have seen, cannot love God whom they have not seen" (1 John 4:20).

The spiritual dimension of human personhood constitutes the 'whole' of the self as a psycho/social unity of embodied personal life. Spirituality, then, is to be seen as more than a religious aspect of the self. The spiritual core of the self is what makes religion possible. Spiritual fitness thus is the basis for authentic religious expression as well as for effective mental health. Lack of mental health, then, can be considered the result of a partializing or splitting of the self, or a lack of spiritual fitness as a holistic expression of the self in relation to self, others, and God.

Theologian Emil Brunner speaks of a 'sorrow-of-heart' that experiences the disharmony of existence without a center that lies outside of the self. To attempt to organize the self around its own center, warns Brunner, produces what might be called spiritual or psychological health, but without a center that gives the self a place of hope in God, this 'health' is itself a form of madness, or insanity. "To place the central point of existence outside God, who is the true Centre, in the 'I' and the world, is madness; for it cannot be a real centre; the world cannot provide any resting-place for the Self; it only makes it oscillate hither and thither."[30]

---

[29] *Ethics* (New York: Macmillan, 1965), 80.
[30] *Man in Revolt* (Philadelphia: Westminster, 1939) p. 235. For further discussion of the social formation of human spirituality, see Ray S.

*Sin or Pathology?*

I have attempted to present a profile of human personhood as a personal, social, and spiritual unity of embodied life, having both an intrinsic value and a developmental drive toward health and maturity. This is how it ought to be. But, as Brunner so well put it, even what can be viewed as normal and healthy often exhibits a perversity and pathology which is akin to madness apart from an anchor in God's gracious preservation. Sin is one way of describing the disorder and disunion of the self—as 'not the way it's supposed to be,' as one theologian put it.[31] Pathology is another. If they are not the same, how are they different?

Some hold that there is a fine line between pathology and sin that both the psychologist and the theologian must respect, allowing pathology to be removed through therapy and sin through grace. To my mind, this is a fundamental disintegration of personhood as a futile attempt at integration. To think in this way is to place pathology and sin on a continuum, which inevitably demands respect for the extremes and leads to confusion and collusion at the center. This is two-dimensional thinking with regard to mental and spiritual health.[32]

For example, when the focus moves to the center of the continuum, there is a tendency to spiritualize symptoms of emotional and mental disorder, even to go so far as to demonize mental illness, with exorcism being the weapon of choice. At the same point, there is a tendency for psychology to pathologize sin, and what cannot be cured by psychotherapy can be managed by psychopharmacology.

This two-dimensional approach can be likened to the classic parable of *Flatland*, where a two-dimensional world was the only one known to its inhabitants.[33] When one of them suddenly discovered the third dimension of height and attempted to convince his fellow two-dimensional creatures of this reality, he

---

Anderson, *Spiritual Caregiving as Secular Sacrament: A Practical Theology for Professional Caregivers* (London: Jessica Kingsley, 2003).

[31] Cornelius Plantinga, Jr. *Not the Way it's Supposed to Be: A Breviary of Sin* (Grand Rapids: Eerdmans, 1995).

[32] See my essay, "Sin: The Third Dimension of Human Spirituality," in *Christian Counseling Today*, Vol. 10, No. 1, 2002, 26-29.

[33] Edwin Abbott, *Flatland: A Romance of Many Dimensions* (New York: Penguin Books, 1998).

was ridiculed and viewed as delusional. From the perspective of the third dimension, the two-dimensional world made sense and had its own place in the structure of reality. From a two-dimensional worldview, however, there was no bridge from the one to the other. Attempts to explain the third dimension as 'just another angle' failed to satisfy the demands of this new perspective.

Sin is not circumstantial, as though it can be accounted for by physical/social environmental factors which afflict the self. Guilt is not a moral failure, to be removed by moral repentance. Sin and neurosis are not two sides of the same coin.[34] Nor is sin existential, an aberration due to angst.[35] Properly understood from a three-dimensional view of human spirituality, sin is *axial*. In art, an axis is an implied line in a painting or sculpture through a composition to which elements in the composition are related. As an adjective, axial means relating to or having the characteristics of having an axis.

Sin is located in the spiritual axis of the human self and can be viewed as representing a third dimension of human spirituality to which the other dimensions of the human self are related. What defies explanation from a psychological and even religious view of the self is the way in which the human will can be so perverse in its motives and actions. Perversity is more than a disease; it is a deliberate and intentional, though not always conscious, deviation from what is good, for the self and others.

The fifth century theologian Augustine lamented the fact that the core of the human self seemed bent on a perversity, which could not be explained other than as a willful grasp for that which gave pleasure only in the fact that it was forbidden. He gave an example from his own youth to make his point when he stole pears off his neighbor's tree: "I willed to commit theft, and I did so, not because I was driven to it by any need, unless it were by poverty of justice, and dislike of it, and by a glut of evildoing. For I stole a thing of which I had plenty of my own and of much better quality. Nor did I wish to enjoy that thing which I desired to gain by theft, but rather to enjoy the actual theft and the sin of theft." After he and his friends stole the pears, he admitted that he had access to better quality pears in his own yard, and rather than eating them

---

34 Ernest Becker, *The Denial of Death* (New York: Macmillan/Free Press, 1973).
35 Søren Kierkegaard, *The Concept of Dread* (Princeton: Princeton University Press, 1957).

to satisfy his hunger, they were given to the pigs. Thus, for Augustine, sin represented a deeper bondage to desire as something perverted; it is something that we are born with.[36] Sin is perverse, not merely problematic.

This perversity of the will, as Augustine termed it, is descriptive but not definitive with regard to sin. It would be safe to say that every human gives evidence of it at some time or other and in some way or other. "At risk is not the existence of sin but our ability to grasp and say something articulate about the presence of sin in our lives and world."[37]

In addition to healing for deep intrapsychic disturbances, emotional pain, and dysfunctional social relationships, the self requires mending at the level of core social spirituality. When the spiritual core of the self is broken at the root, there is need of grace as both spiritual palliative and therapeutic relief. In his play, *The Great God Brown*, Eugene O'Neill has one of his characters say: "We are born broken. We live by mending. The grace of God is the glue."[38]

The Jesuit psychotherapist W. W. Meissner says, "Grace not only alters our theological condition, but it delves into our psychic reality. . . . Grace is the energizing and relational principle on the spiritual level for the proper functions of the ego. Development of spiritual identity, then, is achieved through the same ego-functions that are involved in the natural psychological identity."[39] Facilitating a movement toward health in one sphere may release the self to grow toward health in another sphere. The 'ego' as a specific subject of psychological attention lies between the self and its lived experience in the world. When the self is addressed and responds at the level of its spiritual sphere, the 'ego' of the self is also touched and healed. Effective mediation of God's grace not only is a spiritual means for healing, but also touches the very core of the human self, enabling it and assisting it in the integrative task of becoming whole.

---

[36] Augustine, *Confessions* (New York: Oxford University Press, 1982), 24.

[37] Patrick McCormick, *Sin and Addiction* (New York: Paulist Press, 1989), 3.

[38] Eugene O'Neill. "The Great God Brown," *The Plays of Eugene O'Neill*, Vol.1 (New York: Modern Library, 1982), 318.

[39] W. W. Meissner, *Life and Faith: Psychological Perspectives on Religious Experience* (Washington, D. C.: Georgetown University Press, 1987), 7, 58.

# Ray S. Anderson

## Ethical Issues

In his earliest work on the nature of the human person, Dietrich Bonhoeffer wrote that the "*social ontic-ethical basic-relations of persons*" constitutes the basic reality structure in which humans live. He went on to say, "*the metaphysical concept of the individual is defined without mediation, whereas the ethical concept of the person is a definition based on ethical-social interaction.*"[40] In contrast to Kant, who held that individuals have at their disposal ethical value and that ethics has an epistemological basis in universals, Bonhoeffer wrote that individuals are not 'value-filled,' but 'value-related.' In other words, only in the concrete (ontic) social relation does the individual have personal value and dignity, and only in that relation have ethical obligation. "The person exists always and only in ethical responsibility . . . ."[41]

From Bonhoeffer's perspective, one cannot discuss the nature of human personhood without also understanding that persons exist in a concrete social interaction which constitutes an 'ethical event.' Ethical issues, then, arise out of a discussion of the nature of human persons necessarily and not only incidentally.

For example, critical ethical issues relating to conception of life as well as to termination of life are first of all questions as to what constitutes human life. The most that we can say is that a human person begins as any other creature in a biological process that entails fertilization and cell division. However, even in that process, the resulting life form carries the form of the human, even in its prenatal stage. Once conceived in a human womb, the embryo is essentially human, dependent only upon sufficient bio-chemical support to come to birth as a human person. At the same time, biological life is a necessary but insufficient condition to be human. The human self is contingent upon something more than biological life (*bios*) in order to have vital human life (*zoe*). In the New Testament, *zoe* refers to a person's life made abundantly full, and this life is inseparable from Jesus Christ as the source of life (cf. John 10:10; I Tim. 6:11, 12, 19).[42] The conception of a child is an 'ethical event' because it is the act of human persons,

---

[40] *Sanctorum Communio*, 50. Italics in the original.
[41] Ibid., 48.
[42] See, Robert Nelson, *Human Life—A Biblical Perspective for Bioethics* (Philadelphia: Fortress Press, 1984). Nelson suggests that we might better speak of "zoe-ethics" rather than bioethics (107ff.).

intentionally or accidentally, and as such brings ethical responsibility for the protection and sustaining of human life.

The loss of potential human life is inevitably an ethical event and thus a tragic event. However, Bonhoeffer's view of personhood as an ethical event is not narrowly defined along the lines of abstract principles but in the multi-layered and complex structure of the whole of life. Thus, responsible ethical action is defined first of all in the context of what is, not what ought to be. "In the sphere of Christian ethics it is not Ought that effects Is, but Is that effects Ought."[43] In acting responsibly out of the reality of a person's concrete ontic-ethical social relations, ethical actions are often also tinged with the tragic. "The simple fact," wrote Bonhoeffer, "is that the ethical cannot be detached from reality, and consequently continual progress in learning to appreciate reality is a necessary ingredient in ethical action."[44]

A theological view of human personhood is the underlying moral basis for ethical rules for living and dying. We are to "love our neighbors as ourselves" (Matt. 22:39). The unborn, though not yet persons in the full sense, are "neighbors" in the human sense and thus constitute a moral demand upon the living for preservation of life within the limits of human possibility. Physical life has intrinsic and relative value as possibility, though it does not constitute an absolute value. God upholds the absolute value of human life through the frailties, torments, and trauma of life on this earth. The so-called 'right to die' in this view of human personhood is not first of all an ethical decision but an 'ethical event' in which the immediate social structure of that event is called to uphold life in the very process of dying. I have written earlier on this subject and said, "A so-called 'vegetative' state of bodily existence is virtually a form of death, and can itself become an indignity if artificially prolonged as a monument to medical technology. When a machine and a body have more of a necessary relationship than do the soul and the body, what is being sustained

---

[43] Ibid., 36, 211.

[44] *Ethics*, 360. As a commentary on the sometimes tragic nature of ethical action, Bonhoeffer says that responsible action concerned solely with the other person may of necessity entail guilt. "If any man tries to escape guilt in responsibility he detaches himself from the ultimate reality of human existence, and what is more he cuts himself off from the redeeming mystery of Christ's bearing guilt without sin and he has no share in the divine justification which lies upon this event." Ibid., 238-239.

is not life, but a process of dying."[45] Here again, we discover that an ethical act must also be prepared to accept the tragic aspect of that decision if it is to be a responsible act.

Even as it could be a violation of the value of human life to be forced to live merely at the biological level, so it would be a violation of the value of human life to be forced to live in a role structure (economic, social, or political), which has as a consequence the deprivation of life as a gift to be with and for the other in a relationship of parity and reciprocity. 'Human rights' are thus grounded in the ecological construct of humanity itself, not in an abstract principle mediated through self-determination; other persons have a right to my responsible action in upholding their own humanity, but not the right to kill me for failing in this responsibility. The 'right' to be free from a person or persons who diminish my own quality of life is qualified by my need of persons to uphold the gift of life which constitutes my humanity.

A theological view of human personhood is the positive moral basis for the liberation of human sexuality from degradation, oppression and exploitation; in Christ, "there is neither Jew nor Greek, slave nor free, male nor female," for in Christ all are one (Gal. 3:28). Human personhood is male and female, male or female, equally and mutually human, a polarity and community of personal being manifest through biological sexual differentiation, but under the promise of freedom from such limitations through life beyond death.

Because our humanity is under divine determination, judgment and redemption—from Adam to Christ—a Christian vision of the human is liberating, hopeful, and therapeutic. In life beyond death through the new humanity of Jesus Christ, there will no longer be "mourning, nor crying, nor pain" (Rev. 21:4). The final vision of humanity is more human than human imagination or experience can picture.

---

[45] Ray S. Anderson, *On Being Human: Essays in Theological Anthropology* (Grand Rapids: Eerdmans, 1982), 142.

# Attachment: Bowlby and the Bible

*Robert C. Roberts*
Baylor University

*Introduction*

At the end of the third volume of his magisterial trilogy on the psychology of attachment, John Bowlby declares,

> Intimate attachments to other human beings are the hub around which a person's life revolves, not only when he is an infant or a toddler or a schoolchild but throughout his adolescence and his years of maturity as well, and on into old age. From these intimate attachments a person draws his strength and enjoyment of life and, through what he contributes, he gives strength and enjoyment to others. These are matters, about which current science and traditional wisdom are at one.[1]

One version of such traditional wisdom is the Christian one, which derives from the documents of the New Testament. Bowlby's research supports the biblical view of attachment. However, his concept of attachment, though parallel to the New Testament's in several respects, also diverges in significant ways. I shall compare the two concepts, arguing that Bowlby's concept could be considerably improved by making it more like the New Testament's.

*Attachment in the Bible*

No word, used by any biblical author, has exactly the scope and sense that I shall here attach to "attachment." But I hope to establish that around this word we can construct a concept whose features are all biblical, though never, in the Bible, tied together quite as they are here. If this concept of attachment is, as I intend, a *psychological* concept analogous to the ones that are pivotal for

---

[1] Bowlby, *Loss: Sadness and Depression* (NY: Basic Books, 1980), 442.

standard personality theories, this may explain, in part, why the concept is not found in the Bible. The Bible is not a book of systematic psychology, any more than it is a book of systematic theology. But it does contain concepts that are psychological in a less formal sense, just as it contains analogously informal theological concepts. It is these less formal concepts I shall draw on in constructing the psychological idea of attachment.

Attachment can be to things as well as to people and to God. Because the rich young ruler (Luke 18:18) was attached to his wealth, he was saddened when Jesus told him that to have eternal life he must give it up (detach himself from it); and Jesus invited the ruler to attach himself to Jesus rather than to his "goods" ("come, follow me"). This passage suggests that attachment is a sort of emotional "dependency"—that one's emotional response is conditioned by the state of what one is attached to. Through attachment to something, one becomes subject to the vicissitudes of that thing. The ruler is saddened by the prospect of those goods not being his, and attachment to fellow human beings is evidenced by emotional responsiveness to how they are faring. "Rejoice with those who rejoice; weep with those who weep" (Rom. 15:15) can be read as an exhortation to be attached to one another. Because Paul is attached to the Jewish people ("my brethren, my kinsmen by race") their failure to grasp God's grace occasions "great sorrow and unceasing anguish in [his] heart" (Rom. 9:2-3).

In response to this fact of human nature, the central Stoic prophylaxis against emotional distress is *de*tachment (keeping "emotional distance") from things and persons.[2] Unlike Stoicism and such otherwise diverse psychologies as those of Carl Jung, Albert Ellis, Carl Rogers, and Murray Bowen, the Bible does not commend detachment as an across-the-board policy for personal maturity. Certainly, people may suffer from their attachments, as Paul does from his attachment to his fellow Jews; this is the mischief of being "vulnerable," "dependent," "subject to" the object of attachment. But then emotional suffering is not the worst thing that can happen to a person. In the biblical view, it would be far worse to have no attachments at all—to be without "love." Particular attachments are sometimes unhealthy, as in the ruler's case; but attachment to God and to one's fellow human beings is strongly prescribed (Matt. 22:34-40). This implies something

[2] Epictetus, *The Enchiridion*, tr. T. Higginson & intro. by A. Salomon (Indianapolis: Bobbs-Merrill, 1948).

about the Bible's implicit conception of human nature, a conception similar to Bowlby's: we are not essentially autonomous monads who *happen* to have fellow monads with whom it is convenient and pleasant to live in harmony and some kind of inessential, non-psychological interdependency. We are made for attachments, made to live in terms of things that are not ourselves; it is not a fault in us to have our emotional life subject to the changing conditions of our fellow humans, or to the diverse attitudes and actions of God. Attachment is an essential structure[3] of human personality that calls, not for mitigation or extirpation, but for proper development.

Paul encourages church members to depend on one another for many things (see 1 Cor. 12, Rom. 12:4-5, "membership one of another" being a form of attachment), and the particular kind of attachment to Christ that the apostle Paul calls "faith" is one in which a weak person (a disciple) derives strength from a strong one (the Lord):

> Three times I besought the Lord about [a "thorn" in Paul's "flesh"], that it should leave me; but he said to me, "My grace is sufficient for you, for my power is made perfect in weakness." I will all the more gladly boast of my weaknesses, that the power of Christ may rest upon me. For the sake of Christ, then, I am content with weaknesses, insults, hardships, persecutions, and calamities; for when I am weak, then I am strong. (2 Cor. 12:8-10)

This attachment to Christ is a little bit like that of a small child to its parent, as Bowlby describes it, an attachment in which the child derives security from the ongoing presence of the parent, and thus the ability to explore with confidence. Paul is able to "go on" with his work, despite adversities, living confidently and happily and free from basic anxiety, because Christ is with him; and since Christ's being with him is the paramount blessing, he can even welcome the adversities as accentuating his dependency on Christ. The similarity between the attachment of the human person to God, and that of the child to the human parent, is suggested by Jesus' use of "Abba" ("Father") in addressing God (see Mark 14:36), a use that is picked up in the early church. Thus St. Paul: "When we cry 'Abba! Father!' it is the Spirit himself

---

3 S. Maddi, *Personality Theories: A Comparative Analysis* (Homewood, IL: Dorsey Press, 1980).

bearing witness with our spirit that we are children of God" (Rom. 8:15b-16; see Gal. 4:1-7). The theme of trust in God's fatherly watchfulness, and thus attachment to God, is forcefully struck in Jesus' discourse on the birds and the lilies in Luke 12:22-31.

In the Christian view of persons, it is a basic structural fact of our nature that we get attached to things and persons, a fact not to be resisted, as it is by many modern psychologists. But the Christian psychology agrees with every personality theory I know of, in holding that not all attachments express true human nature. So the trick, for the deepest success in human life, is to get attached *in the right way to the right things*. Jesus says, "Where your treasure is, there will your heart be also" (Matt. 6:21), thus saying, in effect, What you are like at the center of your personality (your "heart") is a function of the kind of thing you are very attached to (your "treasure"). Thus one who is very attached to God will be a different sort of "self" than someone who is very attached to money or power. Similarly, a person who is very attached to her friends will have a different personality from someone deeply attached to her public reputation.

Of course Jesus is not merely remarking here that differing attachments yield differing selves; behind his remark is the supposition that some variants of selves are worthy, healthy, and complete, while others have missed the mark. The Christian virtues are states in which, among other things, proper patterns of attachment are worked out. For example, Christian generosity is a state of relative detachment from wealth and attachment to God, and to friends and neighbors. I shall not try here to elaborate the norms for proper attachment, but such sayings of Jesus as the following will indicate the direction: "Seek first [God's] kingdom and his righteousness, and all these things shall be yours as well" (Matt. 6:33). "Blessed are those who hunger and thirst for righteousness, for they shall be satisfied" (Matt. 5:6). "He who loves father or mother more than me is not worthy of me; and he who loves son or daughter more than me is not worthy of me; and he who does not take his cross and follow me is not worthy of me" (Matt. 10:37-38). "You shall love the Lord your God with all your heart, and with all your soul, and with all your mind . . . . And . . . you shall love your neighbor as yourself" (Matt. 22:37b, 39b). In most of these passages it is acknowledged (if somewhat indirectly) that attachment to property, to son or mother, or to neighbor, is fitting and healthy *provided* that attachment to God and his kingdom is central and overriding in one's emotional makeup.

To summarize: In the Bible, attachment is a psychological relation that a person can have to things, other humans, or God. It is evidenced in emotional responsiveness to the perceived vicissitudes of its object: say, sorrow at the loss of a physical possession, or joy at its retrieval. If the object of attachment is a human being, the response might be satisfaction if the person is perceived as doing well, or anxiety if she is threatened, or anger if she is hurt through someone's action or omission. If the other person is in the role of protector (as a parent is to a child), then attachment to the object will result in anxiety if the protector is perceived as too far away or unable to protect, and relief upon perceiving the object to be near again, or again perhaps anger at the object for not being available. If the object of attachment is God, then again one will experience joy when God's purposes are perceived as fostered, and frustration when they are hindered; one will experience anxiety if God is perceived as distant or even nonexistent, and joy and comfort when he is perceived as near, benevolently watchful, and protective. The Bible regards the attachment disposition as a fact of human nature, not to be resisted wholesale, but to be properly directed, applied, and administered. Thus selective detachment is an important strategy of psycho-spiritual growth. It is proper to be attached (in an appropriate way) to human beings and (in a rather different way) to non-personal things, and proper to be very strongly (indeed, "ultimately" or "infinitely") attached to God. Attachment to inanimate or non-human animate things ("possessions") is consistent with health, but not in the degree of strength or kind appropriate to personal objects, human and divine. To say attachment is a structural feature of human personality is to say that the human psyche is an essentially connected, relational sort of thing; it lives and gains its character, for good or ill, from its connections with things "outside" itself.

*Bowlby on Attachment*

**What Is Attachment?**

In Bowlby's theory the concept of attachment initially seems to have a much narrower scope than its Christian counterpart. The most salient subject of attachment is the infant or young child, and the object is the mother or mother substitute. Bowlby distinguishes attachment as a pattern of relating from attachment behavior; attachment is a strong disposition "to seek proximity to and contact with" the mother, especially when the child is frightened, tired, or ill. Attachment behavior, by contrast, includes all the various forms of behavior by which the child attains or maintains the desired proximity (crying, facial expression, eye contact, clinging, following, calling, etc.).[4] This behavior is "the output of . . . a safety-regulating system, namely a system the activities of which tend to reduce the risk of the individual coming to harm and are experienced as causing anxiety to be allayed and the sense of security to be increased."[5]

Depending on how the mother interacts with her child's attachment behavior, the child's attachment will become secure, or insecure. The quality of the attachment is a function of the quality of the mother's relating to the infant as represented in the infant's "working model" (a cognitive construct) of the mother in her relationship to the infant. The working model is a fairly accurate mental representation of the mother as she has interacted, over time, with the child. If she is represented as *reliable*, the child's attachment is secure; he is happy to be with her, and returns to her regularly as a "secure base" from which to explore, but he is able to explore away from her for periods without anxiety. If she is represented as *not wholly reliable but not, on the whole, unreliable,* the child's attachment is insecure resistant (anxious); he tends to cling to her and to be distraught when she is not very close, and explores with some anxiety. If she is represented *as quite unreliable and thus on the whole a disappointment,* the child's attachment is insecure avoidant; he may cling to her sometimes, but at others will "reject" her, even acting as if he has never seen her.[6] Personal maturity in adult life is, in Bowlby's theory, very largely a result of having had one's attachment needs well satisfied in early childhood, that is to say, having had a reliably warm and solicitous mother.

I say that Bowlby's concept of attachment "initially seems" to have narrower scope than the Christian concept because, although he does not cease interpreting attachment primarily as an infantile system for maintaining safety through spatial proximity to the mother, he broadens the concept to include persons of all ages—to attachments that seem quite remote from any safety-maintaining function. Already in the first volume of his

---

[4] Bowlby, *Attachment*, 2nd ed. (NY: Basic Books, 1982), 371.
[5] Ibid., 374.
[6] M. Ainsworth et al., *Patterns of Attachment: A Psychological Study of the Strange Situation* (Hillsdale, NJ: Erlbaum, 1978).

trilogy he expands the scope of attachment to apply to adults, though he retains the narrow conception of its function:

> That attachment behaviour in adult life is a straightforward continuation of attachment behaviour in childhood is shown by the circumstances that lead an adult's attachment behaviour to become more readily elicited. In sickness and calamity, adults often become demanding of others; in conditions of sudden danger or disaster a person will almost certainly seek proximity to another known and trusted person.[7]

Something like the safety-maintaining function is still evident in the following 1973 passage, though one can detect that the emphasis moves away from survival towards happiness, fulfillment, and the meaning of life:

> Not only young children, it is now clear, but human beings of all ages are found to be at their happiest and able to deploy their talents to best advantage when they are confident that, standing behind them, there are one or more trusted persons who will come to their aid should difficulties arise . . . . Paradoxically, the truly self-reliant person when viewed in this light proves to be by no means as independent as cultural stereotypes suppose. An essential ingredient is a capacity to rely trustingly on others when occasion demands and to know on whom it is appropriate to rely. A healthily self-reliant person is thus capable of exchanging roles when the situation changes: at one time he is providing a secure base from which his companion(s) can operate; at another he is glad to rely on one or another of his companions to provide him with just such a base in return.[8]

And the third volume of Bowlby's trilogy ends with the statement I quoted at the outset of this chapter, which seems to widen both the kind and significance of attachments:

> Intimate attachments to other human beings are the hub

---

[7] *Attachment*, 207-8.

[8] Bowlby, *Separation: Anxiety and Anger* (NY: Basic Books, 1973), 359-60.

around which a person's life revolves, not only when he is an infant or a toddler or a schoolchild but throughout his adolescence and his years of maturity as well, and on into old age. From these intimate attachments a person draws his strength and enjoyment of life and, through what he contributes, he gives strength and enjoyment to others.[9]

Our concept is now very far from that of a safety-regulating control system that functions primarily to insure physical proximity to a protector. It covers the attachment of adult children to parents or grandparents whom they may see infrequently, of spouses, of friends between whom "contact" may be primarily by post and whose function as protectors one of another may be minimal or non-existent. By this broadened concept parents are perhaps typically more attached to their children than children are to their parents—at least this seems to become so as child enter adolescence. Like biblical attachment, broadened Bowlbyan attachment seems to get exemplified (depending on the vicissitudes of the object of attachment) in gratitude, hope, and joy concerning the state of the object fully as much as in feelings of anxiety about the subject's own safety, and feelings of security when the subject perceives himself as safe in object's care.

Bowlby's expanded understanding of attachment differs from the Bible's in scope; in the Bible, meaning-determining attachments can be to sub-human beings as well as to God, while in Bowlby attachments are (it seems) always to human beings. (Bowlby does mention, in passing, attachment to pets. But in most cases these are interpreted as substitutes for attachments to humans, due to either lack or frustration.[10] He also mentions attachment to things and places.[11]) The Bible and Bowlby agree that an attachment-need is a general structural feature of personality, and is not just phase-specific. In the biblical view our personalities are constituted by our attachments, so that our proper functioning as persons is not to be secured by eschewing attachments as such, but by attaching ourselves in the *proper* way to the *proper* objects. For Bowlby our attachment-need is properly satisfied only by human beings, while the Bible posits the need for attachment to God as well; and this latter attachment places

---

[9] *Loss*, 442.
[10] See *Loss*, 174-5, 255-61.
[11] Bowlby, "Separation Anxiety," *International Journal of Psycho-Analysis*, XLI, 1-25.

certain restrictions on what will qualify as healthy attachments to human beings. Bowlby stresses, throughout his writings, the formative power of early attachments, while the Bible concentrates on adult attachments. In accordance with this difference, Bowlby places responsibility for the quality of the attachment almost entirely on the object (whether she is reliable, affirming, etc.), while the Bible tends to place responsibility on the subject of the attachment.

## Explaining Attachment and Attachment Behavior

How did humans, as a species, come to have the attachment *need*? This is a "big" question, about the origins of human nature. But it is legitimate for personality psychology, because *any* kind of explanation may throw light on human nature and the development and constitution of personality. So the question should be asked, even if there is not much hope of an uncontroversial answer to it. Bowlby refers again and again to his functional explanation of the basic human attachment need. I want to point out an inadequacy in the explanation and then suggest that Christianity offers a more satisfactory one; at least it offers the right *kind* of explanation. Then I shall comment briefly on his causal explanation of attachment behavior.

### Functional Explanation of Attachment Behavior

When we look at the kind of explanation that Bowlby favors, we begin to see why he continues to use the infant/mother relationship paradigmatic of his attachment concept—even though he acknowledges that the theory has broader implications than his initial definition would suggest. He distinguishes between

> the *causes* of a particular sort of behaviour and the *function* that that behaviour fulfils. Given the structure of a behavioural system, variables that cause it to become active include such things as hormone level and stimuli of particular kinds from the environment. The function that the behaviour fulfils, on the other hand, is to be sought in the contribution it makes to survival. Male mating behaviour can serve as an example: amongst its usual causes [given the structure of mating as a behavioral

system] are androgen level and presence of female; its function is the contribution it makes to reproduction.[12]

The function of a kind of behavior explains, not why particular *episodes* of the behavior occur, but why a given kind of organism has acquired the *disposition* to behave in this way. But we should note that, despite the difference between these kinds of explanations, functional explanation is a kind of causal explanation; the function of the behavior figures in a causal explanation of the species disposition, whether the explanation is Darwinian or theological. That is, we ask, What caused the species to have the attachment disposition? The Darwinian answer is, Because attachment behavior promoted survival, the physical characteristics that caused instances of it tended to be passed down through the generations. The theological answer is, Because God intended human beings to live a life characterized by love of himself and of fellow humans, he created them with the attachment disposition. Bowlby advocates the Darwinian explanation.

> Among essential features of [Bowlby's theory] are that the human infant comes into the world genetically biased to develop a set of behavioural patterns that, given an appropriate environment, will result in his keeping more or less close proximity to whomever [sic] cares for him, and that this tendency to maintain proximity serves the function of protecting the mobile infant and growing child from a number of dangers, amongst which in man's environment of evolutionary adaptedness the danger of predation is likely to have been paramount.[13]

> In man's environment of evolutionary adaptedness the function of attachment behaviour, which of course promotes proximity to special companions, is protection from predators, and . . . this is as true for humans as it is for other species of mammal and bird. For all groundliving primates, safety lies in being with the band. To become separated from it is to provide a more or less easy meal for

---

[12] *Attachment*, 223, italics added.
[13] Bowlby, *A Secure Base: Parent-Child Attachment and Healthy Human Development* (NY: Basic Books, 1988), 60-1.

a lurking leopard or a pack of hunting dogs.[14]

The causal explanation for our having the attachment disposition is of course that our ancestors' having this disposition contributed causally to their surviving the danger of predators, and thus to their reproducing, and thus to their passing on to us their genetically based disposition to attach.

I suggest that Bowlby emphasizes infantile attachment and its adult counterpart because this kind of attachment behavior lends itself to construal as the output of a safety-regulating system. It is a construal that enables Bowlby to give a Darwinian explanation of our attachment disposition. Attachment behavior that tends to occur in contexts of danger, preceded by anxiety and followed by anxiety reduction, is far more plausibly explained as having a safety-maintenance function than, say, the attachment behavior that consists in two friends writing each other at regular intervals because they enjoy sharing thoughts and experiences and want to keep in touch. Here a Darwinian explanation, even on the behavioral level, is much less satisfying. If we are to explain the letter-writing behavior by reference to the survival-enhancing power of attachments, we must emphasize *other* behavior, like that of the clinging infant or of the friends who seek each other out at news of an approaching hurricane; and then we must treat the letter-writing behavior as somehow secondary or even epiphenomenal, a sort of "frill" that is carried along on the original function of attachment behavior.

On the other hand if, on more Aristotelian lines, we see the letter-writing behavior as *centrally* characteristic or paradigmatic of attachments (an instance of the mature form thereof), and safety enhancing behavior as only an early and primitive form of what reaches its fruition in true friendship, then we will not be satisfied with the Darwinian explanation. A Darwinian will think of spiritual friendship as a vestige of survival-attachment, while an Aristotelian will think of survival-attachment as a primitive prefiguration of spiritual friendship—while agreeing that survival-attachment precedes spiritual friendship both ontogenetically and phylogenetically, and contributes causally to the latter. Clearly, the adequacy of a proposed explanation of attachment is relative to one's *concept* of attachment; conceptual differences here have

---

[14] *Separation*, p. 143. Bowlby goes to some trouble, in the context, to show that safety continues to be the function of attachment, even in older children and adults. See pp. 142-48.

much to do with which cases of attachment one takes to be central and which secondary.

As regards Bowlby's concept of attachment, there seem to be two Bowlbys—the Darwinian Bowlby, who emphasizes psychological phenomena that lend themselves to construal as mechanisms of biological survival; and the increasingly humanistic Bowlby, who wishes to do justice to the multifacial emotional richness and existential significance of human attachments. Bowlby denies that the attachment disposition serves some more basic function such as ensuring a food supply to the infant[15]—as Freudians tend to suggest. He sides with Freud against the Freudians: "Though it might easily be supposed that Freud also held that the function of a child's tie to his mother is mainly to ensure food supply, Freud's position is in fact a little different."[16] Freud held instead that "the function fulfilled by the secondary drive that ties infant to mother [that is, the attachment drive] is, by ensuring the mother's presence, that of preventing the psychical apparatus from becoming deranged 'by an accumulation of amounts of stimulation which require to be disposed of.'[17] Thus, in his own way, Freud opts for a more Aristotelian and less Darwinian account of the function of attachment: Its function is to promote psychic self-realization. Similarly, Bowlby wishes to make attachment a *basic* feature of human nature. "[T]o have a deep attachment to a person (or a place or thing) is to have taken them as the *terminating* object of our instinctual responses."[18] Yet Bowlby's Darwinism pushes him hard to make the attachment object not terminating, but instrumental:

> During infancy and childhood bonds are with parents (or parent substitutes) who are looked to for protection, comfort, and assistance. During healthy adolescence and adult life these bonds persist but are complemented by new bonds, commonly of a heterosexual nature. Although food and sex sometimes play important roles in such relationships, the relationship *exists in its own right* and has an important survival function of its own, namely protection. Thus, within the attachment framework, bonds are seen as neither subordinate to nor derivative from food

[15] *Attachment*, 210-20.
[16] Ibid., 224.
[17] Quoted in ibid.
[18] "Separation Anxiety," 13, italics added.

and sex.[19]

We can see from the quasi-appositive use Bowlby makes of the second "and" in the third sentence that for him the basicness of a structure of human personality is its direct relevance to survival. Food ingestion and sexual activity are no doubt means of survival, and thus so are the drives to them; but attachment has a survival value that is not derived from its relation to food and sex. It is not a means to a means to survive, but *directly* a means to survive. The explanation of everything most basic to human nature by reference to its physical survival function is of course emblematic of Bowlby's ideological Darwinism.

But we can see also an Aristotelian tendency in him, as we see indeed in most personality theorists, to think of proper functioning in terms of a *personal well-being* of a very different order than mere survival. A person's nature determines not just a tendency to survive (or for the race to survive), but for the individual (or the community) *to flourish in a personal way*, to be actualized in the distinctively human manner. It seems to me that in defending the basicness of attachment Bowlby is protesting a reductionism that "dehumanizes" the psyche, making it basically interested in nothing more significant than the satisfaction of bodily needs. We are made for something richer and deeper than that, something found above all in our human attachments. But then the Darwinian in Bowlby cannot be suppressed, and asserts that the function of attachments is after all to facilitate physical survival—survival *is* the richer and deeper something that our attachments are for. Bowlby is in a bind. He has a richly Aristotelian concept of attachment, but the only aspects of attachment he has a functional explanation for belong to the thinner, Darwinian concept, a concept that cannot do justice to the profoundest and most important things he has to say about the relations of attachment to personality.

The Christian psychologist can explain more than the Darwinian about personality because her explanatory framework is ultimately personal: Why do human beings have the attachment disposition? Because they are created by God, who is love. That is, they were created *out of* a kind of proleptic attachment, and *for* attachment of a certain sort to one another and to their God. The Christian psychologist can acknowledge that the attachment of an

---

[19] *Secure Base*, 162-3, italics added.

infant to his mother, which consists, behaviorally, largely in keeping close to her, has a safety-regulating function. Something like an evolutionary process may indeed be the means by which God created the human race. But the Christian psychologist has an added explanatory resource that allows the deeply personal aspects of human life—of which Bowlby too feels the need to make sense—to be themselves, without "reducing" them to something explainable in terms of mere survival function.

Functional Explanation of Attachment Experience

One dimension of human personality insisted on by the Christian psychologist is inwardness (Augustine, Kierkegaard . . . ). When Zeanah and Anders[20] comment that "relationships exist internally as representations, as well as externally as discrete behaviors (interactions)," they make an essential point of New Testament psychology. The Christian psychologist takes seriously, as something requiring development and explanation, the subjective qualities of human life, what it is like to *live* a human life, to *be* a human being, to *experience* the *meaning* of, say, attachments.

Darwinian explanations, inadequate as accounts of human *behavior*, are even less adequate in talking about the psychology of human beings *from within*. The attachment behavior of an infant has a survival function, but it is not chiefly *as* promoting his safety that the two-year-old experiences being close to mother, wanting to be close to her, feeling discomfort at being too long away from her, etc. For example, it is not as promoting his survival that the child experiences mother's return to the house after an absence. It is hard to say what the child experiences here. But it seems to me it is something like, *The world is right again. I was "lost" but now am "found."* The concept of safety shapes only part of this experience. When a child mourns the absence of mother,[21] it is not just safety he longs for (though of course he *may* think, "If Mommy were with me, I wouldn't be in such danger"). He longs, instead, for *her*. Thus his attachment to her is, in his own understanding and feeling, no more conditional on her role as protector than it is on her role as feeder or warmer. This seems to be true even of dogs, of which J. P. Scott says, "separation distress

---

[20] "Subjectivity in Parent-Infant Relationships: A Discussion of Internal Working Models," *Infant Mental Health Journal*, 8, 238.
[21] *Loss*, ch. 1.

is not a response to an anticipated future event but to an ongoing immediate event."[22] The attachment has more the character of love, than of any sort of expediency.

At least this is what will be salient to the Christian psychologist, who starts from a biblical conception of human nature—and, by analogy, of other parts of the creation. Bretherton[23] says that one of the challenges of attachment theory for the near future is to develop "an experiential language akin to that used by other psychoanalytic theories of interpersonal relatedness," and we might predict that, to the degree that this challenge is met, the explanation of attachment as a mechanism of biological survival will come to seem incomplete. Stress on attachment experience would also seem to undermine efforts like that of Ainsworth[24] to restrict the concept of attachment to cases characterized by the secure base and haven functions, and would confirm Bowlby's inclination to allow the concept to range over cases in which safety is not an issue.

If we insist on limiting ourselves to biological or physiological explanations in psychology, then we must treat the meaning of experiences as people experience them, and of personal relationships as people inhabit them, as mere epiphenomena of behavior or other bodily processes. But what right have psychologists to treat the most distinctively *psychological* phenomena as *epi*phenomena? If we are to avoid such reductionism, our explanations must be in personal terms; and if our questions are "big" ones like "Why do people, as people, have the attachment need and the experiences associated with it?" then the theological answer is superior to the Darwinian one. It is, at least, the right *kind* of explanation.

For a critique of efforts to reduce explanations in psychology to biological and physiological ones, see Guntrip,[25] where he shows that the inner logic of the most enduring part of

---

[22] "The Emotional Basis of Attachment and Separation," in J. L Sacksteder et al., eds., *Attachment and the Therapeutic Process: Essay in Honor of Otto Allen Will, Jr.*, M.D. (Madison, WI: International Univ. Pr., 1987), 51.
[23] "The Origins of Attachment Theory: John Bowlby and Mary Ainsworth," *Developmental Psychology*, 28, 771.
[24] "Attachments Across the Life Span," *Bulletin of the New York Academy of Medicine*, 61, 792-812.
[25] *Psychoanalytic Theory, Therapy, and the Self* (NY: Basic Books, 1973), especially chs. 1-4.

Freud's psychology presses toward liberation from biology and neurology, in the direction of a distinctively *psychological* science. But in abandoning purely biological explanations of distinctively psychological phenomena (such as "meaning and motivation that determines the dealings of persons with [one] another, and the way they change and grow in the process,"[26] Guntrip has, it seems to me, left himself without any way of answering the "big" kind of question that Bowlby asks about the origins of the attachment need. Guntrip does not, at least in [*Psychoanalytic Theory, Therapy, and the Self*], offer a theological answer—or indeed, any answer at all. I do not wish to be dogmatic about the matter, but at the moment a broadly theological answer seems to me the only kind that is a real candidate.

Arguments analogous in some ways to the present one, but much more elaborately worked out, can be found in Alvin Plantinga.[27] He argues, first, that the concept of proper function or well-being (of organs as well as organisms, what I have called the Aristotelian idea) is both unavoidable in biology and cannot be coherently developed in a framework of metaphysical naturalism. Second, he argues that it is highly improbable that unguided natural selection would produce an organism with cognitive faculties that fairly reliably produce true beliefs. Since serious inquirers cannot help believing that our cognitive faculties do, or at least can, track truth, it is not rational for serious inquirers to be metaphysical naturalists—e.g. to believe that our cognitive faculties have resulted from unguided natural selection.

Bowlbyan Virtue

We can see the tension internal to Bowlby's psychology in another connection. In accord with his generally Darwinian orientation, the master virtue or trait of personal maturity in his personality theory is *adaptability*, which is defined in terms of *fitness to survive*. According to Bowlby this virtue is facilitated, more than by anything else, by having, in early childhood, a mother who is an excellent attachment figure. The highest degree of adaptability or maturity of character found among a group of 34 seventeen-year-olds was "the rational altruistic," a character featuring a high degree of rationality, friendliness, and altruistic

---

[26] Ibid., 46.
[27] "An Evolutionary Argument Against Naturalism," *Logos*, 12, 27-49; Warrant and Proper Function (NY: Oxford Univ. Pr., 1993).

impulse, social spontaneity and liking of other people, healthy respect for themselves and for others, and firm, internalized moral principles.[28] Notice that while this configuration of traits may adapt an individual to survive (so that its *evolutionary* "goal" might be personal or racial survival), survival cannot be the *individual's own* goal for, or in, having these traits. For if biological survival were his or her overriding goal, the spontaneity, the respect for others, the respect for self, the concern for others, would be undermined. To respect another individual in the way that "rational altruistic" persons do is incompatible with being motivated, ultimately, only by considerations of one's own personal survival or the survival of the human race—or indeed, even of the survival of the person one "respects." In respecting a person, one has in view the *quality* of his or her *individual* life, and that not merely as a biological organism, but as a person in some person-value terms—e.g., the person's dignity as a rational being (Kant) or as a self-determiner (Nietzsche), or the person's status as a child of God (Christianity). The concept of a person operating in the mind of the "rational altruistic" respectful person may be less well defined than any of these philosophical or religious conceptions, but it will always be incompatible with regarding the other person as merely a biological "organism" whose goal it is to survive. If we want to explain, as something legitimate and important, the moral *outlook* of the mature person Bowlby envisages, the goal we ascribe to persons must be something other than survival. And this outlook of maturity is the sort of thing that personality psychologists (as distinct from biochemists, neurophysiologists, biologists) most want to explain.

The question about the function of attachment raises a more general issue of comparison between object-relations psychology and Christian psychology. If we ask, What are object-relations (that is, intimate personal relations) *for?* Bowlby's most basic answer is: For the survival of the race, via the survival of the individual. This answer is in uneasy tension with Bowlby's humanistic concern with psychological maturity and happiness. He is, after all, a psychotherapist, whose goal (function) is to help his clients find fulfillment. In this Bowlby is like the object-relations psychologists. Contrasting the object-relations answer to the question with that of Heinz Hartmann,[29] who says "that

---

[28] *Separation*, 329-33.
[29] *Ego Psychology and the Problem of Adaptation*, tr. D. Rapaport (London: Hogarth Press, 1959).

psychoanalysis is interested in object-relations because they are essential to biological equilibrium," Harry Guntrip comments that

> Without a good mother-infant relationship, the neonate human organism may die, but that is the reason for biology being interested in human object-relations. Psychoanalysis is interested in these relationships for quite different reasons, namely that they are crucial for the achievement of reality and maturity as a person-ego.[30]

Christian psychologists, starting as they do with a view of the universe in which relationships of nurturing, support, and attachment are fundamental to the very nature of God and God's program of creation, regard object-relations as not only for biological survival and the achievement of ego reality, but also as fundamentally important *in themselves*. They are, ultimately, not instrumental to anything; they are their own function. When they are not as they should be, we have not only sick bodies and sick psyches, but sick communities and indeed a sick universe. From a Christian point of view it is dangerous to see right relationships as functioning primarily as instruments or expedients to personal well-being. The danger here is a kind of egoism or perverse individualism. The encouragement to see relationships in this way seems to be one of the liabilities of modern psychotherapy, even if it is not always part of official doctrine. The therapeutic relationship is often one in which the object relation is quite intentionally regarded as instrumental to the psychological well-being of the client and, as Robert Bellah and his colleagues point out,[31] this feature of psychotherapies is probably a significant contributor to the widespread egoism of our culture.

## The Causal Explanation of Attachment Behavior

We have discussed at some length Bowlby's functional explanation of the attachment need in human beings. Let us now look briefly at his causal explanation of attachment behavior. His basic concept is that of a *control system*, that is, some structural

---

[30] *Psychoanalytic Theory*, 109.
[31] *Habits of the Heart: Individualism and Commitment in American Life* (NY: Harper & Row, 1985). For an evaluation and qualification of their thesis, see R. Roberts, Taking the Word to Heart (Grand Rapids: Wm. B. Eerdmans Pub. Co., 1993)

state of the organism such that, when it undergoes impingements of a certain sort, it responds with an adjustment designed to keep the organism within certain physiological or environmental parameters.

> An obvious way to conceptualize the behaviour observed is to postulate the existence of a control system within the central nervous system, analogous to the physiological control systems that maintain physiological measures, such as blood pressure and body temperature, within set limits. Thus the theory proposes that, in a way analogous to physiological homeostasis, the attachment control system maintains a person's relation to his attachment figure between certain limits of distance and accessibility.[32]

Attachment behavior is the output of such a system. The central nervous systems (CNSs) of mother and infant are such that, if the infant moves too far away from the mother, she emits retrieving behavior, and if a certain amount of time has passed without his "checking in" with mother, the infant feels the need to go to her, and does so. Thus Bowlby offers a physiological explanation of attachment behavior. The reference to the structure in the CNS appears to be speculative (it is "postulated," as he says). However, it seems plausible, and unobjectionable from a Christian point of view, that there should be a physiological basis for attachment behavior, and for the extended phenomenon of attachment that Christian psychology sees throughout human life. But the cybernetic version of this that Bowlby proposes seems to apply better to infants (whose behavior we take to be largely determined by hard-wiring) than to older children and adults, in whom the behavior, while still having a physiological *base*, is far more determined by social construction, individual judgment, deliberated attitudes, philosophy of life, etc. So the Christian psychologist's objection to Bowlby's proposal that attachment behavior is physiologically determined really turns on our earlier objection that when Bowlby is wearing his physiological hat he narrows unduly the concept of attachment, and that when he acknowledges the broader, psychological concept, his physicalism no longer serves him plausibly. We acknowledge, of course, that attachment behavior even of the maturest and most distinctively

---

[32] *A Secure Base*, 164.

human kind is based, in some way or other, in our physical constitution. And our learned attachment behavior (say, our "style" of interacting with our dearest friends) is for the most part "automatic" and determined at least in significant part by states of the CNS that have been put there by the learning process.

I do not think, however, that the Christian psychologist will want to admit that our behavior is entirely determined by physiological processes. The concept of agency to which Christians are committed, and to which Bowlby's more humanist side also is committed, seems to require that, to an extent, *we* are in control of our bodies and our behavior . . . The concept of agency is far too complex and subtle to discuss in any detail here, but the recent philosophical literature that locates agency in self-identification, in what Frankfurt[33] calls second-order desires, and in what Taylor[34] calls strong evaluation in terms of evaluative frameworks . . . seems to point in the right direction.

## Bowlbyan and Christian Maturity

God as Attachment Figure

For the humanistic Bowlby, the importance of the vicissitudes of attachment in childhood is their effect on the personality of the resultant adult. Perhaps the most important kind of effect, in Bowlby's view, is the implicit expectations of support from other people that early experiences with attachment figures promote or discourage.

> Thus an individual who has been fortunate in having grown up in an ordinary good home with ordinarily affectionate parents has always known people from whom he can seek support, comfort, and protection, and where they are to be found. So deeply established are his expectations and so repeatedly have they been confirmed that, as an adult, he finds it difficult to imagine any other kind of world. This gives him an almost unconscious assurance that, whenever and wherever he might be in

---

[33] *The Importance of What We Care About* (Cambridge: Cambridge Univ. Pr., 1988).

[34] *Human Agency and Language* (Cambridge: Cambridge Univ. Pr., 1985); *Sources of the Self: The Making of the Modern Identity* (Cambridge, MA: Harvard Univ. Pr., 1988).

difficulty, there are always trustworthy figures available who will come to his aid. He will therefore approach the world with confidence and, when faced with potentially alarming situations, is likely to tackle them effectively or to seek help in doing so.[35]

This sketch of personality maturity is strikingly at odds with the ones offered by many psychologists today, whose personality ideals tend to picture maturity as a matter of detachment from others, autonomy, and emotional independence. For these psychologists the great vice to be avoided is "enmeshment" with others (emotional dependency), but Bowlby says the mature person knows he can depend on others, and has a pretty good idea of where to find them. He is *self*-confident because he is confident that *others* will always be there for him. Proper attachment is not just a phase people pass through on the way to individuation; it is an irrevocable structure of personhood, an abiding feature of true individuation.

In this claim Christian psychologists will agree with Bowlby. But they will see something immature about the person Bowlby sketches as ideal. Is it not unrealistic, in many circumstances, to think there are other human beings who will support one and come to one's aid in time of need? This may be often so, but it is not the sort of generalization on which to build a character-ideal, because it depends on circumstances that may not obtain. Arguably, there are inevitable situations, such as one's own death, in which human help is always at best second-rate. If we affirm, with Bowlby, that by nature we need attachments with persons beyond ourselves, and note, in addition, that human attachments fall short of what we need, it follows that we need another, higher, and more essentially reliable object of attachment by reference to which we can qualify our dependency on human objects. And if, as Christian psychologists believe, the human constitution contains an essential Godward tendency, it will be not only inexpedient, but also a violation of the very order of things to depend on human help to the extent that Bowlby envisions.

The Christian psychologist will grant that the ideally mature person is *willing* to accept support and aid from his fellows, and to do so with gratitude and without humiliation; but he does not always *expect* to get help from others. Furthermore, he

---

[35] *Separation*, 208.

has an attachment need that cannot be satisfied by such others. Part of growing up is coming to the deep realization that in our own finite realm all human support will ultimately (indeed, necessarily) prove undependable. Søren Kierkegaard[36] has this in mind when he speaks of despair as required in the process of psychological maturation. Christians advocate such despair not just because people and circumstances are so unreliable, but because we feel that it fits our nature poorly to rely ultimately on anything but God. God is the ultimate and absolute "attachment figure" for the mature personality; God is the one to whom thanks can be offered in *all* circumstances (1 Thess. 5:18), the one who comforts us in *all* our afflictions (2 Cor. 1:4). The first commandment is that you shall love the Lord your God with all your heart . . . and the *second* is that you shall love your neighbor as yourself (Matt. 22:37-40). He who loves father or mother, son or daughter, more than Christ is not worthy to be Christ's disciple (Matthew 10:37-38). Attachments to other humans are thus compatible with personal maturity, but only when secondary to the attachment to God.

Perhaps the major thesis of Bowlby's entire psychology is that the quality of our early attachments strongly affects our later capacity for mature attachments. What might the Christian say about this? Trust is as important to the Christian psychologist as it is to Bowlby, assuming the ordering of attachments sketched in the above paragraph—a qualified, relative but real trust of people, and an absolute trust of God. The Christian psychologist has reason to agree with Bowlby on the centrality of trust for the mature personality, and to accept the massive evidence he has garnered to the conclusion that trust in mature life is deeply affected by the trustworthiness of one's early attachment figures. Thus the good mother is a deputy of God, one who engenders in her child an implicit sense of the trustworthiness of the universe that, when he is more mature, he can direct to its proper Object.[37] Other things being equal, people who have not enjoyed good mothers are at a spiritual disadvantage. On the other hand, to make human beings the ultimate object of one's trust, as Bowlby

---

[36] *Either/Or*, tr. H. & E. Hong (Princeton: Princeton Univ. Pr., 1987), Vol. II; *The Sickness Unto Death*, tr. H. & E. Hong (Princeton: Princeton Univ. Pr., 1980).

[37] On God as perfect attachment-figure, see G. Kaufman, *The Theological Imagination: Constructing the Concept of God* (Phila.: Westminster, 1981).

proposes, is not fitting, and so it is important to have experiences that remind us of the limits of human trustworthiness, and thus facilitate the "despair" that Kierkegaard talks about. The conjunction and interconnection of these features of the Christian psychology fit it to resolve what we might call "Kirkpatrick's paradox."

Kirkpatrick's Paradox

Kirkpatrick[38] distinguishes two seemingly contrary hypothetical effects of early patterns of attachment on the God-relationship. The *compensation hypothesis* is that attachment to God is a compensation for frustrated attachment to humans (especially one's mother). It predicts that religiosity will vary inversely with the quality of parental relationships. The *correspondence hypothesis*—that the quality of one's relationship with God reflects the quality of one's early attachments, since the God-relationship is modeled on the human one—predicts that the less frustrating one's early attachments were, the better will be one's relationship with God.

Kirkpatrick[39] found support for the compensation hypothesis in a study in which sudden religious conversions occurred four times more frequently among subjects who reported avoidant maternal attachments than among subjects reporting secure or resistant attachments. Several other indicators of religiosity followed a similar pattern among subjects whose mothers were nonreligious, though if the mothers were religious, the quality of attachment showed no effect on religiosity. In a later article[40] Kirkpatrick reviews the evidence for the correspondence hypothesis, such as studies that show loss of faith to be associated with poor parental relationships and anthropological studies that show strong correlations across cultures between nurturing parenting styles and benevolent gods, and between "rejecting" parenting styles and malevolent gods. Thus there seems to be evidence for both kinds of effect, and this fact creates what I am

---

[38] "An Attachment-Theory Approach to the Psychology of Religion," *The International Journal for the Psychology of Religion*, 2, 3-28.

[39] "Attachment Theory and Religion: Childhood Attachments, Religious Beliefs, and Conversion," *Journal for the Scientific Study of Religion*, 29, 315-24.

[40] "Attachment-Theory."

calling Kirkpatrick's paradox. A Christian psychology has ways of resolving the seeming contrariety between these effects.

A Christian psychology posits both analogy and difference between attachments to human figures and attachment to God, and a need for both kinds of attachments. Thus it is unsurprising if one kind of attachment sometimes substitutes for the other, though on the Christian view neither kind of attachment is a fully *adequate* substitute for the other. Lack of an adequate God-relationship can be (partially) compensated for by satisfying human attachments, just as lack of adequate human attachments can be (partially) compensated for by an attachment to God. Also, by way of analogy between the two kinds of attachment, the two kinds of attachment figures can be modeled on one another. Following Bowlbyan cues, Christian psychology will take optimal psychic development to involve modeling of the God-concept on human attachment figures (though one could argue, following Kohutian cues,[41] that the child's early concept of a parent as an omnipotent and perfect caretaker is modeled on the child's innate concept of God). So parental figures will be an important source of our knowledge of God; other things being equal, having better attachment figures prepares the child better for an adequate God-concept and relationship. Thus the Christian psychology predicts that both the compensation hypothesis and the correspondence hypothesis will be empirically borne out.

Though Christians agree with the many psychologists who have pointed out that belief in God often functions as a compensation for deficiencies in human relationships, they will not agree that "to the extent that religious beliefs serve a compensatory role vis-à-vis [human] attachments, an agnostic or atheistic stance would be expected to result from a history of satisfactory (secure) attachment relationships."[42] The assumption behind such an expectation is that humans have no particular and distinctive need for attachment to God—that our attachment needs can in principle be met by human relationships alone. If, as the Christian hypothesizes, we need both kinds of relationships, we would expect that some people who are very secure in their human attachments will still feel the need for God. Even if the compensation effect is universal among human beings, the compensation, when working optimally, may be merely

---

[41] *The Restoration of the Self* (NY: International Univ. Pr., 1977).
[42] "Attachment-Theory," 17.

developmental, in the way that, according to Kohut,[43] t h e developmental mechanism of transmuting internalization is a compensation for "failures" on the part of self-objects. In other words, just as even the best self-object "fails" the child at certain points, and this "failure" is in the child's developmental interest as needed to trigger his autonomy, so a natural stage in the development of attachment to God is the frustrated realization that one's human attachment figures are not just accidentally, but intrinsically, inadequate—that they have in fact been treated (falsely, though necessarily) as substitutes for God.

Why do subjects with rejecting mothers who are *not religious* tend so much more often to find compensation in the God-relationship than children of *religious* non-nurturing mothers? The religious mother, we may suppose, is associated with God in two ways in the mind of her child, the non-religious in only one. In addition to the natural tendency to model God on the mother, the children of religious mothers are exposed to a historical, verbally and behaviorally articulated association of their mothers with God. If both the correspondence hypothesis and the compensation hypothesis are true, then the non-nurturing mother will have *two competing effects* on her child: If the mother is non-nurturing, the child is, on the correspondence hypothesis, more likely to conceptualize God as non-nurturing, and thus to be *deterred* from finding compensation in God for his non-nurturing mother. But if the mother is non-nurturing, the child will also have, on the compensation hypothesis, an extra *impulse* to trust in God, that may overpower the tendency to conceive God as non-nurturing. (We assume that many kinds of social influences affect the child's God-concept, not just the correspondence effect.) But if the mother adds to the normal operation of the correspondence effect by setting herself up as God's associate (talking about God, advocating God, praying to God, claiming God's approval, etc.), she may increase the correspondence effect enough to override the compensation effect in the child's psyche.

In accordance with the fuller concept of attachment that I have been endorsing, the Christian psychologist will want to measure the adequacy of attachment to God on more dimensions than just the secure-resistant-avoidant continuum. A person might have a secure relationship with God which was nevertheless quite immature, or an insecure one that was mature in some ways.

---

[43] *Restoration.*

As attachment figure, God is more than just comforter or protector. God is also a model, an object of admiration, a commander, a judge; and the maturity of one's attachment to him may vary along these dimensions—in terms, e.g., of how seriously one desires to be like him and succeeds in being so, of how deeply one appreciates God's goodness and beauty, of how obedient one is, of how reverently one regards God as moral observer.

## Summary

We have seen that, taking as our standard a concept of attachment constructed from the Bible, the concept with which Bowlby "starts" (both in terms of his conceptual framework and also, it seems, chronologically) is narrower than the Christian concept. Central for Bowlby is a kind of attachment characteristic of infancy and early childhood, characterized by the maintenance of physical proximity between child and mother. On whether the child's need for attachment is well satisfied at this early stage depends much concerning the child's later personality development—his self-confidence as an agent, his ability to trust other people, his disposition to respect others, and his altruism in behavior and attitude. The Bible, by contrast, focuses more on attachments in adulthood and emphasizes strongly the significance of attachments to beings other than humans—in particular, possessions (wealth) and God. The initial narrowness of Bowlby's concept is mitigated to some extent by his increasing acknowledgment that attachments are, throughout the life cycle, deeply important to human beings, indeed the very stuff of life's meaning. The more we emphasize, with the Bible, the attachments of our adulthood and their subjective meaning, the less plausible is Bowlby's explanation of attachment in terms of its survival function and the causal efficacy of the postulated attachment "control system" located in our central nervous system. If we emphasize adult attachments and their depth of meaning, humanistic and theological explanations seem far more apposite. Christian psychology agrees with Bowlby on the basicness of the attachment disposition; it is not just phasic, but fundamental to human nature. Good early attachments prepare us for mature personality, not only by enabling us to trust that other human beings will generally be there for us when we need them, but by readying us to trust God.

# Beyond Bowlby: Attachment Dynamics in Family, Church, and Classroom Relations

*Roger Newell*
George Fox University

*A Clinical Baptism*

In 1989 I was the minister of a United Reformed congregation in the north of England. Being my first pastoral charge, I was eager to do well, but by my fifth year, I was experiencing symptoms of burnout. Seeking to develop a supportive network, I began traveling to seminars at the Scottish Institute of Human Relations in Edinburgh, supplemented by readings in Harry Guntrip. I applied to the Institute's program for pastoral supervision. Following an assessment interview, Brian Lake agreed to supervise my wife and me for the next eighteen months. Our meeting plan comprised bringing whatever pastoral issues with which we were currently wrestling and exploring some of the surrounding psychotherapeutic dynamics, especially where family and personal dynamics intersected with church issues. Personally, I hoped that better insight into these patterns might make the challenges of ministry more life-enhancing and less draining.

The first dilemma I presented regarded "Sarah," an able but rather shy young student who recently graduated from the university. The problem was that she began to telephone relentlessly to request pastoral support, even though she had returned to live with her family over a hundred miles away. Some weeks the calls would come nightly, often when I was just spending some needed time with my young family. My notes from the first session with Lake recalled the atmosphere: "How do you feel?" "Burdened!" "Do you look forward to hearing the phone ring?" "No!" "She seems to evoke a sense of immense responsibility." "Yes!"

In the course of the next ninety minutes, certain themes began to emerge about my style of pastoral care. As we conversed, insights began to dawn, helping me to sense that this dilemma was not simply thrust upon me, but that I had been a kind of co-

conspirator unawares. "I trust only you," she told me over the phone. "How do those words make you feel?" Lake asked. I had to acknowledge that it felt good to be needed. Lake replied that it was also "jolly dangerous," which was why I was feeling so burdened. In the course of our exploratory conversation, it emerged that part of me indeed felt good to be a key source of help for someone. However, another part of me deeply resented this careseeker. I was dreading the ring of the phone, experiencing it as a form of persecution. "You don't express any anger toward her?" "Certainly not!" Why not? Because another highly valued part of me felt obliged to go beyond the normal call of duty, to give sacrificial care as fundamental to my pastoral work. That afternoon we spent some time with each of these parts, exploring their overall impact on me. Thus I was baptized clinically into Fairbairn and Guntrip's object relations theory—with a difference.

## Conceptualizing the Self and its Systems

Over the past twenty-five years, clinicians and researchers Dorothy Heard and Brian Lake have developed a significant extension of and complement to the attachment theory of John Bowlby. They have placed Bowlby's instinctive system for caregiving and careseeking within a theoretical model of the self as a series of integrated, interactive systems. Part of their agenda was to link attachment theory to other aspects of the self-maturation process. Just as in the fifteenth century, when we only knew of the respiratory system while our understanding of the other systems of the body remained largely unexamined, and the co-operation of the systems unexplored, so today the need is for an integration of attachment with other systemic aspects of the self. The written fruit of their collaboration is their 1997 publication, *The Challenge of Attachment for Caregiving*.[1] In this essay I would like to describe some of the themes "beyond Bowlby" that Lake and his wife, Dorothy Heard, have articulated and how I began to experience these as a working pastor. I will also comment on how today in my role as a college professor, certain themes continue to raise relevant questions and provide pedagogical insight into classroom dynamics. The goal in all this is to better understand multiple care systems: how they interact with one another and with the attachment system, in order that

---

[1] Dorothy Heard and Brian Lake, *The Challenge of Attachment for Caregiving* (London: Routledge, 1997).

therapists, pastors, and educators may bring an increasingly comprehensive understanding of the caregiving systems to counseling and teaching.

Their framework begins by acknowledging the attachment group of systems as foundational, providing the infrastructure for regulating and maintaining physical and psychological homeostasis and for consolidating the newly acquired information from which growth and development proceed. In addition to the foundational system, a potentiating group of systems is responsible for furthering personal growth and development. This includes the interest-sharing system, the self-ideal system (and its defenses), and the sexual partnership system as they develop through the emergence of a *supportive companionable* (SC) system.[2] When the primary, instinctive (attachment) system fails to maintain the necessary biologically set level of emotional support, the potentiating and developmental group of systems is impeded. For example, Harlow's surrogate terry towel monkeys never experienced effective caregiving. As a result their developmental and sexual systems were gravely impaired.[3] The point is that these two groups of systems function alongside one another, with the homeostatic attachment system as foundational. However, to some degree, one may exercise conscious control over the relations between the two systems. This occurs through the influence of the potentiating systems as they mature through the experience of caregiving/careseeking partnerships. In other words, the supportive companionable systems can exert a top-down influence to free or alter some of the stimulus-bound, bottom-up responses from the attachment foundation.[4]

*From Object Relations to Internal Models*

Perhaps the place to elaborate further a theoretical integration is the relationship between attachment and object relations theories. Heard and Lake were particularly well-suited to conceptualize in this area. Heard was for many years supervised by John Bowlby and regularly attended his seminars while working as a Consultant in his department at the Tavistock Clinic. Lake, after serving for seven years with his brother, Frank, in the pioneering work of the Clinical Theology Association, had a

---

[2] Ibid., p. 69.
[3] Ibid., p. 71.
[4] Ibid., p. 74.

further training analysis with Harry Guntrip that began in the final stages of Guntrip's own analysis with Winnicott.[5] He went on to work in the National Health Service as a Consultant in Psychotherapy at St. James's University Hospital, Leeds. Briefly stated, Heard and Lake translated "object relations" as "working models" that hold the history of the relations individuals have with any entity or event in their environment. The history of content and quality of interactions exchanged between the participants is represented by "internal models of experience in relationships" (or IMERs).[6] The primary inner system of IMERs is the one individuals have with their parents, or primary attachment figures, and it is a closed system because individuals inherit it unconsciously from interactions with parents from birth. IMERs transmit this inherited attachment system to our present life-situations. The maturational task that counseling seeks to support consists in accompanying the clients as they create a new and open system, rather than simply repeating the closed parental system. For example, in the early years of a marriage within a closed system, a partner may hear the other express a felt need and think, "Here's another bloody demand!" In fact it is heard through the "early warning" defense system which is informed (or deformed) by IMERs, which, being a closed system, is often counter-productive to the present task of building a companionable relationship. From this brief illustration, one can see how such an approach, based as it is in attachment caregiving and careseeking, helps to clarify and interpret the maturing partnership.

*Christian Ministry: Between Ideals and Defensive Idealizations*

Heard and Lake proceeded to explore the connections not only between IMERs and one's parental attachment system but also with other systems of the self, including what has been called the self-ideal or ego-ideal, which individuals carry within and

---

[5] For an introduction to the history of the Clinical Theology Association, see John Peters, *Frank Lake, the Man and his Work* (London: Darton, Longman and Todd, 1989). Guntrip's reflections on his own experiences in therapy are vividly described in his posthumously published essay (1975), "Analysis with Fairbairn and Winnicott (How Complete a Result Does Psycho-Analytic Therapy Achieve?)." See Jeremy Hazel, editor, *Personal Relations Therapy: The Collected Papers of H. J. S. Guntrip* (Northvale, New Jersey: Jason Aaronson, Inc. 1994), pp. 351-270.
[6] Heard and Lake, pp. 85-86.

which has a definitive role in regulating behavior. A self-ideal does not merely consist of defensive, pathological idealizations, especially maligned by Freudians who see it working as the punitive superego by which people "beat themselves up" when they don't live up to its standards. Adler, Jung, and Kohut all granted the ego-ideal a more benign connotation as an internal guide to challenge one to be one's best. At a meeting celebrating Bowlby's eightieth birthday, Lake presented a paper in which he argued for a more empirically grounded discussion of how such ideals actually function in a maturative, as well as in a misguided, defensive manner.[7] For instance, Fairbairn once described how, when functioning in a healthy way, the ideal self incorporates the child's experiences of accepting and supportive parents who serve for the child as an ego ideal. Such ideals channel one's desires to set a course and to reach it. They focus one's resources and energies to accomplish one's vocation.[8]

On the other hand, Fairbairn also theorized that there can be a split off, defensive ego-ideal system that incorporates bad relational experiences with exciting/deserting and rejecting/neglecting parental experiences. These defensive, non-maturative self-ideals arise from a dysfunction of the careseeking system brought on by a failure of appropriate caregiving.[9] Instead of providing internal support that creates standards of cooperative partnerships, exploration, resilience, empathy, and patience, defensive idealizations are reflected either in exaggerated self-responsibility and inappropriate autonomy (doing it one's own way with an assumed superiority over others) or in passive, dependent overvaluing of a group or environment functioning as a protector or potential protector. This dependent overvaluing may involve a part-object or thing (e.g. breast, penis, drugs, money, food, personal possessions) that individuals compulsively seek to obtain and experience, often as a defensive reaction to shame and criticism. The defensive idealization may co-exist with the self-ideal, functioning as compensation, or a closed, shadow system in a strongly defensive system. The oscillation between these two, one conscious and the other unconscious, may explain why overtly sacrificial caregivers are not infrequently reported in the media for their various vulnerabilities to seduction and scandal. All such defensive idealizations involve major forms of exaggeration and

---

7 Ibid., p. 103.
8 Ibid., p. 111.
9 Ibid., pp. 116-117.

distortion of what can realistically be expected of a child or an adult. They are associated with a variety of addictive behaviors.[10] Gerald May has noted the implications for the spiritual life, viewing addictions as misdirecting and depleting desire. "It is like a psychic malignancy, sucking our life energy into specific obsessions and compulsions, leaving less and less energy available for other people and other pursuits . . . These are what we worship, what we attend to, where we give our time and energy, *instead of love*."[11]

Let us recall that defensive idealizations are recorded and passed along to the present in IMERs, more or less segregated from our conscious awareness. Let us also remember that these IMERs, inherited as they are from the early caregiving/careseeking partnerships, are not the whole story. Alongside the most defensive idealizations, there lies a discontented and deep-seated longing to reach new levels of skill and competence in one's work and more maturing experiences of intimacy in one's relationships. Our dilemma is that we are torn between aspiring for further stages of development and defensively maintaining the present homeostatic infrastructure. Sadly, we may simply continue our defensive reactions perpetually.[12]

*Family Systems, Church Systems and Trinitarian Theology*

During my supervision, I began to consider the extent to which an "exaggerated self-responsibility and autonomy ideal" was part of the psychological reality hidden behind my consciously theological ideal of "death to self," the necessary prelude to a deeper union with Christ and a deeper pastoral connection with my congregation. This confusion between two kinds of ideals made it extraordinarily difficult to discern between whether one was being selfish or appropriately taking care of one's self. During this initial time of opening my closed system, Lake raised the possibility that "death to self" might connect more appropriately to "dying to one's internal negative critics," that is, the part of one's IMERs one has inherited from the parental attachment system. Until then, when I translated my theological ideal into pastoral

---

[10] Ibid., p. 120.

[11] Gerald G. May, *Addiction and Grace* (San Francisco: HarperCollins, 1988), p. 13.

[12] Heard and Lake, p. 93.

work, I had included some fairly strong resistances concerning expression of needs and feelings, grounded in the attachment caregiving/careseeking system of my family of origin. In seeking to connect the systems, Lake sought to open and explore the relationship between my pastoral ideal and my ideal for self-care: "If you care for your people the way you're caring for yourself, you're not giving much help." Despite the apparent severity, Lake was challenging me to reframe my goal of giving exemplary, even sacrificial, care to others, because from a systems perspective, it was embedded within a highly conflicted system of self-neglect. How long would such a divided house stand? When might the shadow system become activated and vulnerable to any number of seductions? The challenge was to loosen and renegotiate a closed system of the self-ideal in order to discover a form of pastoral care that felt less burdensome: to wear the authentic gospel yoke that was genuinely light, to offer a kind of caregiving which was something freely given, not squeezed out of me by persecuting parishioners.

Essentially Lake gave me permission to explore the psychodynamics of my self-ideal and pastoral ideal by providing *companionable support.* Only then was I free to construct a pastoral self-ideal which acknowledged that clergy commonly give care out of a perfectionistic model, despite its regularly creating distress in the minister's family system. Formal and informal training combine to engender an imbalanced style in which one overly invests in one's church or service system while neglecting one's family or home system. When this professional model is dominant, God does not miraculously rescue us from its unhealthy consequences.

This perfectionistic model is also linked to a theologically anemic account of God's own pattern of caregiving. One primary piece of evidence of a theological imbalance is an exclusive focus on the sacrifice of Jesus on the cross as our model, isolated from its triune context. For example, the well-known polarity depicted in Nygren's *Agape and Eros* portrays God's love exclusively in terms of sacrificial giving and having nothing to do with receiving. For Nygren, agape *is* self-giving.[13] This could hardly depict God's love more one-sidedly, neglecting the depth context of the *vinicula caritas* where the cross reflects the generous reciprocity of divine life within the holy trinity. This triune giving out of abundant life

---

[13] Anders Nygren, *Agape and Eros* (London: SPCK, 1982), p. 201.

militates against giving out of emptiness in order to find a reward, win approval, or manipulate others to feel obliged to the caregiver. To identify love only with giving collapses the concrete reality of love within God's triune communion into an abstract principle of sacrifice.[14]

When a perfectionistic ego-ideal leaves one feeling that one must go on and on, and hence increasingly depleted, one becomes easily seduced by the next person who makes a demand or subtly disapproves. Faced with too many anxious careseekers, those who are uncooperative, or those whose "getting well rate" is too slow for one's pastoral timetable, an overwhelmed pastor may feel incompetent and powerless. "To regain a sense of control and competence, there is a marked tendency for them to fall back on coercive controlling or avoidant patterns of relating."[15] However, through support and conscious reflection, an alternative self-ideal may emerge, in which one learns to stay connected to careseekers without the need for control or the need for untarnished approval ratings. One may discover the freedom to construct a hardworking but reasonable schedule.

Internalizing a supportive supervisory experience empowers one to migrate from a defensive idealization to a positive self-ideal. Internalizing the *SC* relationship energizes one's nurturing and exploratory capacities. One gradually learns to lower volume on the punitive, guilt-producing internal critic that too harshly condemns one's imperfections and limitations. All parents inadvertently pass on ideals somewhere between healthy and distorted, realistic and maladaptive, impressing them on the highly malleable child. The work of maturity separates one's own ideals from those of our parents (or parental IMERS), transforming defensive ideals into realistic, supportive guides that competently bring forth one's own vocational gifts.

*Everyday Encounters with Defenses*

When one first affiliates with a group, one sets in place the kinds of relationships that mirror the caregiving/careseeking partnerships one has experienced within one's family of origin.[16]

---

[14] For a further discussion of the implications for family and church systems, see Roger Newell, *Passion's Progress: The Meanings of Love* (London: SPCK, 1994), pp. 26-82.
[15] Heard and Lake, p. 92.
[16] Ibid., p. 80.

One does the same with one's peer relationships and romantic attachments. Heard and Lake designate all of these as secondary attachments. All are approached "primed by the history of the primary attachment and other well established defensive habits formed by the activation of their system for interpersonal defense. People therefore tend to behave in secondary and reversed attachment in accordance with what has been learnt from primary attachments."[17] However, the same process of opening closed systems through the supportive, companionable redesigning of IMERs from defensive ideals to mature self-ideals forms a realistic and hopeful path. A crucial moment in maturing towards healthy intimacy involves coming to terms with one another's defenses. What are the patterns of behavior that lead to mistrust? Having identified these, is it possible to accept, or in serious situations to forgive, them? How does one learn to work through the stressors that seduce one to revisit closed-off defensive strategies, including "coercive controlling or avoidant patterns of relating?" Understanding the attachment IMERs from which one's defenses originate can offer a deep understanding of one another's pressure points. Our defenses *are* the pressure points. Can husband and wife, pastor and flock, or teacher and student learn to support and respect each other where one lacks supportive IMERs, especially when there is a chronic area of deprivation?

*Two Alternative Patterns of Relating*

In our first session together, as a most reliable clue of what would follow, Lake refused the role of an expert telling me which course to follow. Though such a *dominance/submission* (D/S) relationship obviously would have seemed benign, taking the form of a protective and even "indulgent dictator," the bottom line would have been a pattern of forcing me to follow the decisions of a controlling leader. To not obey would be to face coercion in various forms, "including being shamed and humiliated."[18] Relying on P. D. MacLean's findings on brain studies, Heard and Lake thought it likely that D/S patterns of relating were sited in the reptilian brain. While varying with previous experience, age, and temperament, evidence suggested that children and adults became dominating to those whom they assessed as likely to become submissive. Bowlby's attachment model pictured the

---

[17] Ibid., p. 84.
[18] Ibid., p. 35.

parent/child relationship as a goal-corrected partnership, with the child's careseeking as half of the process and maternal caregiving as the other half. During the course of the day the mother may have attempted through an attunement process to change the set goals of the child's behavior. The child, in response, may have sought to change the mother's behavior and proximity. In doing so, the child would invariably have adopted some of the methods the mother herself employed. "Therein lies both hope and warning."[19]

With this warning and hope in mind, Lake helped me construct a pastoral caregiving pattern that was not simply set within the pre-existing D/S mold. Lake connected with my own curiosity about problem-solving, to explore alternatives, and to weigh the different parts of myself that were conflicted over how to proceed with Sarah's seeking of care while encouraging my own decision-making. In other words, Lake modeled a *supportive companionable* (SC) way of caregiving that was integrated with interest-sharing and exploration. This style of caregiving is a "protective, explanatory, exploratory form of relating that owes as much to nonverbal signals and tone of voice as to communicating through verbal signals."[20] It is a pattern to which people of all ages seem innately prepared to respond and adopt. When conflict arises, SC caregiving responds by recognizing others' points of view and resolving conflicts through negotiation and compromise. In a supportive, companionable way, parents, teachers, and colleagues treat other adults and children as worthy of respect. From such experiences, children, students, and peers build up new internal models (IMERs) based on the SC pattern.

In this light, one can anticipate self-care and self-management that evolves in one of two ways, depending on the quality of IMERs. One is interdependent, the other is defensive (either overly dependent or independent). Parental caregiving mediated through supportive companionable (SC) patterns enables offspring to feel capable of self-management and to seek help from those whom they trust in situations when they find themselves beyond their competence. When parental figures use dominance/submissive (D/S) patterns of relating, they reduce the child's systemic capacities for careseeking and caregiving, intrapersonal exploration, cooperative interest-sharing, and eventually their capacity for mutually affectionate sexual

---

[19] Ibid., p. 39.
[20] Ibid., p. 34.

relationships and overall self-management.

In the church system, how shall a pastor encourage a shared approach to caregiving/careseeking that reflects a community of mutual respect and a shared partnership in the gospel? That is, how can the church be a priesthood of all believers, not a group dominated by a benign "dictator" or endlessly engaged in territorial conflicts over "who is boss"? How shall one respond to someone, perhaps an elder, who has activated one's defenses? Instead of avoiding and distancing, or seeking to firmly assert control over the situation, can we not negotiate on the basis of a sense of being *companions* (literally, ones who "share bread together")? May we not ground this mutuality in the shared gratitude we acknowledge before a common table of grace? Out of the mystery that God in Christ has embraced our humanity in its imperfections and distortions, we are able to journey together in a supportive, companionable way. Out of the reality of the unique theological attachment revealed in the gospel—grace growing through love—we grow in confidence to journey together as fellow disciples, not masters and servants.

*The Relevance of Companionable Interest Sharing in the Classroom*

For the past five years, my primary SC role has moved from the sanctuary to the classroom, so I will comment on the relevance of the SC model for teaching and for creating classroom community. Heard and Lake helpfully distinguish the goals of an interest-sharing system (which has priority in teaching) from the attachment system goals of either caregiving or careseeking. With the latter, the main sensation is satisfaction or relief. The careseeker's goal is to feel that the caregiving partner understands one's predicament and is prepared to protect, until the environment or internal state no longer evokes careseeking and the careseeker acquires the skills necessary to cope with the predicament. The caregiver's goal is to seek satisfaction in knowing that the careseeker is now able to cope. However, the goals of interest-sharing go beyond felt relief to create a "heightened sense of vitality and intimacy."[21] This bears closer scrutiny.

---

[21] Ibid., p. 54.

We know that attachment realities can and do interrupt the exploratory mode. Ainsworth has identified how missing a loved one arouses a sense of insecurity.[22] Heard likens this "attachment dynamic" to Winnicott's description of a child's play that becomes overridden by anxiety, but which is then re-established when a mother "holds the situation."[23] Heard and Lake consider the pursuit of interests by peers, that is, people of broadly similar intelligence, stamina, and competence in the pursuit of interests, to be the equivalent of mutual play. In fact they report that this observation led to their notion of complementary instinctive behavioral systems—the exploratory interest-sharing systems. "This system is activated initially by the supportive interest of parents, then of peers, and consists of skills that further the understanding and enjoyment of a joint interest extended and new competencies discovered."[24]

Educators might be curious about what activates the interest-sharing system. Heard and Lake call attention to the following triad: a new level of understanding regarding an interest, a new achievement in a related skill area, and an opportunity to see others doing the same. Mutual interest-sharing between peers may begin at the point of communication of one's "eureka" experiences, which evoke in interested companions a wish to discover more. The mere sharing of interests leads to a common delight in the achievement of new insights and skills. A state of comfort is created "akin to feeling in rapport (or not) with someone."[25] Clearly, arranging time and creating space for this quality of interaction is an important pedagogical ingredient in moving beyond a D/S format into an SC learning community. Though the traditional lecture format apparently resembles a D/S structure, lectures do not necessarily embody this quality any more than group discussions are magically free of D/S elements. A lecture may meaningfully share interests when the instructor's approach to the material shapes an environment that invites mutual exploration and encourages dialogue.

The task of a therapist, says Bowlby, "is to help [the client] review the representational models of attachment figures that without his realizing it are governing his perceptions, predictions

---

[22] Ibid., p. 52.
[23] Ibid.
[24] Ibid., p. 53.
[25] Ibid.

and actions."[26]  When a teacher engages students in a manner informed by attachment theory, part of one's effort will include helping them explore the working models they bring to class and how these are currently functioning to create both a class atmosphere and an internal learning environment, for better and for worse.  In other words, what Lake provided for me in the counseling context has a classroom analogue.  In comparing the D/S model to pedagogy, one immediately sees parallels with Paulo Freire's "banking model," with the teacher performing the role of "sage on stage."[27]  Students are the empty vessels, their knowledge purses empty and in need of pure receptivity in order to be filled. From the teacher's perspective, should learning and testing evaluations reveal meager increments of knowledge gained, the fault lies in the lack of receptivity of the student. "Sit still so I can pour the knowledge in."  The student's revenge on the D/S paradigm turns the tables and blames the faulty knowledge dispenser.  Of course, if one compliantly accepts the dominance, an unsuccessful student dutifully absorbs the blame of being a poor receptor.  One who consciously self-blames may simultaneously and unconsciously resent one's learning partner. By contrast, the SC approach would anticipate that there are potentially as many ways to master a subject and as many learning styles as there are personal uniquenesses and combinations of one's own set of "multiple intelligences."[28]

To summarize, a classroom experience congruent with the exploratory system will express empathic support integrated with exploratory interest-sharing.  Such a learning atmosphere will indwell an inner motivation and an external structure to which both student and teacher are committed.  Without this shared commitment, one cannot encourage shared responsibility.  The more one prepares for learning—having read the assignment, having invested one's own mental and emotional resources—the more satisfying results the learning community achieves.  Unless students are persuaded that their own preparation for class is vital, there is no shared belief and only a coerced connection.

---

[26] Ibid., p. 46, quoting Bowlby, *Attachment and Loss: Volume 2. Separation: Anxiety and Anger* (London: Hogarth, 1973), p. 148.
[27] Paulo Freire, *Pedegogy of the Oppressed* (New York:  Herder and Herder, 1970), pp. 39, 60.
[28] Howard Gardner, *Frames of Mind:  The Theory of Multiple Intelligences* (New York: Basic Books, 1983).

Further, an SC approach will acknowledge the personal coefficient in all knowledge, seeing the knower and the known connection not as a scandal to eradicate but as a reality in which we may participate to the limits of our curiosity, imagination, and energy. Polanyi has written, "I have tried to demonstrate that into every act of knowing there enters a tacit and passionate contribution of the person knowing what is being known, and that this coefficient is no mere imperfection, but a necessary component of all knowledge."[29] An example of this cooperation in my area of teaching is the increased sensitivity in biblical hermeneutics to the act of reading itself and to "reader response" criticism in biblical studies.[30] Since readers bring a diversity of gifts and insights to the text, one hopes to encourage students to creatively and actively perform the reading role in such a way that their lives are both informed and transformed by an encounter with the reality of God.

Paramount in this SC style is that the instructor maintains an exploratory collaborative stance in relation to the inquirer of any age. In this way one may respectfully acknowledge students' starting place and seek to connect sensitively to their preparedness to extend their knowledge. At the same time, one seeks to create a real meeting with the material in all its angularity and distinctness, particularly when it does not simply conform to our preconceptions. Thus, for example, when instructors introduce new material, they may choose not to dominate or overwhelm their students by rushing through their lectures, especially if the state of students' interest and attention signals disconnection. SC teaching entails the art of tuning or attunement with students' states of mind. It seeks to regulate both overarousal and underarousal.[31] Should instructors sense the waning of student interest, they may adapt accordingly, perhaps using humor to help re-engage interest.

Of course, inattention is not always a laughing matter.

---

[29] Michael Polanyi, *Personal Knowledge. Towards a Post-Critical Philosophy* (Chicago: University Press, 1958.), p. 312. A contemporary educator who has read Polanyi most helpfully is Parker Palmer. See his *To Know as we are Known* (San Francisco: HarperCollins, 1993), pp. 28, 29.

[30] For a thorough introduction to contemporary hermeneutics, including reader response criticism, see Anthony C. Thiselton, *New Horizons in Hermeneutics* (Grand Rapids: Zondervan, 1992).

[31] Heard and Lake, p. 90.

Suppose that certain individuals appear drowsy during an afternoon class. At such moments I have been torn between ignoring this (avoidance, flight) and firmly confronting it (aggression, fight), inevitably choosing the former course but with an aftertaste of swallowed frustration. Recently I have begun to interact with drowsy or inattentive students after class, sometimes inquiring by email that I had noticed their lethargy and wondered if they were feeling unwell and if they knew the procedure to access medical attention. If it was a simple matter of sleep deprivation, I have asked if there might be a more cost-effective way to organize sleep patterns, especially given the high cost of tuition! Judging by the responses I have received, students are quite open to this feedback and appreciate my interest. It also has a positive effect on attentiveness thereafter.

It would seem more preferable to explore issues of class vitality and attention immediately and directly. The problem is how to make the attuning adjustments in a non-embarrassing way. Though ostensibly engaging in dialogue, it could easily become a form of humiliation and shaming, thus reinforcing a D/S pattern. Good questions to ask might include: "I am curious if you can identify what specific moment or event triggered your disengagement?" "What questions from your own life cause this material to be relevant to you?" "What do others find relevant or meaningful about this material?" "Are there identifiable stressors in the classroom environment which are making exploratory behavior unlikely?"

Finally, it is worth inquiring what discomforting threats to interest-sharing exist in the classroom, which upon reaching a certain level of intensity renders interest-sharing defensive. When interest-sharing becomes defensive, there follows a loss of well-being, low self-esteem, and the anxiety, depression, and despair that is associated with failing to meet the desired goals.[32] I would suggest that one crucial stressor is the imminent reality that education continually involves assessment and evaluation, which create the nagging fear that one might not reach one's goal. Since fear of failure is never far from any kind of work, how can interest-sharing maintain vitality and not suffer extinction? Here the D/S and SC styles surely affect both the way one experiences assessment and how it is administered. Crucial to a SC evaluative experience, which is not permeated with dominance/submissive

---

[32] Ibid., p. 170.

overtones, is the felt experience of supportive feedback. Supportive evaluation gives one confidence to grow and improve one's skills, keeps exploration vital and honest, and energizes students to reach their goals in a realistic and truthful manner. It follows that one can experience competition in the classroom in one of two ways. In the SC classroom, competition seeks to increase ability and skill relative to a shared interest. In D/S contexts, competition seeks to maintain the status and power of the competitors.[33]

*The End of Session One and a New Beginning*

My initial session with Lake ended without him telling me what to do with Sarah. We did consider ways to support Sarah while encouraging her to find care closer to home, grounded more realistically in her current living situation. We explored ways of expressing this to Sarah in a manner that would not be rejecting, but supportive and encouraging, firmly leading her to create an environment of self-care and support appropriate for life in a new setting. The bottom line of Lake's mentoring of me was this: having spent time with all the different aspects of how I felt about this pastoral situation (including the previously unacknowledged part of me which felt good about being needed and valued so highly), I must do what I felt was right. I now see that Lake modeled for me a companionable, supportive style of caregiving. Had he simply told me what I should do, he would have functioned in a dominant/submissive style, in which Lake as the expert in human relations administered the prescription that I should follow. Though I may have wanted such expert advice, he did not offer it. I left his office that day sensing I had begun a journey into a new way of giving care to others—and receiving it as well. At times I would need more support (Bowlby), and at other times I would be secure enough to explore significant issues that would increase my skills and insight into the multiple systems involved in pastoral care.

Conceptualizing the self and the processes that lead to a maturing identity are exceedingly difficult tasks. Heard and Lake have illuminated this important work by broadening attachment theory to include the role of interest-sharing and companionable support in one's maturing ego-ideal. Parents, pastors, and

---

[33] Ibid., p. 90.

teachers may consider, then, how to give supportive care and how to create a feeling of belonging and community to their children, parishioners, and students. As another has reminded us, "there's nothing so practical as a good theory."[34]

---

[34] Ibid., p. 135 (quoting Jock Sutherland). I would like to close by thanking my wife, Sue Newell, L.C.S.W., for her careful editorial skill and supportive feedback on an earlier version of this essay.

# On Becoming a Person of Character: Behavioral, Social-Cognitive, and Developmental-Contextual Perspectives

*Kaye V. Cook, Daniel Larson, and Maren Oslund*
Gordon College

Marissa, a 14-year-old girl in the 8th grade, has lots of friends but is failing her schoolwork. Extremely charming, she is known as someone who will do "anything" for her friends. Indeed, she seems to be a slightly different person with each of her friends. Despite considerable strengths and talents, despite being well-liked, she would not be described as a person of character. Someone who saw her in therapy would describe her as having a disorganized sense of self.

Marissa and other children like her who lack a solid sense of self are difficult to treat effectively in therapy. Yet these are the children who demonstrate, by their lack, the central importance of the self in personality development and, by their progress in therapy, that the self grows and develops.

Although it may seem odd to have a chapter on character emergence in a volume about personality theory, we believe that the self is best conceptualized as a multi-faceted complex of organized characteristics, to which character is integral. Within this paradigm, one's character is central to a well-organized self. In this chapter, we will argue for a unitary and developmental model of an organized self in which character and self are inextricably combined.

We will first review behavioral and social-cognitive theories of character development and then present a paradigm that builds on the strengths of both while addressing some of their weaknesses. Our paradigm will attempt to integrate theoretical and research perspectives from several sources, primarily research on conscience development by Kochanska,[1] self-regulation research, theorizing about the emergence of the moral self in

---

[1] G. Kochanska, "Beyond Cognition: Expanding the Search for the Early Roots of Internalization and Conscience," *Developmental Psychology*, 1 (1994): 20-22.

infancy,[2] and a developmental-contextual paradigm developed by Rutter and Sroufe.[3]

Using this paradigm, we will discuss the emergence of character—the moral self. We believe that this paradigm describes better than behaviorist and social-cognitive theories our creation in the image of God, our fallenness, and our potential for hope and redemption. We will end the chapter with some practical suggestions for therapists (primarily therapists who work with children and their parents) and for parents who wish to nurture moral development in their children.

We would like to start by briefly reviewing the behaviorist paradigm. This review is not meant to be comprehensive, but to highlight concepts relevant to the self and character development.

*Behaviorism*

In the behaviorist model, the person is the passive recipient of environmental stimuli. Learning takes place by either *operant* or *classical* conditioning techniques, and therapists use the principles of learning, based on these techniques, to modify behavior. According to this model, the self is a collection of learned associations between behavior and context.

Basic Concepts. The learning of associations between stimuli marks classical or respondent conditioning. Classical conditioning is sometimes called Pavlovian conditioning because Pavlov first and notably conditioned a dog to salivate when a bell was rung.[4] This kind of learning involves the modification of an organism's behavior by replacing an unconditioned stimulus (UCS) that naturally elicits a behavior with a conditioned stimulus (CS) that comes to trigger a behavior similar to that elicited by the UCS. Food, for example, is a UCS that elicits salivation in a

---

2 R. N. Emde, Z. Biringen, R. B. Clyman, & D. Oppenheim, "The Moral Self of Infancy: Affective Core and Procedural Knowledge," *Developmental Review*, 11 (1991): 251-270.

3 L. A. Sroufe & M. Rutter, "The Domain of Developmental Psychopathology," *Child Development*, 55 (1984): 17-29. M. Rutter & L. A. Sroufe, "Developmental Psychopathology: Concepts and Challenges," *Development & Psychopathology*, 12 (2000): 265-296.

4 I. P. Pavlov, *Conditioned Reflexes: An Investigation of the Physiological Activity of the Cerebral Cortex*, translated by G.V. Anrep (London: Oxford University Press, 1927).

hungry dog. As Pavlov showed, a bell paired with food becomes a CS because it comes to elicit salivation in a hungry dog.

A well-known example of classical conditioning is the case of little Albert, who was conditioned to fear white rats by repeated exposure to a white rat paired with a loud noise.[5] His response to loud noises is labeled the unconditioned response (UCR) because loud noises naturally (i.e., without conditioning) elicit a fearful response. His response to white rats is labeled the conditioned response (CR), learned by association with loud noises.

Classically (and operantly) conditioned responses are *acquired*. For example, Pavlov's dogs salivated more reliably in response to the bell as conditioning proceeded. These responses *generalize*, as shown by the fact that bells of similar but not the same tone elicited salivation. Similarly, little Albert generalized his fear of white rats to other furry animals. Acquired responses also illustrate *discrimination*; sounds that were quite different from the original tone failed to elicit salivation in Pavlov's dogs.

Conditioned responses generally involve the learning of emotional associations—for example, pleasure in Pavlov's dogs and fear in little Albert's case. We all show classically conditioned responses to mealtimes, holidays, and a host of other experiences.

Operant or instrumental conditioning was pioneered by E. L. Thorndike,[6] who called it the "law of effect," and elaborated by B. F. Skinner[7] into principles of behavioral control. Operant conditioning is based on the premise that the frequency of a behavior can be altered depending on its consequences. Consequences include reinforcers and punishers. Reinforcing consequences increase the frequency of a behavior, while punishing consequences (in theory if not always in practice) decrease the frequency of a behavior.

Reinforcers are of two types. Positive reinforcements such as food for a hungry dog and praise for a school child increase the likelihood that a behavior will occur again. Negative reinforcements increase the likelihood that a behavior that avoids the negative experience will recur. Thus, studying avoids low grades, increasing the frequency of studying; teenagers who meet

---

5 J. B. Watson & R. Rayner, "Conditioned Emotional Reactions," *Journal of Experimental Psychology*, 3 (1920): 1-4.

6 E. L. Thorndike, "The Newest Psychology," *Educational Review*, 28 (1904): 217-227.

7 B. F. Skinner, *The Behavior of Organisms: An Experimental Analysis* (New York: Appleton-century-Crofts, 1938).

parental curfews avoid their parents' wrath, making responsibility more likely.

Reinforcers can be delivered on a continuous schedule (i.e., each time a behavior is produced, it is rewarded) or a schedule of partial reinforcement (i.e., only some behaviors are rewarded).[8] A child who is rewarded each time he obeys his parents is likely to learn obedience quickly but not to be very obedient once rewards are no longer provided. A child who is rewarded intermittently for obedience learns the association more slowly but is more likely to continue to obey once rewards are no longer provided. Recommended, of course, is continuous reinforcement early in the acquisition process and intermittent reinforcement as the association becomes established.

Punishers are of less predictable effect than are reinforcements.[9] For example, spanking children is a controversial practice because, in some cases, spanking seems to increase rather than decrease aggressive behavior, particularly for children whose behavior is measured at a later time rather than immediately.[10]

All behaviors—whether observable or internal (e.g., thoughts)—follow these principles of learning. Thus, according to behaviorists, cognitions do not shape behaviors but co-occur with external behaviors and are equally as much a product of reinforcements.

Treatments. Behaviorism has given rise to a range of therapeutic interventions. Best known among these are behavior therapy, relaxation techniques, and systematic desensitization, all of which are useful with children.

Behavior therapy[11] begins when a behavior, perhaps cleaning one's room or going to bed on time, is targeted for change using operant conditioning techniques. Rewards and/or punishments are then used to shape the behavior, in these cases to

---

[8] Ibid.

[9] R. D. Parke, "Rules, Roles, and Resistance to Deviation: Recent Advances in Punishment, Discipline, and Self-control," in A. D. Pick (ed.), *Minnesota Symposia on Child Psychology* (Minneapolis MN: University of Minnesota Press), pp.111-143.

[10] J. H. Laub & R. J. Sampson, "The Long-term Effect of Punitive Discipline, "in J. McCord (ed.), *Coercion and Punishment in Long-term Perspectives* (Cambridge, England: Cambridge University Press), pp. 247-258..

[11] C. M. Franks, *Behavior Therapy: Appraisal and Status* (New York: McGraw-Hill, 1969).

encourage it. The type of reward or punishment is individually selected, depending on the person's likes and dislikes and the behavior to be modified. Indeed, it is worth noting that there are few universal rewards and punishments; rather, rewards and punishments are selected by their effectiveness (i.e., do they increase or decrease the behavior as desired?) and for each individual (i.e., what works for one person may well not work for another).

The second kind of therapy, relaxation techniques,[12] uses classical conditioning to reduce stress and anxiety. Children are taught to relax either by focusing on muscle groups (feet, legs, knees, etc.) or by meditation training (focusing on a syllable or an image). Certain environments or calming tones or textures (e.g., blankets) may also be used. With minimal modification, relaxation techniques can generally be used with children as young as 8 or 9 years of age.

Systematic desensitization[13] techniques use imagery to help children older than 8 or 9 years of age deal with certain phobias or anxieties. The child and the therapist together establish a hierarchy of fears, beginning with least fearful and continuing to the highest level of fear. For a child who fears dentist visits, the least fearful event to imagine might be seeing a picture of a toothbrush. More fearful might be seeing a picture of the dentist's office. Most fearful to imagine might be sitting in the dentist's chair. The therapist leads the child in visualization of each level of the hierarchy of fears, beginning with the lowest level. When the child has habituated to fear (i.e., no longer reports feeling fearful) at each level, he or she progresses to the next level. When the highest level of fears is reached and successfully visualized without fear, the therapist might have the child actually participate in the fear-producing situation while doing relaxation exercises.

View of Self. In behavioral theory, the self is atomistic, i.e., a collection of learned associations between behaviors and the environment.[14] Behavior can be changed by altering the context (e.g., moving a child from one troublesome context to another

---

[12] H. Benson, *The Relaxation Response* (New York: Morrow, 1975).

[13] J. Wolpe, "The Systematic Desensitization Treatment of Neurosis," *Journal of Nervous and mental Disease*, 132 (1961): 189-203.

[14] Skinner argued that some form of an inner world exists but that its activities are private and have no place in scientific psychology unless they can be operationalized (i.e., measured by objective means); behavioral theorists, however, act as if the self is atomistic.

context that is more rewarding of positive behaviors) and the consequences that the environment provides. Character, according to this model, is a loose collection of learned associations that can be readily modified by new learning.

According to behaviorists, the person is a behaving organism that functions in a mechanistic or machine-like way. The organism increasingly produces those behaviors that are rewarded and ceases to produce behaviors that are punished. The self is a passive agent, not a responsible or cognitive agent.

This metaphysic has proved a powerful way of understanding human learning. If all behaviors (including cognitions and other complex behaviors, e.g., language) can best be understood using the same principles of learning, then any behavior can be readily modified. It does not, however, describe well what it means to be human.

The person of behaviorism learns pro-social and aggressive behaviors. This self is a collection of learned but not organized or integrated associations. In contrast, character intuitively seems to be made up of organized, not isolated, behaviors, and some behaviors seem more desirable than others. A person has a particular nature, perhaps described as kind or patient, in which pro-social or aggressive behaviors appear and are organized. Behavioral theory does not allow exploration of this higher order of organization; rather, it explores the learning of even complex behaviors, such as language and cognition, by the same principles of learning, association and reinforcement, no matter how complex the behaviors.

Of further concern is that this model presumes a passive, incoherent self, subject to environmental or other controls, which redefines the meaning of morality. In this kind of model, there are no criteria for what "ought" to be; there is only what "is."[15] Without criteria, how are virtues chosen? What differentiates worthy respondents from unacceptable ones? Either the criteria for the "good" (i.e., what is moral) come from external sources, not explored by behavioral theory, or behaviorists commit the naturalistic fallacy, confounding "what is" with "what ought to be." In behaviorist theory, those associations are "good" that can be acquired. There are no other criteria for identifying the good, leaving us with an unacceptable and seriously deficient view of

---

[15] O. Flanagan, *The Science of the Mind* (Cambridge, MA: MIT Press, 1984).

character. Thus, with behaviorist theory, we are left searching for a way to understand the self that better represents what we know of the self and of ultimate reality.

As we will see later on, our model utilizes the basic concepts of behaviorist theory but applies these concepts to a unified self. We thus accept the methodological contributions of behaviorism but not its metaphysical assumptions. First, however, we need to review social-cognitive theory.

*Social-cognitive theory*

In the social-cognitive model, the self is active and cognitive, shaping and being shaped by others. Reinforcements can be indirect, and learning can occur by observing others. Therapeutic intervention focuses on modifying specific behaviors and cognitions (e.g., cognitive-behavioral therapy) and on modifying the interactions in which problem behaviors occur (e.g., parent management training).

Character education manuals typically recommend that character be developed as outlined by the social-cognitive model. Parents are encouraged to use the learning principles of behaviorism as well as vicarious reinforcement, observational learning, and modeling (basic concepts of social-cognitive theory that we will soon define) to modify undesirable behaviors and develop character.

Major concepts and personalities. The social-cognitive model, developed by Bandura, Rotter, Mischel, and others, builds on the strengths of behaviorism while addressing some of its weaknesses. Albert Bandura, its best known advocate, was well-trained in learning theory. As a clinician, he was interested in exploring clinical phenomena with experimental techniques.

Bandura's primary focus was on family patterns and their effects on children's development, specifically on their aggressive development. As a result, he and his first graduate student, Richard Walters, began to explore the central role of *modeling* (i.e., learning through observing others) in personality development. Using inflatable clown ("bobo") dolls in their now-classic research design, they demonstrated that children who observed violent behaviors being directed at the bobo doll subsequently copied these behaviors.[16] It is significant that the

---

[16] See, e.g., A. Bandura & R. Walters, *Social Learning and Personality Development* (New York: Holt, Rinehart and Winston, 1963).

powerful learning effect observed here occurred as a result of *observational learning* (i.e., imitation of another's behavior) and *vicarious reinforcement* (i.e., reinforcement delivered to an observed other) rather than by direct, overt reinforcement. Neither observational learning nor learning as a result of indirect reinforcement is predicted by classic learning theory.

From these experiments and others, Bandura developed his concept of *reciprocal determinism*. Thus, in contrast to behaviorism's unidirectional emphasis (i.e., environment shapes behavior), reciprocal determinism describes a transactional system in which such outcome-determining factors as the environment, cognitions (i.e., beliefs and perceptions), and behavior all exert reciprocal influences on each other. Bandura particularly focused on the reciprocal nature of cognition; in other words, he argued that cognition plays an active role in the perception of behavior and environment at the same time as it shapes both.

In Bandura's approach to personality, the self is not passive or atomistic. Rather, the self is a collection of cognitive processes and structures concerned with thoughts, feelings, and perceptions. This move from the mechanistic model of behaviorism to a more cognitive model, he argued, was necessary to explain the efficacy of vicarious reinforcement and observational learning. The learner must be actively engaged in cognitively processing information about the occurrence and results of events, including the possibility of future actions, for modeling to occur.

A central element of Bandura's cognitive model is the concept of *perceived self-efficacy*. Self-efficacy refers to the ability to successfully negotiate a situation, accomplish a task, or cope with a challenge.[17] Each person makes subjective evaluations of his or her own abilities. These evaluations form a person's *perceived self-efficacy* and have a strong influence on his or her behavior and self-image. People with high perceived self-efficacy believe they are good at a task and will do better on the task than those who have low perceived self-efficacy, even if their abilities are the same. As importantly, those with high self-efficacy produce more positive self-evaluations of task performance, thus enforcing their

---

[17] A. Bandura, "Self-efficacy," in V. S. Ramachaudran (ed.), *Encyclopedia of Human Behavior* (vol. 4). New York: Academic Press. (Reprinted in H. Friedman, ed., *Encyclopedia of Mental Health*, San Diego: Academic Press, 1998), pp. 71-81

perceptions of high self-efficacy. In contrast, those with low perceived self-efficacy evaluate comparable task performances more negatively.

Even more strongly than Bandura, Julian Rotter[18] emphasized the cognitions, feelings, and beliefs of persons. He suggested that we perceive ourselves as conscious beings, able to make decisions that shape our lives. Reinforcement is important, but its effectiveness depends on our own cognitions. According to Rotter, behavior is influenced by several factors, including our *expectancies* of its consequences (i.e., our subjective evaluation of the outcome of the behavior in terms of the reinforcement that will follow it), the *reinforcement value* of the consequences (i.e., our judgment of the relative worth of various reinforcements), and our individually selected *goals*.

Walter Mischel[19] observed the same phenomenon: that one person may exhibit significantly different responses to similar situations. Trait theorists, who believe that people possess distinctive internal attributes that produce unique behavioral patterns, cannot explain this fact. Behaviorists attempt to explain this by invoking an individual's history of reinforcements. Mischel, even more effectively, explains this variability by suggesting that differences in thinking about situations (e.g., expectancies) leads to different behaviors within those same situations, a relationship he refers to as person * situation (P * S) interactionism.[20] Cognition is not an epiphenomenon, parallelling behavior but not causing it, as behaviorists argue, but mediates the nature of reinforcement.

A recent focus within social-cognitive theory has been on self-regulation.[21] Self-regulation is the mechanism by which one gains control of the effects of one's perceived self-efficacy on

---

[18] J. B. Rotter, *The Development and Application of Social Learning Theory* (New York: Praeger, 1982).
[19] W. Mischel, "Assessment from a Cognitive Social Learning Perspective," *Evaluacion Psicologica*, 1. 1-2 (1985): 33-57.
[20] R. Mendoza-Denton, O. Ayduk, W. Mischel, Y. Shoda, & A. Testa, "Person * Situation Interactionism in Self-encoding (I am . . . when . . .): Implications for Affect Regulation and Social Information Processing," *Journal of Personality & Social Psychology*, 80.4 (2001): 533-544.
[21] A. Bandura, "Social Cognitive Theory of Self-regulation," *Organizational Behavior & Human Decision Processes*. 50.2 (1991): 248-287; R. F. Baumeister & T. F. Heatherton, "Self-regulation Failure: An Overview," *Psychological Inquiry*, 7.1 (1991): 1-15.

behavior.[22] Self-regulatory skills such as cognitive reframing, self-reinforcement, and achievable goal-setting allow persons to improve their self-efficacy and performance.

<u>Implications for therapeutic intervention</u>. The therapeutic approaches developed within social-cognitive theory, similar to those developed within behaviorism, are characterized by a practical emphasis on the learning of more adaptive behaviors (or responses) in specific situations through the use of a range of techniques. Social-cognitive theory is distinctive, however, in its emphasis on the central role of cognition in behavior. This emphasis is evident in cognitive-behavioral therapy.

In cognitive-behavioral therapy, intervention focuses in part on behavioral change. Both behavior and cognitive-behavioral therapists often ask that clients keep a *behavioral record*, noting when a problem behavior occurs and what its antecedents and consequents are. With a child, parents might be asked to record this information, but teenagers keep their own behavioral records. Behaviorists then attempt to change the antecedents and consequents of problem behaviors. In addition to this, however, cognitive-behavioral therapists ask that clients keep a record of what their feelings and thoughts are in association with the event. Thus, cognitive-behavioral therapists address not only behavior but also cognition and emotion, using the behavioral record as a guide to thoughts and feelings that need to be addressed.

Cognitive-behavioral therapists thus focus, unlike behavior therapists, not only on what people do, but also on what people think. Self-efficacy judgments influence expectancies and beliefs, emotions, and self-evaluations, all of which influence behavior. The ability to modify one's perceived self-efficacy changes behavior from the "inside out."

A social-cognitive model that attempts to describe the faulty functioning of families of aggressive children is the coercion model, developed by Patterson[23] and his colleagues. This model is based on the premise that aggressive behavior is shaped by family interaction. Patterson suggests, for example, that some parents get into "reinforcement traps," in which they reinforce their children for undesirable behavior. These parents commonly pay attention to their children when they misbehave, an experience that is actually reinforcing for children. In other cases, parents and

[22] Bandura, 1994.
[23] G. R. Patterson, *Coercive Family Process*, Vol. 3, Series: *A Social Learning Approach* (Eugene, OR: Castalia Publishing Co, 1982).

children may experience "coercion cycles," in which parents threaten to punish their child for misbehavior, but their punishments are extreme. When their children misbehave, it becomes impossible to impose the promised punishments. When parents don't follow through, children misbehave even more, perpetuating a cycle that leads to further misbehavior.

One of several intervention models based on these principles, Parent Management Training (PMT),[24] was developed to modify the negative interaction patterns documented by Patterson's coercion model. Using social-cognitive principles of modeling and reinforcement, PMT teaches parents to use their attention to child behavior selectively as a reward for positive behavior, to use reinforcers and punishers wisely, and to give more effective and clearer commands.

In summary, although the behaviorist and social cognitive models share many features, including the basic learning processes of conditioning and reinforcement, the social cognitive model addresses some of the weaknesses of the behaviorist model. Most significantly, social-cognitive theory opens the door to learning without direct reinforcement through the operation of cognitive processes. By highlighting the effects of cognitive variables interacting with and mediating the relationship between behavior and the environment, the social-cognitive model introduces cognition as an important and relevant factor in human behavior and character development, painting a more accurate and holistic picture of human experience. Finally, social-cognitive theory allows for a more versatile and useful version of therapy than the limited stimulus-response occurrences of the behaviorist approach provide. By presenting a conception of the person as an active cognitive agent, social-cognitive theory arms individuals with the ability to self-regulate in the absence of external reinforcement through the operations of the cognitive system and to behave responsibly, abilities required for the development of character.

*Developmental-contextual model*

Marissa, the case with which we began this essay, was referred for treatment. Her therapist, if he or she were a

---

[24] R. A. Barkley, "Behavioral Inhibition, Sustained Attention, and Executive Functions: Constructing a Unifying Theory of ADHD," *Psychological Bulletin*, 121.1 (1997): 65-94.

behaviorist, would select several behaviors for shaping—e.g., good study habits, defined perhaps as time spent reading and number of assignments completed. Contingencies would be established to encourage the frequencies of these behaviors. As a result, Marissa would perhaps read more and study better, at least while the rewards were in place. This approach is useful but limited.

From a social-cognitivist perspective, cognitive-behavioral therapy might be used to modify Marissa's unhealthy thinking or self-evaluative patterns and to encourage change. Cognitive-behavioral therapy begins with a behavioral record to identify those behaviors that occur and in what context they occur. In Marissa's case, she and her parents might record when she begins and stops studying, what she does during the time, and how she thinks and feels about it. With this information, the therapist can modify the contexts and consequences to maximize positive behavior and address problem thinking and behaviors. Thus, for example, the therapist might realize that Marissa believes she can't learn and so sabotages her own study plans and might challenge this belief by demonstrating that some things come easily to her. Or the therapist might set up a regular time to study, during which all distractions are minimized. Again, we believe this approach is useful but inadequate.

From a developmental-contextual perspective, as the name implies, more information is needed about Marissa's past experiences and the patterns of abilities the child currently possesses and formerly possessed to design appropriate intervention. The developmental psychopathology model (also called the ABCD, affective-behavioral-cognitive-dynamic model[25]) studies the origins and course of individual patterns of behaviors. Originally, maladaptive patterns of behavior were studied;[26] more recently, the paradigm has been extended to study adaptive and prosocial patterns of behavior as well.[27] We believe

---

[25] M. T. Greenberg, C. A. Kusche, & M. Speltz, "Emotional Regulation, Self-control, and Psychopathology: The Role of Relationships in Early Childhood," in D. Cicchetti & S. L. Toth (eds.), *Internalizing and Externalizing Expressions of Dysfunction*, Vol.2, *Rochester Symposium on Developmental Psychopathology* (Hillsdale, NJ: Laurence Erlbaum, 1991).

[26] Sroufe & Rutter, 1984.

[27] See, e.g., A. S. Masten & W. J. Curtis, "Integrating Competence and Psychopathology: Pathways toward a Comprehensive Science of Adaptation in Development," *Development and Psychopathology*, 12

that this model more readily lends itself to the study of character and the self, as we will demonstrate in the pages to follow.

The developmental-contextual paradigm has several components. It:

(1) values historical over categorical explanations of behavior;
(2) values contextual and holistic understandings of behavior over assessment of isolated abilities;
(3) defends the primacy of organic or synthetic models of ontogenesis over strictly analytic or linear ones;
(4) values transactional over unidirectional explanations of behavior.

*The developmental-contextual model values historical over categorical explanations of behavior.* DSM-IV,[28] for example, represents a categorical explanation of maladaptive behavior, and the statements, "She's a smart little girl," or, relevant to this paper, "He has a solid sense of self," represent categorical explanations of intelligence. In contrast, a historical explanation does greater justice to the continuity of the self. Perhaps, in this example, a historical explanation might add to the statement that "he has a solid sense of self" the more nuanced understanding that, whereas he earlier showed strong skills in group leadership (presumably because he has a solid sense of self), he has more recently become particularly able to negotiate interpersonal conflicts.

Historical explanations of behavior are assumed to be continuous if not behaviorally consistent. Behaviorists assume behavioral consistency, i.e., that individuals will produce similar behaviors in similar contexts. In situations similar to those situations in which certain behaviors have been rewarded in the past, similar behaviors will be produced. Social cognitivists also assume behavioral consistency, with any inconsistencies explicable by understanding the cognitions of the behaving individual. Developmental contextualists assume continuity but not behavioral consistency. Thus, an individual's behaviors may

---

(2000): 529-550; A. S. Masten, "Resilience Comes of Age: Reflections on the Past and Outlook for the Next Generation of Research, in M. D. Glantz, J. Johnson, & L. Huffman (eds.), *Resilience and Development: Positive Life Adaptations* (New York: Plenum, 1999): 251-57.
[28] American Psychiatric Association, *Diagnostic and Statistical Manual of Mental Disorders*, 4th ed. (Washington, D.C.: Author, 1994).

change, but his or her behavioral *patterns* show relative stability. Thus, a prosocial child at three years of age may point and hold up objects frequently. A prosocial child at eight years of age may navigate interpersonal relationships easily. The child's overall patterns of performance show continuity, but the individual behaviors may not.

*The developmental-contextual model values contextual and holistic understandings of behavior over the assessment of isolated abilities.* Behaviorists examine the conditioning of isolated behaviors, with the goal of nurturing those behaviors that facilitate community. Behaviors, however, are never isolated. A child who is hyperactive is overly active in some contexts and not others. Further, his or her activity level affects characteristics of their lives, such as how much homework they finish, whether they learn in class, and whether they are socially adept or awkward. In every case, although a categorical analysis of isolated abilities does indeed describe something accurate about the child, it does not do justice to the complexity of the child's functioning.

Further, behaviors are not isolated but patterned. A child diagnosed as hyperactive may also be talkative and impatient. As he matures into adolescence, he may become less impatient and less talkative but manifest his hyperactivity by participation in organized sports or by engagement in intense, creative, marathon writing sessions. In each case, hyperactivity is best described as a pattern of behaviors, rather than as individual, isolated behaviors. Also, this child, as he matures from childhood to adolescence, shows continuity in behavior (hyperactivity), but the isolated behaviors that manifest this behavior may change or be reorganized, forming a new pattern.

*The developmental-contextual model defends the primacy of epigenetic models of ontogenesis over strictly analytic or linear ones.* Behaviorist and social cognitive theories describe development as a linear process, with later abilities depending on earlier competencies and learning. The nature of development is, however, much more complex than this, a complexity better recognized by the epigenetic models of the developmental psychopathologist. According to Waddington's epigenetic model,[29] development is characterized by increasing differentiation and specialization of abilities. Thus, adequate social skills at one age are nuanced, reorganized, and supplemented by maturationally

---

[29] C. H. Waddington, *Principles of Development and Differentiation* (New York: Macmillan, 1966).

emerging social skills at another age.

*The developmental-contextual model values transactional over unidirectional explanations of behavior.* Although social cognitive models recognize the transactional nature of development (i.e., that a child both shapes and is shaped by their relationships with others), the transactional component of a developmental-contextual model is much more complex. Within the developmental-contextual model, what is important in behavioral understanding is not only a person's immediate context but also the history of that context and the place of that interaction within the child's larger context and complex of behaviors.

In sum, the self of developmental-contextual theory is active and cognitive, as is the self of social-cognitive theory, but with a history and a context from which it organically emerges.

In a more practical vein, consider the diagnosis of social abilities. A typological, or diagnositic, psychologist might assess a child's social abilities and deficits, comparing these to, perhaps, Eysenck's Five-Factor Personality Model or the DSM-IV criteria for Asperger's and autism or even the twenty-four virtues outlined by positive psychologists (a relatively recent movement with psychology that focuses on using psychology to improve the lives of others).[30] A psychologist who uses the developmental-contextual paradigm, in contrast, would assess a child's current social abilities, attempt to assess earlier performance, and return to assess their abilities at a later time, paying attention to individual social abilities and the pattern among them as they grow and change with age. Thus, developmental-contextual psychologists recognize the history of a particular behavior, its place in the child's larger complex of behaviors, and its dynamic nature.

Intervention is similarly theory-driven. Learning theorists intervene by modifying the context and the contingencies. Social-cognitive theorists intervene by assessing behavior and self-evaluation and attempting to change these. The developmental-contextual intervention includes these perspectives but again is much broader. Consider Marissa. Within the developmental-contextual model, it becomes important to know what her educational history has been and what her family situation is. It also becomes important to know the pattern of her performance. Is she struggling in math as well as reading, for example? What

---

[30] Information about positive psychology can be accessed on their webpage: http://www.positivepsychology.org.

can be found out about her school performance during the early grades, and was her pattern of performance at that time similar to her current functioning? With this added information, a psychologist might come to the same conclusion as without this information, i.e., that the best intervention is strengthening her reading ability. Or a psychologist might reach other conclusions. With this information, the psychologist might conclude that Marissa would benefit as well from some counseling focused on her troubled family life, or some special attention in science, in which she earlier showed particular aptitude but more recently has performed poorly.

The developmental-contextual therapist recognizes the role of classical and operant conditioning in learning and that rewards and punishments shape behavior. This therapist, therefore, has at his or her disposal all the techniques of the behaviorist and social learning theorist, including systematic desensitization, cognitive-behavioral therapy, and reinforcements.

The goal of the developmental-contextual therapist is understanding the abilities that children possess and documenting their strengths and weaknesses. Developmental-contextual therapists therefore begin with assessments that explore competencies, such as self-regulation and social skills. They look for patterns of behaviors and how those patterns have changed. Assessment is followed by treatment planning, in which therapists select where to focus and intervene. During assessment and intervention, the focus is not on individual behaviors but on patterns of behaviors.

A brief description of Collaborative Problem Solving,[31] a model that incorporates some of the principles of the developmental-contextual model, might help to sharpen understanding of this model.

Greene and his colleagues developed Collaborative Problem Solving (CPS) as an alternative paradigm to PMT[32] in the treatment of oppositional defiant children (ODD, DSM-IV, 1994). Greene argues that children with this diagnosis are typically easily frustrated, chronically inflexible, and explosive because they are compromised in the domains of self-regulation and/or affective modulation and because they are poorly parented. Intervention

---

[31] R. W. Greene, *The Explosive Child: A New Approach for Understanding and Parenting Easily Frustrated, Chronically Inflexible Children*, 2nd ed (NY: HarperCollins, 2001).
[32] Barcley, 1997.

requires that parent and child are actively engaged in a process of "collaborative problem solving" in order to resolve issues of parent-child conflict. In other words, if parents respond to child noncompliance with rigid rule expectations, then, if the noncompliance depends in part on deficient child competencies, parent and child become locked in a maladaptive cycle that perpetuates oppositional behavior. If, on the other hand, parents respond more appropriately, the cycle can be broken.

Although Greene et al.[33] describe their model as cognitive-behavioral, their emphasis on studying "pathways" makes this a developmental-contextual model. Greene et al. outline treatment goals in CPS that begin with a focus on increasing parental understanding of the development of child self-regulation and/or affective modulation skills. Then they suggest that parents, in any given situation, use one of three basic approaches to handling events in which parental expectations are not met: (1) parents require obedience (the nonnegotiable events), (2) parents are willing to negotiate (negotiable events), and (3) parents are willing to back down (events that aren't worth fighting over). By describing events in terms of these categories, or baskets, as Greene calls them, parents can easily see that far too many interactions (particularly experiences that challenge their child's deficient abilities) are in the first category. Interactions in the second category are those that can be negotiated between parent and child and provide opportunities for collaborative problem-solving and thus for effective and lasting intervention with children who show oppositional defiant behaviors. Parents who decide that more interactions belong in the third category find more time and energy to nurture learning during the interactions in the crucial second category.

CPS, then, identifies child strengths and weaknesses in the areas of self-regulation and affective modulation and attempts to develop skills in these areas by collaborative problem-solving. In contrast, Parent Management Training (PMT), as developed by Barkley[34] and described earlier in this paper, uses reinforcers and punishers to increase compliant behavior. The focus in CPS on

---

[33]R. W. Green, J. S. Ablon, M. Monuteaux, J. Goring, L. Raezer-Blakely, A. Henin, G. Edwards, C. Moore, & J. Biederman, *Comparison of Two Forms of Psychosocial Treatment for Affectively Dysregulated Children with Oppositional Defiant Disorder: Outcomes at Four Months Post-treatment* (in press).
[34]Barkley, 1997.

patterns of behaviors and on developing strengths and skills, rather than the focus in PMT on reinforcing and punishing individual behaviors, seems intuitively more appropriate for addressing problem behaviors and more effective in bringing about growth in competencies and self-regulatory abilities. Preliminary research indicates that this is true.[35]

This model can be more broadly applied. Therapists who use this model follow several steps:

(1) **Assess** the child's current level of functioning in multiple areas, the child's past performance in the problem area, and the meaning of the problem behavior in the larger context of the child's life.

(2) **Select** areas of focus. Consider, for example, Tom, a child who is aggressive. This child may also be hyperactive, learning disabled, and have sleep problems. At the same time, Tom is charming, friendly, and eager to please. In the complex of the child's life, which strengths can be nurtured and which problem behaviors—conceptualized as patterns of behaviors not as individual behaviors—are most important to address?

(3) **Decide** which behaviors are required, which behaviors are negotiable, and which behaviors aren't worth the fight. Perhaps Kaia's parents struggle with her being manipulative and demanding. Kaia, in a grocery store, demands candy. At the same time, Kaia's mother, Ellen, is trying to pay the cashier and keep an eye on Kaia's younger brother. Ellen gives in, then berates herself for doing so. After all, in traditional behaviorist theory terms, she is reinforcing an undesireable behavior.In developmental-contextual terms, however, Ellen's response to individual infractions is less important than a more comprehensive understanding of Kaia's competencies and performance. In behaviorist and social-cognitive terms, behaviors are shaped by rewards and punishments. Every event matters. In developmental-contextual terms, however, individual incidents matter less than parental willingness to engage the child in collaborative problem-solving experiences.

Ellen might recognize that Kaia has trouble with self-regulation and therefore, in the future, try to avoid the situation

---

[35] Greene et al., in press.

(therefore putting it in category three) or, deciding that it is a category one event, prepare Kaia beforehand when it next occurs in order to maximize the likelihood of positive behaviors. Or, she might decide this is a category two, problem-solving event, in which she needs to talk with Kaia and problem-solve about how best to maximize positive behavior. She might recognize, for example, that Kaia has problems with self-regulation in crowded areas (e.g., grocery stores) but benefits from clear guidelines (e.g., she might suggest that Kaia "go have a seat on that bench just the other side of the cashier"). She and Kaia might decide together that if Kaia sits quietly her mother will take her to the park afterward.

(4) **Focus** on the negotiable interactions. From these category 2 events, children learn more positive social behaviors than as a result of the other two kinds of interactions.

In tandem, these characteristics—historical, contextual, organic, and transactional—mean that the developmental psychopathology model, although coherent with both behavioral and cognitive-behavioral models, is broader than either theoretical tradition.

We now come to our view of early moral development, character emergence, and the social self. We will see that this paradigm is helpful in understanding these components of the self.

*The Emerging Moral Self*

The self. As we have seen, the self of behaviorism is atomistic. The self of social cognitive theory is also not an organized self but has agentic, transactional, and cognitive characteristics. The developmental-contextual paradigm, however, assumes an organized or unitary self made up of skills critical for the development of character, including self-regulation and internalization.[36] By assuming a unitary self, we can explore such questions as when and in what context these abilities emerge, how they are organized, what the developmental trajectories of these abilities are, and what the interrelationships among these are.

The developmental-contextual self is agentic, transactional, and cognitive, as is the social-cognitive self, but it

---

[36] See, e.g., Emde et al., 1991; Greene, 2001.

also shows "social fittedness," has a history, and is dynamic. First, the self shows "*social fittedness,*"[37] meaning that it enters the world pre-adapted for social interaction. The self is present from birth, progressively emerges from social interaction, and understands itself in relationship to other selves. Second, the self is *historical*. It has a past and a future. Selves have a continued identity through time that shapes and constrains contemporary manifestations of the self and visions for its future. Third, the self is *dynamic*. It is continuously changing, within constraints. Young people have a different sense of self than older people; married people than unmarried; parents than non-parents; siblings than only children. Such a self is a responsible agent, unlike the "selves" of behaviorism and social learning theory, and is coherent with Christian affirmation of humanity as created in the image of God.

The emerging social and moral self. The human infant is embedded in an enlarging web of relationships that shape and modify the organization of the self.[38] Sander[39] outlines a series of phases in a child's development from initial regulation in the first three months of life to the emergence of an organized self around three years of age. In this sequence, social transactions parallel and promote the development of an inner organization of the self. As the self participates in larger and larger social circles, and with increasing abilities, the self is reorganized. As a result, the self is continuously emerging, rather than fully formed at any one point in time.

Parents modify their child's sense of self as they caregive and play with their infants. Parents may modify the nature of the organization (i.e., whether the child's sense of self is well-organized or not), validate and modify children's feelings and the meanings they develop of their experiences, and shape children's expectations of responsivity and warmth. All of these experiences

---

[37] Emde et al., 1991.

[38] D. Cicchetti, "Fractures in the Crystal: Developmental Psychopathology and the Emergence of the Self," *Developmental Review*, 11 (1991): 271-287.

[39] L. W. Sander, "Infant and Caretaking Environment: Investigation and Conceptualization of Adaptive Behavior in a System of Increasing Complexity," in E. J. Anthony (ed.), *Explorations in Child Psychiatry* (NY: Plenum Press: 129-66.

affect the "oughts" or standards for appropriate and desirable behaviors that children come to hold.[40]

Further, children's social world expands and, concomitantly, the self is reorganized.[41] By nine to twelve months of age, the infant has begun to internalize experiences with caregivers and to organize the self. By the first half of the second year of life, the toddler begins to realize that his goals may conflict with the caregiver's goals, setting the stage for an independent self. Also during this period, the toddler's awareness that her caregiver understands her internal state moves the child toward self-constancy. By eighteen to thirty-six months of age, the burden of self and emotion regulation shifts from parent to child. As the child's circle of relationships widens, as symbols become available, children develop increasingly complex and differentiated, inescapably moral selves.

<u>Self-regulation</u>. The self, then, is organizing and developing, as is the moral self. Central to the moral self is a child's abilities in self-regulation.[42] For children who are often *not* moral, a lack of self-regulatory abilities is of clinical significance, as shown by interest in the development of both the PMT and CPS models, discussed earlier.

Theorists within the behaviorist paradigm study self-regulation in terms of learned self-control.[43] According to this paradigm, experiences—both planned and unplanned—teach children the value of rewards. Over time, children learn to maximize rewards by developing self-control.

As described earlier, the social-cognitive paradigm has contributed significantly to our understanding of self-regulation. According to this paradigm, adaptive self-regulation is central to the establishment of personal control and to perceived self-efficacy. Interventions using this paradigm have proved useful for ameliorating specific self-regulatory failures. Nevertheless, considerations of the longer-term development of self-regulatory abilities and of moral behaviors indicate the limitations of this

---

[40] J. E. Grusec & J. J. Goodnow, "Impact of Parental Discipline Methods on the Child's Internalization of Values: A Reconceptualization of Current Points of View," *Developmental Psychology*, 30 (1994): 4-19.
[41] These changes are summarized by Cicchetti, 1991.
[42] R. F. Baumeister & J. J. Exline, "Virtue, Personality, and Social Relations: Self-control as the Moral Muscle," *Journal of Personality*, 67.6 (1999): 1165-1194.
[43] A. W. Logue, *Self-control* (Englewood Cliffs, NJ, 1995): Prentice-Hall.

approach.

The developmental-contextual paradigm addresses these weaknesses by using a process, rather than an information-processing, approach.[44] Kochanska,[45] for example, in her study of the roots of internalization and conscience development, documents that early self-regulatory abilities appear in the first three years of life and remain important in later moral development. Early markers of self-regulation include children's awareness of standard violation, evident during the second year of life when children start saying, "Uh oh," or showing distress at another's misbehavior.[46] These perceptions of standard violation appear at about the same time as children's organized self and are connected with children's developing cognitive abilities, developing social abilities, and developing sense of self.

As the self emerges, acts of wrongdoing become significant emotional events.[47] Children hesitate on the verge of wrongdoing,[48] experience distress and sometimes amusement[49] with standard violation, and show developing knowledge of rules and their abilities for compliance.[50]

Self-regulation also depends upon parent-child communication, including social referencing. Social referencing[51] occurs when a child, in an uncertain situation, looks to the parent to clarify the situation for her and shape her response. From social referencing, children also learn their first prohibitions,

---

[44] Greenberg, Kusche, & Speltz, 1991.

[45] Kochanska, 1994.

[46] J. Kagan, *The Second Year: The Emergence of Self-awareness* (Cambridge: Harvard University Press, 1981).

[47] P. M. Cole, K. C. Barrett, & C. Zahn-Waxler, "Emotion Displays in Two-year-olds During Mishaps," *Child Development*, 63 (1992): 314-324.; J. Dunn, "The Beginnings of Moral Understanding: Development in the Second Year," in J. Kagan & S. Lamb (eds.), *The Emergence of Morality in Young Children* (Chicago: University of Chicago Press): 91-112.

[48] H. Lytton, "Child and Parent Effects in Boys' Conduct Disorder: A Reinterpretation," *Developmental Psychology*, 26 (1980): 683-697.

[49] J. Dunn, *The Beginnings of Social Understanding* ( Cambridge: Harvard University Press, 1987).

[50] J. H. Gralinski & C. B. Kopp., "Everyday Rules for Behavior: Mothers' Requests to Young Children," *Developmental Psychology*, 29 (1993): 573-584.

[51] K. C. Barrett & J. J. Campos, "Perspectives on Emotional Development: II. A Functionalist Approach to Emotions," in J. D. Osofsky (ed.), *Handbook on Infant Development* (NY: Wiley, 1987): 555-578.

prohibitions which children very quickly become able to access even in the absence of the parent.[52] Children, in addition, receive affective information from parents, which affects their sense of guilt, as documented by Zahn-Waxler & Kochanska.[53]

*Conclusion*

Our view of the moral self shapes our view of character. The atomistic self of behaviorism has no character. The social-cognitivist self behaves consistently in similar situations (Mischel) but is not assumed to be unitary. The developmental-contextual self is organized, dynamic, and historically continuous, even if not behaviorally consistent.

Developing character is a process, and character is never fully formed. We resonate with the definition of character proposed by Hay, Castle, and Jewett: character is "an individual's general responsiveness to the dilemmas and responsibilities of social life, based on any number of sensitivities, skills, conventions and values."[54] This is a broad definition that allows study of the stability and integrity of character, without assuming either one.

This definition of character is psychologically useful because it recognizes (unlike Kohlberg's theory of moral development[55]) that morality is emotional and embodied as well as cognitive. It assumes an organized and unitary self. In this definition, character is grounded in modern developmental theory, rather than in trait theory. According to trait theory, character is made up of traits, which are internal to a person and largely in-built. According to developmental-contextualists, character is observable in the individual's responses to others, acquired, internalized, relatively stable, and inherently social.

Admittedly, this definition of character is not enough, because it doesn't specify which are positive social behaviors (i.e.,

---

[52] Emde et al., 1991.

[53] C. Zahn-Waxler & G. Kochanska, "The Origins of Guilt," in R. Thompson (ed.), *The 36th Annual Nebraska Symposium on Motivation: Socioemotional Development* (Lincoln: University of Nebraska Press, 1990): 183-258.

[54] D. F. Hay, J. Castle, & J. Jewett, "Character Development," in M. Rutter & D. Hay (eds.), *Development Through Life: A Handbook for Clinicians* (Oxford: Blackwell Scientific Publications, 1994): 319.

[55] L. Kohlberg, *Stages in the Development of Moral Thought and Action* (New York: Holt, 1969).

virtues) or how to encourage them. By redefining character as a social process, however, it provides a definition that we think is useful for parents and therapists.

Describing character as a process may seem to move away from traditional Christian definitions of character, definitions that are reflected in the *Oxford English Dictionary* (OED) definition of "character." According to the OED, the term "character" comes from a Greek instrument for marking or impressing a distinctive mark on something. One example of the use of the word "character" presented in the OED is the phrase "signed with the character of Christ in baptism."[56] Similarly, Kierkegaard describes character as "engraved" and not easily changed.[57]

We do not think that a process model obviates character in the sense of a "distinctive mark"; rather, our model is similar to Kierkegaard's meaning of character as "engraved." Development can be stable and continuous even in a process model. "Character," as the term is generally used, refers to a snapshot taken at one point in time of a person's developing character in a longer-term, more patterned, more comprehensive sense.

The process nature of character is captured by Wolterstorff's concept of "tendency learning," which refers to "changes in one's inclination or disposition as the result of learning or training."[58] Character education nurtures the development of pro-social or virtuous tendencies.

Change is always a possibility in one's character, although the rate of change may vary, with rapid change in childhood and slower change in adulthood. We would like to be able to demonstrate that character in adulthood, and perhaps quite a bit before adulthood, is relatively stable, but the Hay, Castle, & Jewett definition doesn't assume it. Even for adults without mature character, character development is possible.

Implications for practice. In some ways, developmental-contextual recommendations for character development are consistent with behaviorist and social-cognitive recommendations. Parents need to model prosocial behaviors (a principle consistent

[56] J. A. Simpson & E. S. L. Weiner (Preparers), *Oxford English Dictionary*, 2nd ed., Vol. 3, (Oxford: Clarendon Press, 1989): 30

[57] S. Kierkegaard, *Two Ages: The Age of Revolution and the Present Age: A Literary Review*, H. V. Hong & E. H. Hong, eds., trans. (Princeton, NJ: Princeton University Press, 1978): 77.

[58] N. P. Wolterstorff, *Educating for Responsible Action* (Grand Rapids MI: Eerdmans, 1980): 4.

with social-cognitive theory), to encourage and reinforce positive behaviors (a behaviorist recommendation), and to set achievable standards (i.e., goals in social-cognitive theory).

The developmental-contextual model makes further suggestions for parents wishing to nurture character in their children. Parents struggle, for example, with questions such as: Why is it that some children seem to be more cooperative and kindly, whereas others are less cooperative and more difficult to parent? Yet, the complex web of abilities required for demonstrating character is itself a process. Parents who understand where an individual child is in that process and who appreciate the process are more effective in nurturing character.

It is tempting to believe that the model is only useful for children whose character needs significant development, perhaps even for children who potentially fit one or more DSM-IV diagnostic categories. All children, however, have a range of skills, in self-regulation and in abilities. It is helpful to think of character development not as an all-or-none phenomenon (i.e., children either have strong character or they don't) but as progress in a range of abilities, some of which may be strengths, and others weaknesses. This paradigm is much closer to the realities parents experience in their daily lives and much more effective in bringing about change.

The developmental-contextual model is a powerful model for character development. Parents and therapists need to understand the developmental pathways for the abilities that constitute character, including self-regulation and emotional regulation. Parents and therapists need to be aware that interactions in which pro-social behaviors can appear represent one of three categories: non-negotiable expectations for positive social behaviors, negotiable expectations, and unnecessary expectations. For children and clients in whom character does not seem "automatic"—and it isn't automatic for anyone, but for many the requisite abilities emerge as expected without targeted intervention—parents and therapists need to recognize that too many expectations are non-negotiable. They need to focus on negotiable interactions. Rather than seeing these interactions as "problem" times, they need to see these as opportunities for nurturing the growth of character. When they do, they provide for their children and their clients real opportunities for becoming persons of character.

Effective character development hinges on having an adequate model. Of the three models presented in this chapter, the developmental-contextual model best describes the self and thus best reflects our creation in the image of God, our fallenness, and our potential for hope and redemption. Simply put, behaviorists remind us that we are like God in our ability to learn; social-cognitivists remind us that we are cognitive, emotional, and social beings; and developmental-contextualists recognize these characteristics but also remind us of the larger historical and ecological context in which we live and move. To developmental contextualists, we do not ever have character that is finished and complete, but we are continually developing character. All of us are fallen and therefore capable of sin, and all of us have the potential for growth and change and redemption. It is this hope, captured to some degree in developmental-contextual theory, that makes it worth our while to serve as parents and therapists who nurture character in others.

# Family Systems Epistemology:
# The Evolution of a Perspective on Persons and Relationships

*Cameron Lee*
Graduate School of Psychology
Fuller Theological Seminary

The well-known opening line of Tolstoy's *Anna Karenina* reads: "Happy families are all alike; every unhappy family is unhappy in its own way." Would present-day family therapists agree? *Contra* Tolstoy, much of modern psychology looks for what unhappy families share in common. Universal principles of health and pathology are the intellectual ground of a therapist's professional expertise, and by extension, the basis upon which to build a psychotherapeutic approach. By contrast, however, the growing "postmodern" trend of recent years views such technical expertise as suspect. Taking a more collaborative and non-expert position, the postmodern therapist helps families find happiness as they define it for themselves.[1]

This chapter will explore the constantly evolving discipline of family therapy, with particular attention to the movement from the modern to the postmodern. It is impossible, of course, to encompass the entire field in a single chapter. "Family therapy" is a term that embraces a diverse set of concepts and methods. I have chosen therefore to narrow the discussion by focusing on a

---

[1] The term "postmodern" has been used in various ways across numerous disciplines. In this essay, "modernism" refers to a dominant attitude in the Western world that arose after the European Enlightenment, namely, that the systematic use of human reason (as, for example, in empirical science), grounded in universally-recognizable truths, could be the basis of social progress and the betterment of humankind. "Postmodernism" refers to an intellectual countermovement which views reason itself as bounded by local customs of language and belief, so that claims to universal truth are seen as the attempts of one group to dominate another. The practical implications of this should become clearer as the chapter proceeds.

central theme: the evolution of a therapeutic *epistemology* and its effect upon how therapists understand their role.

Traditionally, epistemology is that branch of philosophy that deals with questions of the nature and limits of human knowledge. In the family therapy literature, the word usually has a more limited sense, referring roughly to habits of thought and the assumptions that lay behind them, whether in the minds of therapists or family members themselves.[2]

Early family therapists understood themselves to be advocating an important epistemological shift regarding diagnosis and treatment. Moving away from explanations based on individual models of psychic structure, they emphasized the importance of interactional processes. At the core of the *family systems* perspective, therapists share a fundamental assumption:

> [I]f the individual is to change, the context in which he lives must change. The unit of treatment is no longer the person, even if only a single person is interviewed; it is the set of relationships in which the person is imbedded.[3]

Parents, for example, may bring a child into therapy believing that the child is the "problem." From an individual perspective, therapy might proceed with the diagnosis of the child's difficulties and the implementation of an appropriate treatment plan. To a family therapist, however, the child is not the problem, but the family member with the most overt symptoms of distress. Her difficulties are seen as rooted in and sustained by disordered patterns of interaction in the family. The therapist's goal, therefore, is to locate these patterns and change them, anticipating that the child's symptoms will also disappear.

The identity of family therapy as a distinct profession has always relied to some extent on the sense of being founded on a new idea. Therapists committed to a systemic perspective generated a host of new intervention strategies, many of which

---

[2] For the varying uses of the word "epistemology" in the family therapy literature, see Paul Dell, "Understanding Bateson and Maturana: Toward a Biological Foundation for the Social Sciences," *Journal of Marital and Family Therapy*, 11 (1985):1-20; and Barbara S. Held and Edward Pols, "The Confusion about Epistemology and 'Epistemology'—and What to Do About It," *Family Process*, 24 (1985): 507-522.

[3] Jay Haley and Lynn Hoffman, *Techniques of Family Therapy* (New York: Basic, 1967), p. v.

brought dramatic changes to cases that were previously considered intractable. For many, this confirmed the sense that systemic approaches were superior, a more accurate description of therapeutic reality. In the public eye, however, family therapy was known more for its attention-grabbing interventions than its epistemological commitments.

It took about two decades for the field to enter a self-critical phase that brought epistemological questions back to center stage. Today, the modernist impulse that supported the therapist's expert knowledge and power is being steadily eroded and replaced by a postmodern orientation. We will explore the contours of a family systems perspective through an overview of three broad, overlapping stages, in which the movement from modern to postmodern ideas can be clearly seen.

The early family therapy movement organized around what is now referred to as a *first-order cybernetic* paradigm, in which therapists used their expertise to intervene directly in pathogenic patterns of family interaction. The work of the Mental Research Institute and Jay Haley's *strategic therapy* will be used to represent this first stage of development. For some family therapists, this evolved into a *second-order cybernetic* perspective, a transitional phase in which therapists began to recognize their own participation in a larger system that included both the family and the therapist. Therapists began to question the privileged status of their own expertise vis-à-vis the family, and pursued more collaborative models of therapy. The evolution of the Milan approach illustrates this transitional stage. In the third and current stage, first-order perspectives still exist, but the postmodern worldview is gaining influence. This is exemplified by *narrative therapy* and related approaches. These carry forward the collaborative model of the therapist-family relationship, and seek to help individuals and families "rewrite" the restrictive stories they have learned to tell about themselves.

Following this selective review, we will also look briefly at three alternative models: the evolutionary theory of Murray Bowen, the psychoanalytic approach of *object-relations family therapy*, and the ethical theory of Ivan Boszormenyi-Nagy's *contextual therapy*. These theoretical approaches raise additional questions and insights regarding the scope and definition of a family systems epistemology.

Despite the differences between the theories examined here, I will suggest that their central ideas can be integrated into a more comprehensive metatheory, a "bigger picture" that gathers together important insights from the various approaches.  The essence of a systemic view, in all its forms, is its inherently relational anthropology: an understanding of human nature and existence that is social to its core.  Each "school" of family therapy, to a greater or lesser extent, can be treated as a midrange theory that describes another aspect of that sociality.  This, I believe, is the theological and philosophical value of a family systems approach.[4]

The history we will review here is complex and multifaceted.  I will attempt to present that history from a neutral stance, and reserve theological reflection for the concluding section.  Of necessity, I have left out many important voices, and encourage the interested reader to consult the footnotes for additional sources.  I hope the approach adopted here will serve as a useful introduction to key intellectual issues in the field, while paving the way for interdisciplinary dialogue.

## The Origins of Family Therapy

The psychotherapy movement we know as family therapy began in the United States in the late 1950s, though precedents existed well before its advent.  Ministers, attorneys, physicians, and other professionals had long been advising families on marriage and parenting.  Courses on family life were taught at the high school and college levels from the early decades of the 20th century.  Marriage counseling centers existed in the United States as early as 1929, and a professional organization, the American Association of Marriage Counselors, was formally established in 1945.[5]

Before the family therapy movement, therapists were already becoming increasingly aware of family influences on individual pathology.  Those who worked with children observed how the quality of the family environment seemed inextricably entwined with a young patient's progress.  In some cases, children who appeared to make progress in individual treatment often regressed dramatically when placed back into their family contexts.  In others, a child's movement toward health seemed to

---

[4] For the purposes of this essay, questions of the clinical utility or validity of different approaches will be bracketed as secondary.

[5] In 1978, the organization changed its name to the American Association for Marriage and Family Therapy, signifying the absorption of marriage counseling into the family therapy movement that was to follow.

trigger a reactive response, sending another family member swirling into pathology.

The prevailing canons of psychiatric treatment, based on psychoanalytic assumptions, insisted that individuals and not families were the patients. If multiple family members needed treatment, they were to be seen individually in separate sessions and by different therapists. Little by little, this restriction eased, so some therapists began seeing more than one individual from the same family, but still in separate sessions. Later, therapists began to experiment with conjoint sessions, where more than one family member was present in the room simultaneously.

As history would have it, some of this innovation was based on accidental misunderstanding. In 1951, John E. Bell of Clark University was staying at the home of John Sutherland, the medical director of London's Tavistock Clinic. Sutherland casually mentioned that one of their psychiatrists, John Bolwby, had been seeing entire families in therapy. The conversation was interrupted, and Sutherland never had the chance to explain his comment. He had meant that Bowlby was seeing family members individually, and only occasionally holding sessions with the entire family present. Bell took him to mean that the family was present at every session. Intrigued with the idea, he began to include whole families in his therapeutic interviews. His work resulted in the book *Family Group Therapy,* one of the founding documents of the field.[6]

Another precedent was the research on schizophrenia being conducted at different centers from the late 1940s and throughout the 50s.[7] Extant theories understood the disorder as an individual pathology, potentially traceable to such physiological sources as brain lesions. Researchers, however, began to highlight

---

[6] John E. Bell, *Family Group Therapy.* Public Health Monograph No. 64. (Washington, DC: U. S. Government Printing Office). The incident with Sutherland is reported in Carlfred Broderick and Sandra S. Schrader, "The History of Professional Marriage and Family Therapy," in Alan S. Gurman and David P. Kniskern, Eds., *Handbook of Family Therapy*, Vol. II (New York: Brunner/Mazel, 1991), pp. 21-22.

[7] In common usage, the term "schizophrenia" refers to what should be called multiple-personality disorder, or even everyday ambivalence. In psychiatric nomenclature, however, the term designates a class of thought-disorders, as exemplified in delusional and hallucinatory states. The causes are still not fully understood, though researchers generally agree that genetics plays an important role.

the relational contexts in which the disorder made sense. Theodore Lidz and his colleagues at Yale, for example, produced a series of papers suggesting that withdrawal and reality-distortion in schizophrenic patients reflected the craziness of the family environment. In Lidz's studies, family interaction was characterized by strife in the marital relationship, and general patterns of irrationality and disturbed communication.[8] Other researchers, including Lyman Wynne and his colleagues at the National Institute of Mental Health, put forth similar ideas.[9]

Such trends suggested the need for a new paradigm. Similar shifts were already occurring in other disciplines. In theoretical biology, Ludwig von Bertalanffy had developed *General System Theory* to transcend the limitations of reductionist thinking in scientific method.[10] We cannot understand living organisms by dissecting them into constituent parts, he argued. They are "open systems," characterized not only by internal relationships, but active external interaction with an environment. Physicist Fritjof Capra sums up the essence of systemic thinking this way:

> The systems view looks at the world in terms of relationships and integration. Systems are integrated wholes whose properties cannot be reduced to those of smaller units. Instead of concentrating on basic building blocks or basic substances, the systems approach emphasizes basic principles of organization. . . . The activity of systems involves a process known as transaction—the simultaneous and mutually interdependent interaction between multiple components.[11]

By extension, a family is more than the sum of its

---

[8] See Theodore Lidz, Stephen Fleck, and Alice R. Cornelison, *Schizophrenia and the Family* (New York: International Universities Press, 1965), a collection of papers dated as early as 1942.

[9] In particular, see Lyman Wynne, Irving M. Ryckoff, Juliana Day, and Stanley I. Hirsch, "Pseudomutuality in the Family Relationships of Schizophrenics," *Psychiatry*, 21 (1958), pp. 205-220.

[10] See, for example, von Bertalanffy's "An Outline of General System Theory," *British Journal of the Philosophy of Science*, 1 (1950), pp. 134-165; and General System Theory (New York: George Braziller, 1968).

[11] Capra, *The Turning Point* (Toronto: Bantam, 1983), pp. 266, 267.

individual members: it is also a pattern of interaction between the members, as well as an organism adapting to its environment.

A similar, and perhaps more influential, line of thinking came through the work of anthropologist Gregory Bateson, who was also studying schizophrenia in the mid-50s. Bateson had been intrigued with the developing field of *cybernetics* throughout the 1940s, and sought to apply this way of understanding to human communication. Both the cybernetic and systemic perspectives shared a common emphasis on the importance of interaction. "Systems" was by far the more popular term, and Bateson was certainly familiar with the literature in both fields. But it is the direct application of cybernetic metaphors to the understanding of families that gives rise to the first major stage in our review of the development of a family systems perspective.

*The Cybernetic Metaphor: The Therapist as the Expert Agent of Change*

Mathematician Norbert Wiener used the term "cybernetics" to describe the study of self-governing, information processing systems, like missile-guidance mechanisms and household thermostats.[12] The central idea is that systems can regulate their own behavior through a *feedback loop* of information, where data regarding the system's previous behavior (output) are routed back into the system (input) and acted upon according to pre-established rules.

Prior to his research on schizophrenia, Bateson had already begun applying cybernetic principles to anthropology, describing tribal behavior in terms of communicative feedback loops. In 1954, in Palo Alto, California, he received a grant to study communication in the families of schizophrenic patients. Two years later the research team, which included Jay Haley and psychiatrist Don Jackson, published a seminal paper on the "double-bind" theory, which explained schizophrenic behavior as a reasonable response to an unreasonable environment.[13]

---

[12] Wiener, *Cybernetics, or Control and Communication in the Animal and the Machine* (New York: Wiley, 1948). The term derives from the Greek word for one who steers a boat.

[13] Gregory Bateson, Don D. Jackson, Jay Haley, and John H. Weakland, "Toward a Theory of Schizophrenia," *Behavioral Science*, 1 (1956), pp. 251-264.

The paper contained a case description of a complex interaction between a schizophrenic son and his mother. The mother's communication was fraught with contradictory verbal and non-verbal signals. When she visited her son in the hospital, he was glad to see her and spontaneously put his arm about her shoulders. She stiffened, giving a clear non-verbal signal that she did not want to be touched. Predictably, the son withdrew his arm. Her response, however, was oddly condemning: "Don't you love me anymore?"

From an outside observer's point of view, it was the mother who could not accept the son's gesture of affection. Unable to admit this, she engaged in a confusing communication sequence that made it seem as if the son were the problem. The son could have escaped the dilemma by pointing out the conflicting messages in her communication: "Look, Mom. First I hug you and you act like you don't want me to. Then you scold me for not showing you affection. What am I supposed to do?" Bateson and his colleagues hypothesized, however, that the son had learned that this kind of *metacommunication*, or communication about communication, would not be tolerated. Thus, caught in a no-win relationship pattern, the boy could escape only by withdrawing into pathology.

The double-bind theory recast schizophrenia as a problem in communication. Such work by the Palo Alto group led to the establishment of the Mental Research Institute in 1959, with Jackson as its founding director. Over time, its staff boasted nearly every luminary of the early family therapy movement, including Virginia Satir, Paul Watzlawick, and John E. Bell. Books associated with the MRI quickly became the classics of the field.[14]

The MRI's intellectual calling card was the application of cybernetic metaphors to family process. This is clearly seen in a 1963 excerpt from Haley:

> Insofar as family members set limits for one another, it is possible to describe their interaction in terms of the self-corrective processes in the total system. The family members respond in an error-activated way when any

[14] Three are of particular note: Jay Haley's *Strategies of Psychotherapy* (New York: Grune & Stratton, 1963); Virginia Satir's *Conjoint Family Therapy* (Palo Alto, CA: Science and Behavior Books, 1967); and Paul Watzlawick, Janet H. Beavin, and Don D. Jackson's *Pragmatics of Human Communication* (New York: Norton, 1967).

individual exceeds a certain limit. This process of mutually responsive behavior defines the "rules" of the family system. In this sense the family is a system that contains a governing process. However, there is not just a single governor for the system; each member functions as a governor of the others and thus the system is maintained . . . . In the family no outsider sets the limits of family behavior, although the culture might be said to partially function in that way. The limits of the family system are set by the members of the family as they influence each other.[15]

At a simplistic level, the family can be seen as operating like a household thermostat. The thermostat is an error-activated cybernetic mechanism. When the temperature in a room exceeds the limits set by the occupants of the house, the heating/cooling system is automatically activated, and stays active until the error has been corrected.[16] Similarly, therapists viewed families as rule-governed systems that seek to maintain *homeostasis*, a steady state of internal balance that resists change.[17]

There are both internal and external pressures on any family to change and adapt its organization. Internal pressures include the maturation of family members. As children grow, parents must adapt their parenting style to the child's expanding competencies and social network. External pressures include the death of a member of the extended family, or the loss of a paying job. Families experience problems when pressures for change are stalemated by the family's homeostatic tendency to remain the same.

In order to help families toward constructive change, therapists must identify the rules of organization that block adaptation. Some family rules are obvious and consciously held. Others are more automatic and difficult to articulate, though just

---

[15] Jay Haley, *Strategies of Psychotherapy* (New York: Grune & Stratton, 1963), pp. 159-160.

[16] In cybernetic terminology, this is known as a negative feedback loop. The goal of such a loop is the control and reduction of deviations from the norm.

[17] The term was coined by Walter Cannon to describe the self-regulating processes of human physiology. Its application to families was an important part of Don Jackson's work, q.v. "The Question of Family Homeostasis," *Psychiatric Quarterly Supplement*, 31 (1957): 79-90.

as powerful. These must be inferred from the family's pattern of interaction. There are subtle rules about power, intimacy, and communication that govern how family members respond to one another, even when they cannot openly say what they are.

Therapists, for example, can infer much from a family's behavior in the first session. Mom and Dad enter the room first and greet the therapist. Their son Johnny, an only child, follows silently. He meets the therapist's gaze only briefly, then returns to looking resolutely at the floor. The parents seat themselves, huddling close together on one end of a sofa, while the boy slumps in a separate chair. After a brief opening statement, the therapist turns to the boy and asks him why he thinks the family is here. The boy is silent, and the therapist asks again, gently. Johnny glances up, making eye contact with his mother, who blinks slowly and nods, almost imperceptibly. Quietly he begins to speak, and the session begins in earnest.

What does the therapist observe? She already knows that Johnny is the *identified patient,* the one defined by the family as being the problem. This seems to be reflected in the parents' openness and confidence as they enter the room, and the sullen silence of the boy. She notes how the parents sit closely with Johnny separate from them, a visual metaphor of the patterns of closeness and distance in the family. Johnny looks to his mother before answering the therapist's question, suggesting that he needs his mother's permission before speaking.

The therapist holds these and other observations in mind as the session proceeds, formulating hypotheses about the rules that govern this family's relationships. The family may not be conscious of any of these rules, any more than a thermostat "knows" the settings that govern its behavior. At some level, of course, as Haley suggests in the quote above, the thermostat metaphor breaks down (as do thermostats). In a family, there is no single "setting" which is established unilaterally from outside the feedback system. Rather, family members regulate each other in a complex communicational dance.

The use of cybernetic metaphors encouraged a somewhat mechanistic view of problems as something to be fixed by the appropriate and direct use of therapeutic expertise. The therapist's goal was not necessarily to change individuals directly, but to interrupt the problematic patterns of interaction that created and sustained symptomatic behavior. Past behavior and trauma were largely irrelevant; families did not need insight to change. All that mattered was that the therapist find and break the pattern that kept the problem going in the present.

From the 1960s through the 1980s, models built on cybernetic assumptions dominated family therapy. The *communication theory* approach grew out of the work of the Mental Research Institute and was most influential in the 1960s. Recall the insight of the double-bind theory. When viewed on an individual level, schizophrenic behavior appeared bizarre and difficult to explain. In the wider social context of a crazy-making family's disordered communication, however, the behavior made sense.

More generally, individual pathology was to be studied in its social context, lest the behavior be misunderstood:

> [A] phenomenon remains unexplainable as long as the range of observation is not wide enough to include the context in which the phenomenon occurs. Failure to realize the intricacies of the relationships between the event and the matrix in which it takes place, between an organism and its environment, either confronts the observer with something "mysterious" or induces him to attribute to his object of study certain properties the object may not possess.[18]

Individuals, in other words, might be misdiagnosed as crazy when the actual problem was in the family system. Furthermore, if individual behavior was to be understood against the backdrop of patterns of relationship, then relationship in turn was to be understood through the study of communication:

> The observer of human behavior then turns from an inferential study of the mind to the study of observable manifestations of relationship. *The vehicle of these manifestations is communication.* . . . [A]ll behavior, not only speech, is communication, and all communication—even the communicational clues in an impersonal context—affects behavior.[19]

Note that "communication" is here broadly defined as any verbal or non-verbal behavior that has "message value" in a

---

[18] Watzlawick, Beavin, and Jackson, *Pragmatics*, pp. 20-21.
[19] Ibid., pp. 21-22, emphasis in original.

relationship.[20] We take for granted, for example, that speech has message-value, but often forget that silence has meaning as well.

The therapist's task in these early models of family therapy was to change problematic patterns of communication. As we have seen in the double-bind example, there can be a lack of congruence between what a person says and what he does, between the words used and how they are spoken. A person who scowls while saying "I love you" places the recipient in an awkward and confusing position.

This is more than a matter of two equal but contradictory types of messages. There is also a hierarchy of levels in communication. At one level is the information or message one wishes to transmit, which is usually done verbally. At a higher level of abstraction, how the information is delivered sends an additional message about how the sender views the relationship. Bateson called these the *report* and *command* aspects of a communication, respectively.[21] Two spouses argue. At the report level, they express their own opinions and communicate that the other person's opinion is wrong. At the command level, however, the message may be "You are wrong for arguing with me in the first place." Frequently, spouses become hopelessly entangled in the former, when metacommunicating about the latter would be more fruitful.

The presence of these different types and levels makes debilitating paradoxes like the double-bind possible. Haley reinterpreted symptoms themselves as a type of paradoxical communication, a means to gain the tactical advantage in a relationship.[22] A humorous example of this could be seen repeatedly in the classic television comedy *Sanford and Son*. Fred Sanford, played by Redd Foxx, had a heart condition that he would use to his advantage. Whenever he felt he was losing an argument, he would suddenly clutch his chest, look up to heaven, and call out to his departed wife, "I'm coming Elizabeth!" The ruse frequently worked, and he would get his way.

This illustrates the paradox that a symptomatic person can

---

[20] Raphael and Dorothy Becvar, *Systems Theory and Family Therapy: A Primer* (Washington, DC: University Press of America), p. 13.

[21] In *Conjoint Family Therapy*, Satir uses the terms denotative and metacommunicative; in *Pragmatics*, Watzlawick and his colleagues refer to this as the content and relationship aspects of communication.

[22] See Haley, "Symptoms as Tactics in Human Relationships," in *Strategies of Psychotherapy*.

gain control of a relationship through a display of helplessness. Families in therapy might say they wish to be rid of a particular symptom, but the therapist understands that the symptom itself plays a crucial role in maintaining the balance of power. *Strategic* approaches, which pervaded family therapy of the 1970s and 80s, offered a therapeutic countermove. The *paradoxical prescription* often took the form of suggesting that the family not try to extinguish the symptom, sometimes with the added directive that the symptom be expressed in a more constructive way.

In one case study, an eight-year-old child was brought to therapy for a chronically infected wound that would not heal because he continued to stick pins into his waist.[23] Occasionally, the boy would also try to stick pins into other people. Instead of trying to directly eliminate the behavior, the therapist explained matter-of-factly that the child needed to learn a more proper way of sticking pins into things. She gave the mother an assignment. Every evening for a week, the mother was to sit in private with her son and help him stick 100 pins, one at a time, into a rubber doll. They would then remove the pins one by one at put them back into the box. The mother complied, and her son's symptom vanished by the next session. Why?

The therapist understood the son's odd behavior as a metaphor for the mother's problems. She was grossly overweight and refused to listen to her doctors' orders about her eating. The son's self-inflicted wound to his waist symbolized the mother's self-destructive behavior, while at the same time providing her with a helpful distraction. The paradoxical intervention succeeded in changing both the role of the symptom and the quality of the mother and son's interaction around the symptom.

This illustrates the *functionalist* understanding of symptoms, wherein symptomatic behavior serves an important systemic purpose. It is not necessary for the therapist to understand the history behind the symptom's formation; all that is needed is to understand how symptoms help maintain the family's homeostatic balance. By changing the way the boy stuck pins, the behavior no longer served the purpose of drawing his mother's attention away from her own self-destructiveness. This left the door open for the therapist to deal with the mother's needs through more direct and conventional means. Thus, the therapeutic goal in this case was not to tackle the symptom

---

[23] The case of "The Self Inflicted Wound," in Cloé Madanes, *Strategic Family Therapy* (San Francisco: Jossey-Bass, 1981), pp. 97-99.

directly, but to change the system in such a way that the pin-sticking behavior was no longer necessary or helpful.

As should be apparent, these ways of understanding families lent themselves to highly directive interventions. The therapist was active in locating and changing pathogenic processes. From the early MRI point of view, the therapist's job was to change how people communicated, correcting discrepancies between verbal and non-verbal messages, as well as the report and command aspects:

> We call an individual dysfunctional when he has not learned to communicate properly. . . . If illness is seen to derive from inadequate methods of communication (by which we mean all interactional behavior), it follows that therapy will be seen as an attempt to improve these methods. . . . [T]he emphasis will be on correcting discrepancies in communication and teaching ways to achieve more fitting joint outcomes.[24]

A similar stance can be seen in Haley's definition of "strategic." He coined the term to describe the work of hypnotherapist Milton Erickson, whose seemingly counterintuitive approach to therapy produced remarkable results. Haley's study of Erickson opens with these words:

> Therapy can be called strategic if the clinician initiates what happens during therapy and designs a particular approach for each problem. . . . [T]he initiative is largely taken by the therapist. He must identify solvable problems, set goals, design interventions to achieve those goals, examine the responses he receives to correct his approach, and ultimately examine the outcome of his therapy to see if it has been effective. The therapist must be acutely sensitive and responsive to the patient and his social field, but how he proceeds must be determined by

---

[24] Virginia Satir, *Conjoint Family Therapy*, pp. 92, 96. Satir was the first training director of the MRI. Lynn Hoffman notes that while Satir used cybernetic terminology, her approach was broader in ways that sometimes irritated her colleagues at the MRI. See Hoffman, *Family Therapy: An Intimate History* (New York: W. W. Norton, 2002), pp. 6-8.

himself.[25]

In a modernist vein, the therapist acts as an expert diagnostician, taking the initiative to create change.

Haley in particular viewed family members as motivated by the desire for power and control in relationships, and advocated that therapists cultivate their own base of influence to have the leverage needed to change stuck systems. In cybernetic terms, "If a therapist is going to change the 'setting' of a family system, he must become a metagovernor of the system."[26] This meta-position is an Archimedean point maintained by careful control of information received from family members:

> To be in a position to reveal or conceal information between groups is to be in a *meta-*, or power, position in relation to those groups. . . . [A] therapist's position in a hierarchy is largely determined by his or her control of information . . . . Given this view, it follows that a therapist who seeks power and influence over an individual or group should establish himself as a gatekeeper of information between that group and a larger one. . . . [H]is power is enhanced if he is provided with secrets to be protected. . . . It also follows that a therapist not only should see a whole family together but should also see members and factions alone. He must have, or appear to have, information that he controls at a boundary.[27]

It should be noted that Haley's is not the only voice in strategic therapy. His own work was influenced not only by the Bateson/MRI tradition, but also by his later association with Salvador Minuchin, whose *structural family therapy* was highly influential in the 1970s and early 80s.[28] Nevertheless, approaches

---

[25] Haley, *Uncommon Therapy: The Psychiatric Techniques of Milton H. Erickson, M.D.* (New York: W. W. Norton, 1973), p. 17.
[26] Haley, *Strategies*, p. 174.
[27] Haley, *Problem-Solving Therapy*, 2nd ed. (San Francisco: Jossey-Bass, 1987), pp. 240-241.
[28] See, for example, Minuchin's *Families and Family Therapy* (Cambridge: Harvard University Press, 1974), and *Family Therapy Techniques*, co-authored with Charles Fishman (Cambridge: Harvard University Press, 1981). The two approaches shared much in common, so

deriving from cybernetic metaphors tended to view therapists as outside experts who bore the responsibility for creating change in the families that sought their help. As we shall see shortly, it is precisely this image of expert control that became a matter of controversy in the 1980s, leading to a shift toward more collaborative models of the therapeutic relationship.

The influence of the MRI and strategic approaches was not limited to the United States. In Milan, Italy, Mara Selvini Palazzoli had already established herself as a prominent psychoanalyst with a specific interest in anorexia. She was disenchanted, however, with analytic work, which seemed to require too long to produce even small improvements. In the 1960s, she heard of the family therapy movement, and traveled to the U.S. to study the methods of Haley and the MRI. Returning to Italy, she established an institute to study family process and experiment with new treatment approaches. In 1971, Palazzoli and three other psychiatrists, Luigi Boscolo, Gianfranco Cecchin, and Giuliana Prata, broke off from the rest of the group to form an association that would focus more deeply on the cybernetic principles they had learned from the American movement.

In just a few brief years, the group was a tremendous success. Their reputation for clinical wizardry spread throughout the country; some clients traveled long distances for treatment. By 1975, in response to growing demand for a report of what they were doing, Palazzoli and her colleagues published *Paradox and Counterparadox*, a book which demonstrates both their allegiance to the cybernetic-communications model, as well as their willingness to innovate.[29]

The title of the book itself shows their dependence on the strategic use of paradoxical methods. The opening paragraphs clearly show a cybernetic understanding of family process:

> [T]he family is a self-regulating system which controls itself according to rules formed over a period of time through a process of trial and error. . . . [F]amilies in which one or more members present behaviors traditionally diagnosed as "pathological," are held together by transactions and, therefore, by rules peculiar to the

---

that many family therapists identified themselves as "structural/strategic" in orientation.

[29] The book was originally published in Italian; the English translation appeared in 1978.

pathology. . . . Since the symptomatic behavior is part of the transactional pattern peculiar to the system in which it occurs, the way to eliminate the symptoms is to change the rules.[30]

The early work of the Milan group, however, was known for the unique way in which therapy was conducted. Prior to the family's arrival, the four therapists would meet to discuss their systemic hypotheses about the family. When the family arrived, two therapists, one male and one female, would interview them directly, while the other two watched from behind a one-way mirror which closed them off from the family's view. This arrangement allowed the observers to maintain a greater emotional distance from the family drama, and thus to notice details that the therapists in the room might miss. When necessary, the observing team would call one or both therapists out of the room for a mid-session consultation.

Before the close of the session, the four would meet together behind the mirror while the family waited. They discussed their observations, and formulated an appropriate intervention, which usually contained two elements: a *positive connotation* and a *paradoxical prescription*. The latter is derived from the strategic practice described earlier. When therapists prescribed the symptom back to the family, they set up a *therapeutic double bind*.[31] To disobey the injunction meant to cease behaving symptomatically. To obey the injunction meant that the symptom was now revealed to be a conscious choice, making it impossible to exert covert control through a display of helplessness.

The positive connotation was designed by the Milan group to provide the rationale for the paradoxical prescription. Following a functionalist understanding, therapists carefully framed a convincing statement that would show how the symptom kept the family in balance. The paradoxical prescription followed, with the logic that since the symptom served a beneficial purpose, it should not be changed. Once the entire team had decided the details, the two therapists would deliver the intervention. The four would meet once more after the family's departure to discuss the

---

[30] Palazzoli, et al., *Paradox and Counterparadox*, translated by Elisabeth V. Burt (New York: Jason Aronson, 1978), pp. 3-4.
[31] See, for example, the discussion in Lynn Hoffman, *Foundations of Family Therapy* (New York: Basic Books, 1981), pp. 235 ff.

session.

One can trace the influence of Bateson, Haley, and Watzlawick in the Milan team's early work, and because of this they are often classified as a strategic approach. As in strategic therapy, the Milan therapists' intervention provided a counterparadox that disrupted the way the symptom functioned in the family system. Yet they had taken what they had learned from the American family therapy movement and made it uniquely their own. Milan-style treatment teams began springing up across Europe, as well as in training centers in the U.S.

By the late 1970s, however, the team had begun to question some aspects of their own work. Even though the presenting symptom was given a positive connotation, family members still felt blamed and pathologized by the therapists, and frequently resented it. Trainees delivered the required intervention, and fearing the family's reaction, promptly ushered them out. What the Milan therapists would discover, through a fresh and unmediated reading of Bateson, was that his understanding of cybernetics was in some respects antithetical to Haley's. This realization would change their way of practicing therapy.

*Transitions: The Second-Order Cybernetic Critique*

Bateson died in 1980, and the decade that followed was a time of ferment in the field. Family therapists had spent twenty years justifying their existence, focusing on what made them different. As the field became more stable and grew in influence, critical voices emerged from within the ranks. Some put forth a new understanding of cybernetics, arguing that Bateson had been misunderstood. Others, especially those concerned with women's issues, argued that cybernetic metaphors themselves were problematic.

Of particular interest for the first group was Bateson's notion of *cybernetic circularity* (or *circular causality*), that challenged assumptions of power and control. Imagine an island inhabited by foxes and rabbits. As the rabbits multiply, there is more food for the foxes, and the fox population can increase. But if the foxes kill too many rabbits, their food supply dwindles, and the number of foxes decreases. The organization of animal life in this island ecology is thus made up of two highly interdependent species. If foxes could talk, they might brag about their superiority over the rabbits. Likewise, the rabbits might boast of their cleverness in evading the foxes. But in terms of the larger ecology, neither species has power over the other: they are mutually part of the same web of events.[32]

Haley, as we have seen, was fond of metaphors of power, and this characterized the early work of the Milan group as well. In their central metaphor, family members were locked into a destructive *family game*, each compelled to play and win by their own hubris. In the strategic view, family members were engaged in a power struggle, and the therapist had to be more powerful still, using his expertise to leverage change. Bateson, however, fundamentally disagreed with Haley on this point.[33] He believed that power was a mythical abstraction, an inappropriate application of physicalist metaphors to the realm of ecological interaction. In the appendix to his book, *Mind and Nature,* Bateson wrote:

> It is not so much "power" that corrupts as the *myth* of "power." It was noted above that "power," like "energy," "tension," and the rest of the quasi-physical metaphors are to be distrusted and, among them, "power" is one of the most dangerous.[34]

This meant that family members did not actually "control" one another, and neither did therapists. To believe that such unilateral control was possible was to make the same mistake as the boastful foxes and rabbits in the illustration above.

It is this more circular understanding of systems that lay behind the Milan team's change of approach. Abandoning the hierarchical and directive bent learned from Haley, they developed a new therapeutic style. Strategic therapists unilaterally hypothesized about the function of symptoms in the family's organization. In contrast, the Milan group came to view hypotheses as something constructed by families and therapists

---

[32] The illustration is adapted from the opening pages of Watzlawick et al., *Pragmatics of Human Communication.*

[33] See, e.g., Bradford Keeney, "What is an Epistemology of Family Therapy?" *Family Process,* 21 (1982): 153-168, where he highlights the importance of this difference. Keeney had spent some time with Bateson shortly before the latter's death in 1979. See also Lynn Hoffman, "Beyond Power and Control: Toward a 'Second Order' Family Systems Therapy," *Family Systems Medicine,* 3 (1985): 381-396.

[34] Bateson, *Mind and Nature: A Necessary Unity* (New York: E. P. Dutton, 1979), p. 223.

together. Whether or not the hypothesis was "true," what mattered was that it made sense to the family and helped encourage them to change in a desired direction. The group also translated Bateson's notion of circularity into an interviewing style called *circular questioning*. Previously, questions in a family session meandered until the therapist began to develop a hypothesis, then the questions would focus on eliciting the information needed to confirm what the therapist was thinking. In circular questioning, however, therapists incessantly asked questions to elicit differences in perspective between family members. A therapist might ask one of the children, "Who noticed the problem first, you or your mother?" and follow with a question to the father: "Would you agree with this, or do you think someone else noticed the problem first?" The more alternative perspectives could be generated, the freer family members would be to develop new hypotheses about the problem that brought them to therapy.[35]

This marks an important conceptual shift that was beginning to take hold in the field at large, as others questioned strategic notions of the therapist's power. The 1982 volume of family therapy's premier journal, *Family Process*, opened with three provocative essays that challenged the status quo.[36] Like the Milan group, the authors advocated a return to the ecological vision that Bateson had proposed, and cited a literature base that many therapists found unnecessarily abstruse.

A number of these sources had been written by acquaintances of Bateson and each other, who together sought to reform cybernetic thought. The group included cybernetician

---

[35] See Mara Selvini-Palazzoli, Luigi Boscolo, Gianfranco Cecchin, and Giuliana Prata, "Hypothesizing-Circularity-Neutrality," *Family Process*, 19 (1980): 73-85. See also Luigi Boscolo, Gianfranco Cecchin, Lynn Hoffman, and Peggy Penn, *Milan Systemic Family Therapy* (New York: Basic Books, 1987). In 1980, Boscolo and Cecchin split from the group to focus on training, taking the name "The Milan Associates." The two women, Palazzoli and Prata, emphasized research to develop the notion of the family game. Palazzoli and Prata eventually separated as well.

[36] Bradford P. Keeney and Douglas Sprenkle, "Ecosystemic Epistemology: Critical Implications for the Aesthetics and Pragmatics of Family Therapy," *Family Process*, 21 (1982): 1-19; Paul F. Dell, "Beyond Homeostasis: Toward a Concept of Coherence," *Family Process*, 21 (1982): 21-42; and L. Allman, "The Aesthetic Preference: Overcoming the Pragmatic Error," *Family Process*, 21 (1982): 43-56. Some mark 1961, the first year of the journal's publication, as a candidate for the birth of the family therapy movement. Jay Haley was the journal's first editor.

Heinz von Foerster, linguist Ernst von Glasersfeld, biologist Humberto Maturana, and cognitive scientist Francisco Varela. Were families really like mechanisms that could be fixed? Cybernetic metaphors and the success of strategic interventions seemed to suggest so. These writers, however, disagreed. Their work contributed to the perspective known as *constructivism,* which took the notion of circularity to a new level.[37]

Much of constructivism is based on physiological answers to the classic epistemological questions "What is knowledge?" and "How do we know what we know?" Constructivists assert that we cannot know what is "really out there" directly. We are accustomed to believing that our concepts have some objective referent in the world outside our minds; though imperfect, there must be some reliable correlation or correspondence between what we know and what actually exists. Constructivists, however, while not directly denying the existence of extra-mental reality, relegate it to secondary importance. Research on the biology of perception in humans and animals suggests that while external events may prod perception, what matters is the organism's maintenance of internal coherence. What we know as "reality," in short, is a product of our nervous systems.

Maturana's theory of *structure determinism* was well-publicized in the family therapy literature. Bateson himself had acknowledged the Chilean biologist as his most prominent successor in matters of epistemology.[38] Maturana viewed the human organism as a closed system that could only behave in ways intrinsic to its biological structure. This undermines the concept of unilateral causality, or what Maturana called *instructive interaction.* Event A may result in response B from an organism, but A is only said to "select" B, which is determined solely by the organism's own biology. As Paul Dell illustrates:

> Selecting is akin to pushing the Sprite button on a Coke machine. Pushing the button selects the response of the machine (it gives you a Sprite), but it does not determine that the machine gives Sprites when the button is pushed.

---

[37] Or "radical constructivism," a term introduced by von Glasersfeld. See Paul Watzlawick, ed., *The Invented Reality* (New York: W. W. Norton, 1984), which contains essays by von Glasersfeld, von Foerster, and Varela.

[38] Paul Dell, "Understanding Bateson and Maturana," p. 5, citing unpublished conversations between Bateson and Brad Keeney.

In essence, Maturana is claiming that our everyday use of the word "cause" always implies or threatens to imply a determining in the sense of instructive interaction—whereas causation is always only a selecting.[39]

The organism, in other words, is pre-wired to respond in particular ways when perturbed. In this it has no choice: it simply cannot produce a Coke when the Sprite button is pushed.

Maturana had been writing about the biological coherence of individual organisms, but others were quick to use his concepts to assail the strategic stronghold. Therapists cannot directly cause families to change; at best, they can provide an environment in which change might occur. But no therapist, no matter how brilliant nor determined, can make families change in ways that are not already permitted by their structure.[40]

Constructivist doctrine and concepts of circularity supported the shift to what Maturana and his colleagues were calling a *second-order cybernetics*. In first-order cybernetics, a seemingly neutral observer watches the functioning of a system from the outside, analyzing its feedback loops. In a second-order model, however, the observer is included in the loop. Epistemologically, a first-order stance supports the idea that the observer can have objective knowledge of the system. But by bringing the observer into the loop, a second-order stance raises the matter of the observer's contribution to what is "known."

How does this apply to therapy? In first-order approaches, therapists unilaterally applied cybernetic principles to families from outside the system. They operated as change-making experts, and did not easily question the objectivity of their diagnoses. From a second-order stance, however, the therapist and the family are both seen as parts of a larger ecology—a treatment system of therapist plus family, and any others that contribute to the definition of the problem. At this higher level of abstraction, cybernetic concepts become self-reflexive, for the therapist must now consider her own role in the system. As Lynn

---

[39] Dell, "Understanding Bateson and Maturana," p. 8.

[40] For further reading on structure determinism, see Humberto Maturana and Francisco Varela, *The Tree of Knowledge: The Biological Roots of Human Understanding* (Boston: New Science Library, 1988). For an attempt at a consistent application of Maturana's theory to therapy, see Jay S. Efran, Michael D. Lukens, and Robert J. Lukens, *Language, Structure, and Change* (New York: W. W. Norton, 1990).

Hoffman notes, this shift affects how she understands her role as a change agent:

> A first-order view in family therapy would assume that it is possible to influence another person or family by using this or that technique: I program you; I teach you; I instruct you. A second-order view would mean that therapists include themselves as part of what must change; they do not stand outside. This view allows a whole new picture to appear. For one thing, the very notion of "fixing problems" can be seen to be part of the problem . . . .[41]

In the first-order view, families come to therapists because they have problems, and it is the therapist's job to fix them. In the second-order view, at least part of the reason families have problems is because they are in a therapist's office—in other words, they are participating in a social setting that defines the therapist as the paid expert, who in turn defines their situation as problematic. The dilemma for the practitioner is that what was previously taken for granted as expert knowledge loses its privileged status, making the therapist's role more ambiguous. Second-order advocates argue that since control is an illusion and therapists and families occupy an epistemologically level playing field, then the therapist-family relationship should take on a less hierarchical and more collaborative form.

The matter has been vigorously debated in the family therapy literature. Some have expressed concern that the new epistemology will have a chilling effect on therapeutic practice, as practitioners become uncertain of their ability to create change. Some have proposed compromise solutions, allowing some second-order insights to influence therapists' attitudes, while retaining directive first-order practices.[42] Still others have raised doubts as to whether therapists can really practice non-hierarchically, arguing that the therapist's actual influence will be masked by second-order language. As Stuart Golann has stated,

---

[41] Hoffman, "Constructing Realities: An Art of Lenses," *Family Process*, 29 (1990): 5.
[42] George Simon, "Having a Second-Order Mind While Doing First-Order Therapy," *Journal of Marital and Family Therapy*, 18 (1992): 377-387.

"Power obscured eventually emerges—a therapeutic wolf clad as a second-order sheep."[43]

One response to such criticisms is that second-order cybernetics "is not a method of therapy but something more like a stance."[44]    Including the therapist in the treatment system relativizes his expertise.  The new epistemology thus presses toward greater therapist humility, regardless of how this is actualized in practice.  The second-order therapist adopts a non-instrumental and collaborative approach that avoids thinking too highly of his own idea, or too judgmentally about the families that seek his help.  Even the non-instrumental attitude needs to be held lightly, as Gianfranco Cecchin has suggested with his concept of *irreverence* toward all therapeutic concepts:

> To believe too much in non-instrumentality could result in one being trapped, restricted, unable to act . . . .  We postulate that it is appropriate to act as long as the therapist is willing to accept responsibility for his actions . . . .  Irreverence is to never accept one logical level of a position but, rather, to play with varying levels of abstractions, changing from one level to another.[45]

Put this way, much of second-order cybernetics might be interpreted as limiting the excesses of first-order practices, but without proposing an intervention-specific alternative.[46]

During the theoretical tumult of the 1980s, not only did second-order theorists criticize their first-order heritage, but feminist scholars found fault with both first- and second-order cybernetics.  Cybernetic descriptions of family interaction were ahistorical and abstract, poorly suited to questions of gender injustice.  Strategic and structural interventions, concerned with

---

[43] Stuart Golann, "On Second-Order Family Therapy," *Family Process*, 27 (1988): 51-65.

[44] Lynn Hoffman, "Beyond Power and Control," p. 393.

[45] Gianfranco Cecchin, Gerry Lane, and Wendel Ray, *Irreverence: A Strategy for Therapists' Survival* (London: Karnac Books, 1992), pp. 7, 10, 11.

[46] Perhaps the best-known therapeutic strategy to emerge from the second-order ideology is the reflecting team approach, where the therapist team discusses their observations about the client family while family members look on. See, e.g., Tom Andersen (ed.), *The Reflecting Team* (New York: W. W. Norton, 1990).

reestablishing appropriate boundaries and hierarchies between family members, could unwittingly play into a family's gender politics.

The second-order approach, moreover, which eschewed the language of power, risked closing the therapist's eyes to the presence of real disparities of power in family relationships. Deborah Anna Luepnitz is worth quoting at length on this point:

> Some dialectical relationships do not involve a power difference (e.g. thermostat and room temperature; Tweedledum and Tweedledee) but others do—master and slave, parent and child, employer and employee. It is true that the less powerful can almost always influence the more powerful, but the difference between influence and legitimate power is not trivial . . . . Some family therapists, following Bateson, have tried to do without a concept of power. They maintain the idea that a complementary system should never be described in terms of the relative power of its constituents. The result can be the familiar sophistry that men who batter their wives are in a "complementary dance" with them. The complementary dance theory presumably affords therapeutic leverage, but it misses the point that the social institutions with the power to name things like psychiatry and law privilege the male partner.[47]

Cybernetic metaphors, whether of the first- or second-order variety, seemed too abstract and narrowly focused to deal with such large-scale social concerns. Rape, incest, and battering, feminists argued, together with less extreme forms of gender injustice, are abuses of power. Any clinical paradigm that blinded therapists to these social dynamics, or worse yet, colluded with them, should be revised or abandoned.[48]

---

[47] Luepnitz, "Bateson's Heritage: Bitter Fruit," *The Family Therapy Networker*, 12 (September/October 1988): 53. The article is adapted from her book, *The Family Interpreted: Feminist Theory in Clinical Practice* (New York: Basic Books, 1988).

[48] Morris Taggart, "The Feminist Critique in Epistemological Perspective: The Questions of Context in Family Therapy," *Journal of Marital and Family Therapy*, 11 (1985): 113-126; Gerald Erickson, "Against the Grain: Decentering Family Therapy," *American Journal of Marital and Family Therapy*, 14 (1988): 225-236. For further reading on feminist

To many, another paradigm shift seemed necessary. Could the more circumspect second-order therapeutic stance be maintained, while recognizing dynamics of power and dominance? Yes, if therapists were willing to adopt a more postmodern worldview. Indeed, some feminist scholars were already turning in that direction.[49]

*The Postmodern Turn*

In retrospect, the turn toward postmodern thought in family therapy seems like a natural consequence of the second-order critique. An important change in root metaphors had already taken place. First-order therapists had implicitly viewed families as cybernetic mechanisms, systems in need of treatment. With the second-order shift, as we have seen, therapists were newly included in the scope of the treatment system. But the epistemological implications of that simple adjustment altered the very understanding of the system itself. Lynn Hoffman expressed it this way:

> The treatment unit looks vastly different than it did before. The old idea of treating a psychiatric symptom was based on the medical notion of curing a part of the body. The illness is "in" some spatially defined, out-there unit. We can no longer say that it is "in" the family, nor is it "in" the unity. It is "in" the heads or nervous systems of everyone who has a part in specifying it. The old epistemology implies that *the system creates the problem*. The new epistemology implies that *the problem creates the system*. . . . The problem is the meaning system created by the distress and the treatment unit is everyone who is contributing to that meaning system. This includes the treating professional as soon as the client walks in the door. . . . I would prefer the formulation that the *problem*

---

perspectives in family therapy, see Deborah Anna Luepnitz, Monica McGoldrick, Carol Anderson, and Froma Walsh, eds., *Women in Families: A Framework for Family Therapy* (New York: W. W. Norton, 1989); and Marianne Walters, Betty Carter, Peggy Papp, and Olga Silverstein, *The Invisible Web: Gender Patterns in Family Relationships* (New York: Guilford Press, 1988).

[49] See, e.g., Rachel T. Hare-Mustin, "Discourses in the Mirrored Room: A postmodern analysis of therapy," *Family Process*, 33 (1994): 19-35.

is an ecology of ideas and dismiss the thought that what comes in the clinician's door is ever a family organization per se.[50]

In the first half of the quotation, we see familiar themes: the inclusion of the therapist; the movement away from a modernist understanding of the professional role; and the reference to "nervous systems," which represents the constructivist influence on Hoffman's thought. The crucial new idea, however, is in the second half of the passage.

In the older epistemology the family system, like a broken machine, creates the problem that brings the family to therapy. In the new way of thinking the "problem" is radically redefined. Families still suffer distress and come for treatment, but the family is not the system of interest. Instead, the therapist focuses on the "meaning system"—the "ecology of ideas" created by how everyone who encounters the family's distress thinks about it. A "family organization," in this view, does not have an objective existence independent of the professionals who perceive and name it.

The underlying displacement of mechanism by meaning needed more explicit theoretical expression. Once again, therapists turned to existing developments in other fields for inspiration. A growing number of therapists have adopted a postmodern and *social constructionist* epistemology, through which they emphasize the role of language and *narrative* in creating and sustaining meaning. We will discuss each of these intellectual commitments in turn.

Family therapists, of course, were not the first to question their modernist belief in detached objectivity. The majority of the most influential philosophical sources, by thinkers such as Jean Baudrillard, Jacques Derrida, Michel Foucault, and Jean-Francois Lyotard, were published in French in the 1970s. Some even trace the postmodern movement to the 19th century writings of Friedrich Nietzsche.[51] Today, the influence of postmodern ideas extends across the academy, from philosophy to literature, history, law, and of course, psychology.

A commitment to postmodernism in psychotherapy carries forward the second-order skepticism about the possibility of therapeutic objectivity, and places a high degree of emphasis on

---

[50] Lynn Hoffman, "Beyond Power and Control," pp. 386-387.
[51] See Jürgen Habermas, *Philosophical Discourse of Modernity* (Cambridge, MA: MIT Press, 1987).

the power of language. The modernist takes for granted that words are a reflection of reality, even though the correspondence may be imperfect. The postmodernist argues instead that words create reality, and that because of this, language can be an instrument of power. For example, do psychiatric diagnoses reflect reality or create it? A modernist therapist believes the former. A particular diagnosis may be incorrect, but in principle, it is possible to match a diagnostic term to an entity that exists within the patient. A classic study by David Rosenhan, however, suggests that diagnostic labels create the reality they appear to name.[52]

Eight individuals, including Rosenhan, posed as "pseudopatients" to gain admission to the psychiatric wards of twelve hospitals. During the intake interviews, they gave false names and employment information, and alleged that they were hearing voices. All other questions about life history and relationships, however, were answered truthfully. Every pseudopatient but one was admitted with a diagnosis of schizophrenia. After admission, they stopped pretending to have any symptoms whatsoever and behaved normally. Other patients on the ward seemed to realize that there was nothing wrong with these individuals, but the hospital staff never questioned their diagnoses. Clinical reports interpreted normal behavior as symptomatic, in accordance with the "known" diagnosis. In short, once these eight people had been labeled as schizophrenic, their normality became invisible to the staff.

What makes such a startling result possible? Taken as an objective truth, the diagnosis blinds the practitioner to competing interpretations of reality. Nietzsche had written about the "will to power"; Foucault wrote about the "will to truth."[53] A society and its institutions, in the name of truth, allow some ways of speaking but suppress others. Truth is embedded in privileged discourses, and discourses undergird the exercise of institutional power:

> There can be no possible exercise of power without a certain economy of discourses of truth which operates

---

[52] David L. Rosenhan, "On Being Sane in Insane Places," in Watzlawick, ed., *The Invented Reality*, pp. 117-144. The original study was published in 1973.

[53] See, e.g., the 1970 lecture "The Discourse on Language," in the Appendix of Foucault's *The Archaeology of Knowledge*, translated by A. M. Sheridan Smith (New York: Pantheon Books, 1972).

through and on the basis of this association. We are subjected to the production of truth through power and we cannot exercise power except through the production of truth. . . . Power never ceases its interrogation, its inquisition, its registration of truth: it institutionalizes, professionalises and rewards its pursuit.[54]

Thus, from a postmodern point of view, Rosenhan's study illustrates the coercive power of therapeutic discourse. Diagnoses are linguistic practices that are meant to reflect the truth about a patient's mental health. These practices, however, also confer power upon the experts who use the language, supporting the practical dominance of therapists over their clients.

Postmodernists subject all claims to knowledge and truth to an ideological critique: how does a particular discourse represent the power of one group over another? What alternative voices are being suppressed? Feminist theorists, for example, find postmodernism congenial because it provides an intellectual frame for asking how various texts and practices support white-male dominance over women and people of color. In Lyotard's well-known phrase, the spirit of postmodernism is summed up as "an incredulity toward metanarratives," or roughly, a posture of skepticism toward grand explanatory systems and received traditions of knowledge.[55] Knowledge, truth, and power are of a piece: metanarratives are *totalizing discourses,* that is, uses of language that define all of reality according to the will of the dominant group.

This orientation is supported by *social constructionism,* which must be distinguished from the constructivist theory described earlier. Constructivism is the biologist's answer to the epistemological question, "How do we know what we know?" Social constructionism is the sociologist's answer: knowledge is a social achievement, accomplished through language. The theory was given early expression in the mid-60s by sociologists Peter

---

[54] Foucault, *Power/Knowledge: Selected Interviews and Other Writings, 1972-1977,* edited by Colin Gordon (New York: Pantheon Books, 1980), p. 93.

[55] From Lyotard's *The Postmodern Condition* (Minneapolis: University of Minnesota Press, 1984), as cited by Hoffman, Family Therapy: An Intimate History, p. 132. The original edition of Lyotard's book was published in French in 1979.

Berger and Thomas Luckmann; since that time, its chief exponent has been psychologist Kenneth Gergen.[56]

In Berger and Luckmann's view, language originally arises out of the need to streamline and organize social interaction. Words have agreed-upon meanings, but eventually take on a life of their own. Their social origins recede from view; meanings become institutionalized and take on an objective quality. Through the customs of language, parents socialize children into a world of pre-existing meanings that teach them "the way things are."

Subgroups within society are maintained by the knowledge and use of specialized lexicons. From a modernist perspective, psychology is an empirical science and therapy its practical arm. A social constructionist, however, sees how the use of psychological terminology and therapeutic jargon is self-legitimating. The existence and continued use of such language, through institutional practices of dissemination (e.g. publication, education, and licensure) helps preserve the status and existence of the profession itself. Moreover, the therapeutic lexicon serves the larger societal purpose of maintaining a boundary between health and pathology. Psychological theories are thus an example of what Berger and Luckmann called "universe-maintaining conceptual machinery":

> Therapy entails the application of conceptual machinery to ensure that actual or potential deviants stay within the institutionalized definitions of reality, or, in other words, to prevent the "inhabitants" of a given universe from "emigrating." It does this by applying the legitimating apparatus to individual "cases." . . . This requires a body of knowledge that includes a theory of deviance, a diagnostic apparatus, and a conceptual system for the "cure of souls."[57]

In this light, therapists are not simply advocates of their own profession, nor of their clients' well-being: they are agents of

---

[56] See Berger and Luckmann, *The Social Construction of Reality: A Treatise in the Sociology of Knowledge* (New York: Anchor/Doubleday, 1967); Gergen, *Realities and Relationships: Soundings in Social Construction* (Cambridge, MA: Harvard University Press, 1994) and *An Invitation to Social Construction* (London: Sage Publications, 1999).

[57] Berger and Luckmann, *The Social Construction of Reality*, pp. 112-113.

the dominant culture.

Postmodern and social constructionist perspectives on language have had two related effects on the field of family therapy. The first was to encourage further movement toward non-hierarchical and collaborative models of the therapist-client relationship. A prime example of this is the *not-knowing* stance recommended by Harlene Anderson and the late Harold Goolishian. For them, as with Hoffman above, the interaction of therapist and client is a meaning-generating linguistic system. The primary root metaphor for the relationship is conversation or dialogue:

> Therapeutic conversation refers to an endeavor in which there is a mutual search for understanding and exploration through dialogue of "problems." . . . People talk "with" one another and not "to" one another . . . The emphasis is not to produce change, but to open a space for conversation.[58]

This kind of collaborative mutuality requires a particular attitude of openness on the part of the therapist, in contrast to the expert and directive approach of first-order family therapies:

> The not-knowing position entails a general attitude or stance in which the therapist's actions communicate an abundant, genuine curiosity . . . a need to know more about what has been said, rather than convey preconceived opinions and expectations about the client, the problem, or what must be changed.[59]

Anderson and Goolishian are not suggesting that therapists should have no knowledge. They argue, rather, that therapists will always be prejudiced by what they think they already know, and must therefore work to not let this pre-knowledge hamper listening with full respect to the client's own account. Through a process resembling a Socratic dialogue, therapists ask questions that bring the "not-yet-said" possibilities to light so that these can

---

[58] Harlene Anderson and Harold Goolishian, "The Client is the Expert: A Not-Knowing Approach to Therapy," in Sheila McNamee and Kenneth J. Gergen, eds., *Therapy as Social Construction* (London: Sage Publications, 1992), p. 29.

[59] Anderson and Goolishian, "The Client is the Expert," p. 29.

become a part of the conversation.[60] Because "problems" are held to be matters of meaning, the creative generation of new meanings in therapeutic conversation allows problems to dissolve.

The second and closely related effect was the turn to narrative models of treatment (which include Anderson and Goolishian's collaborative approach). A person's identity and sense of self are not given at birth. They are socially constructed through continual interaction with others. Moreover, humans construe their lives in narrative forms; they implicitly understand themselves as characters in a story that proceeds according to a particular plotline. Narrative therapists work on the assumption that people in therapy are struggling with what Michael White calls "dominant narratives," echoing Foucault:

> [W]e make the general assumption that persons experience problems, for which they frequently seek therapy, when the narratives in which they are "storying" their experience, and/or in which they are having their experience "storied" by others, do not sufficiently represent their lived experience, and that, in these circumstances, there will be significant aspects of their lived experience that contradict these dominant narratives.[61]

Some therapists place particular emphasis on the way parents burden their children with restrictive narratives from which they must be freed as adults.[62] But the dominant narrative that constrains an individual can also be internalized from the culture at large, including normative expectations about gender roles, appearance, or even success in one's career.

Typical narrative interventions include *externalizing*, in which the therapist helps the family to give the presenting problem a name and then speak of it as if it were a separate character in the family drama. A family with an anorexic teenager, for example, might give the problem the obvious name of "Anorexia." After mapping the influence of Anorexia in the

---

[60] Anderson and Goolishian, "Human Systems as Linguistic Systems: Evolving Ideas About the Implications for Theory and Practice," *Family Process*, 27 (1988): 371-393.

[61] Michael White and David Epston, *Narrative Means to Therapeutic Ends* (New York: W. W. Norton, 1990), pp. 14-15.

[62] See, e.g., Alan Parry and Robert E. Doan, *Story Re-Visions: Narrative Therapy in the Postmodern World* (New York: Guilford Press, 1994).

family's life, the therapist will ask questions about the family's influence on it, looking especially for forgotten or neglected instances in which the family was successful in its campaign against Anorexia.

The intervention serves two purposes. First, anthropomorphizing the problem creates new narrative possibilities. Instead of anorexia being an internal part of me, a burden over which I have no control, the externalized Anorexia becomes my antagonist, someone against which I have some freedom of choice. Second, looking for exceptions to the problem-saturated dominant narrative lays the foundation for a new story line, one that is more in accordance with the family's wishes.

Narrative therapists use a number of means to "thicken" the preferred narrative, to make it seem more realistic and true. One of the most inventive and effective is the creation of *leagues*, or groups comprised of others who have overcome similar problems. This is a practical embodiment of the principle that new narratives must also be socially constructed. A client may be given the names of several people who have volunteered to participate in an Anti-Anorexia League. Their encouragement and sharing of their own struggles help give realistic support to the client's own process of restorying.

Despite such distinctive interventions, however, narrative therapists do not emphasize technique. To do so would reflect the mistaken modernist notion that there is a "right" way to practice. The therapist's attitude is key:

> Perhaps the most important feature of the worldview that informs narrative therapy is a certain attitude about reality. . . . Adopting a postmodern, narrative, social constructionist worldview offers useful ideas about how power, knowledge, and "truth" are negotiated in families and larger cultural aggregations. It is more important to approach people and their problems with attitudes supported by these ideas than it is to use any particular "narrative technique."[63]

In other words, first, be a postmodernist—then practice in a manner that makes the most sense.

---

[63] Jill Freedman and Gene Combs, *Narrative Therapy: The Social Construction of Preferred Realities* (New York: W. W. Norton, 1996), pp. 19, 22.

In such postmodern practices, the field has come a long way from where it began. The family therapist's epistemological commitments have always been of explicit importance, but these have evolved, and with them the tenor and principles of practice. Early cybernetic views were modernist in orientation, confident in the superiority of the new paradigm. Theories of family pathology replaced notions of individual pathology. Therapy was hierarchical and sometimes mystifying, but justified by the therapist's expertise and ability to coerce change from stuck family systems.

With the growth of a postmodern orientation, family therapy has become less and less about families. Some early family therapists, convinced of the family's role in the maintenance of individual symptomatology, insisted that all members of the family living under the same roof attend the sessions together. The second-order, feminist, and postmodern critiques, however, undercut allegiance to narrow mechanistic theories and turned the field toward broader issues of meaning. To the postmodern contingent, family therapy is not about the treatment of pathogenic family systems; it is about the adoption of a new kind of self-reflexive systemic attitude that holds all theories lightly.

That is not to say that postmodernism has itself become the dominant discourse in family therapy. In an era of managed care, brief therapy approaches have become a practical necessity; this is the cornerstone of the continuing influence of the MRI.[64] Nevertheless, it is likely that postmodern perspectives will continue to gain in importance, redefining therapeutic attitudes and practices.

The movement from first- to second-order cybernetics, and on to postmodern and constructionist approaches, can be seen as a vine springing from a Batesonian root, sometimes doubling back on itself, and sometimes extending in new directions. The next section will review three alternative theories that provide still more ways to interpret what it means to think systemically.

*Beyond Bateson: Alternative Models of Family Systems*

Many of the pioneers of the family therapy movement had

---

[64] See, e.g., John H. Weakland and Wendel A. Ray, eds., *Propagations: Thirty Years of Influence from the Mental Research Institute* (New York: Haworth Press, 1995).

been trained in psychiatry, and particularly in psychoanalysis. Some, like Nathan Ackerman, developed explicitly psychoanalytic approaches to family treatment.[65] But a growing discipline needed a distinctively different paradigm, and psychoanalytic conceptions seemed to symbolize the past that was to be left behind. As the cybernetic metaphor gained in popularity, psychodynamic theories were marginalized, though they remained as a recognizable undercurrent. Three such theories will be reviewed below: *Bowen theory*, *object relations family therapy*, and *contextual therapy*. Each suggests important insights for extending systemic theory beyond the Batesonian line of development.

*Bowen Theory*

Murray Bowen was a psychoanalytically-trained psychiatrist. During the 1950s, like Lidz, Wynne, and Bateson, he conducted research on schizophrenics and their families. His analytic background led him to expect fused, symbiotic relationships between schizophrenic patients and their mothers. What he observed, however, was a cyclical pattern of emotional fusion and distance. When patients retreated, they would fuse with someone else, whether another member of the family or the hospital staff. The experience stimulated Bowen to look beyond the boundaries of the nuclear family. The resulting theory is comprised of eight interlocking concepts.[66] Two of the concepts, *differentiation* and *triangling,* are widely used by family therapists regardless of their theoretical orientation.

Bowen distinguished between intellect and emotion, and between *basic* (or *core*) *self* and *pseudo-self.* He posited that people driven by emotion were more socially reactive. They had a higher level of pseudo-self, meaning that more of their identity was negotiable under social pressure. The more differentiated a person, the greater their dependence on intellect as opposed to

---

[65] Ackerman, *The Psychodynamics of Family Life* (New York: Basic Books, 1958). See also the collection of papers written by Helm Stierlin from 1963 to 1976 entitled *Psychoanalysis and Family Therapy* (New York: Jason Aronson, 1977).

[66] The key texts are a collection of Bowen's papers entitled *Family Therapy in Clinical Practice* (New York: Jason Aronson, 1978), and a later work, Michael E. Kerr and Murray Bowen, *Family Evaluation* (New York: W. W. Norton, 1988). The latter was written by Kerr; Bowen contributed only the epilogue. He died in 1990.

emotion, and the higher the level of basic (non-negotiable) self as opposed to pseudo-self. Early in the development of the theory, Bowen imagined a scale of differentiation from low to high, and described the accompanying characteristics:

> People in the lower half of the scale live in a "feeling" controlled world in which feelings and subjectivity are dominant over the objective reasoning process most of the time. They do not distinguish feeling from fact, and major life decisions are based on what "feels" right. . . . People in the upper half of the scale have an increasingly defined level of basic self and less pseudo-self. Each person is more of an autonomous self: there is less emotional fusion in close relationships, less energy is needed to maintain self in the fusions, more energy is available for goal-directed activity, and more satisfaction is derived from directed activity. Moving into the upper half of the scale one finds people who have an increasing capacity to differentiate between feelings and objective reality.[67]

Thus, level of differentiation affects how people relate to others. Well-differentiated people have emotions but are better able to avoid being controlled by them. They are free, for example, to disagree in relationships, to take separate stands, and still maintain intimate ties. Those who are poorly differentiated, by contrast, find it difficult to disagree with others: the pull for togetherness overcomes their ability to maintain and voice a separate opinion.

Triangling describes how poorly differentiated people manage such relational pressures. When tension threatens the relationship between A and B, they deflect the threat by talking about a third person (or thing) C. B might even engage C by telling her an unfavorable story about A, rerouting the conflict to A and C. Bowen hypothesized that entire extended families were made up of such interlocking triangles, which lay dormant until a crucial event triggered the family's anxiety. Family therapy often resembled a coaching process: one key individual would be trained to anticipate and avoid relational triangles, thus forcing the rest of the system to reconnect in more direct ways. In this regard, one of the most useful tools to emerge from the Bowenian tradition is the

---

[67] Bowen, "On the Differentiation of Self," in *Family Therapy in Clinical Practice*, pp. 473-474.

*genogram,* a diagram used to map patterns of fusion, distancing, conflict, and triangling across several generations of a family.[68]

Bowen was a restless intellect who valued theory above practice or technique. His lifelong quest was for a comprehensive "science of human behavior" that would incorporate his concepts.[69] To that end, Bowen turned to evolutionary theory. Though much of his thinking and writing had been shaped by psychoanalytic paradigms, he had schooled himself broadly in evolution and biology. His early papers made scant reference to Darwin. By the publication of *Family Evaluation* in 1988, however, evolutionary theory had taken center stage. The pressures of emotional fusion, he held, originated from more primitive brain structures, while the capacity for reflective rationality and differentiation was centered in more recent evolutionary developments like the prefrontal.

Some of Bowen's terms have been common coin in the family therapy realm throughout most of its history. Near the end of his life, however, Bowen would complain that family therapists had little patience for theory, had ignored the importance of evolution, and had misunderstood what he meant when he used the word "system." Survey textbooks of family therapy tend to make little mention of the evolutionary thrust of Bowen's thinking, and therapists often lift his terms out of their theoretical context for descriptive use.

For our purposes, however, Bowen theory leaves two important legacies to the development of a comprehensive view of systems, which he expressed as background assumptions: first, "that emotional illness is directly related to the biological part of men"; and second, "that emotional illness is a multigenerational process."[70] The former is embodied in his evolutionary approach, the latter in his theory that it took three generations of poorly differentiated interaction in a family to produce a schizophrenic child. These two assumptions have important anthropological implications, to which we will return in the final section of this chapter.

---

[68] See Monica McGoldrick and Randy Gerson, *Genograms in Family Assessment* (New York: W. W. Norton, 1985).

[69] Bowen, in the epilogue to Kerr and Bowen's *Family Evaluation*, p. 386.

[70] "Society, Crisis, and Systems Theory," in *Family Therapy in Clinical Practice*, pp. 417, 418. The paper was first presented in 1973.

*Object Relations Family Therapy*

As suggested earlier, the family therapy movement in its early decades turned firmly away from psychoanalysis, even though many of the field's founders were trained analysts themselves. To some extent, this was a necessary but unfortunate part of establishing a unique professional identity. Advocates of the new systems view could be strident, polarizing therapists into warring camps:

> Family therapists saw themselves as forward-looking progressives, liberating the field from a fossilized view of mental disorder, namely that problems are firmly embedded inside people's heads. If at times they sounded a little self-righteous, perhaps that was due to the vehemence of the resistance they encountered from the psychiatric establishment. Understandable or not, the result was a prolonged and unfortunate rejection of depth psychology.[71]

In the 1980s, however, a rapprochement began to take place. By then, family therapy had attained a more secure position of respectability, which blunted the defensiveness that had characterized earlier years. As we have already seen, it was a decade in which the cybernetic mainstream was under fire; this opened a space for a reconsideration of other models. Changes were occurring within the psychoanalytic community as well, as a broad spectrum of more relational interpretations of Freudian theory gained in popularity. By mid-decade, it was possible to speak of *object relations family therapy*, as represented in textbooks by Samuel Slipp and the team of David and Jill Scharff.[72] Only a few years prior to that time, the term could scarcely have been imagined.

Since object relations theory has already been discussed in two earlier chapters of this volume, I will forgo its exposition here

---

[71] Michael P. Nichols and Richard C. Schwartz, *Family Therapy: Concepts and Methods*, 5th ed. (Boston: Allyn and Bacon, 2001), p. 199.

[72] See Slipp, *Object Relations: A Dynamic Bridge between Individual and Family Treatment* (New York: Jason Aronson, 1984) and *Technique and Practice of Object Relations Family Therapy* (New York: Jason Aronson, 1988); David E. Scharff and Jill Savege Scharff, *Object Relations Family Therapy* (New York: Jason Aronson, 1987).

and focus on its contribution to family therapy.[73]  Let me begin by noting that to some extent, the opposition of individual and systemic perspectives in first-order cybernetics had been disingenuous.  The strong emphasis on systemic interaction tended to mask the fact that therapists still operated with assumptions about the role of individual motivation.  Haley assumed that family members wanted power over others; Madanes thought family members were trying to protect one another; the Milan group proposed that everyone was driven to win the family game.  Such assumptions were crucial to how they understood the relationship between family process and therapeutic change.

Is there room, then, for recognizing the place of the psychology of the individual in the dynamics of the system?  At one level, MRI and cybernetic approaches simply declared individual approaches to be wrong: psychopathology was not like an individually-borne disease, but the manifestation of a disordered system of interaction.  The startling changes brought about by cybernetic interventions seemed to prove the point.  But this would be a circular argument.  Seemingly pathological behavior may admit of more than one explanation.  The success of strategic interventions tells us that what appears to be an individual malady can be changed through systemic means, and confirms the suspicion that individual explanations are incomplete.  It cannot tell us that individual factors do not exist, nor that they are irrelevant to the process of change.

Systemic therapists have begun to reconsider what individuals bring to family interaction.  Once again, Palazzoli's professional journey is a case in point.  Originally, she had turned to systems thinking out of frustration with the results of her analytic work.  But this does not mean that she completely rejected her psychoanalytic training.  Note the pragmatic emphasis in the following excerpt from an interview with Palazzoli, published in 1980, where she stated,

> [T]he psychoanalytical approach has impeded the adoption and application of the systemic method.  The temptation to interpret, to be more or less didactic, is always strong, but nowadays I am becoming more and more convinced that families must be induced to *do*, before they can be made to

---

[73] See chapters six and seven.

*understand.* Insight into one's own condition serves no purpose in itself but can prove useful *after* a revealing experience.[74]

Here, a systemic approach corrects the didactic and insight-oriented style of the psychoanalyst, but does not strictly replace a psychoanalytic view of persons. Indeed, she does not reject the role of insight, but argues that systemic change may be the necessary precursor if insight is to have value.[75]

It was necessary for a time, Palazzoli argues, to adopt an aggressively systemic approach in order to unlearn the habits that came with a limited individualistic approach. She discovered, however, that this could constitute a logically equivalent mistake in the opposite direction:

> [W]e realized we had gone from the frying pan into the fire, that is, from psychoanalytic reductionism, which disjoins the individual from his interactions, to holistic reductionism, which disjoins the system (family) from its individual members. Indeed, so wary had we been in the past of explicitly focusing on the individual, his intentions and aims, that for lack of "real, live people" we found it necessary to "personify" the system, endowing it with all the intentions and finalities of which we had so carefully dispossessed the individuals! . . . We were forced to acknowledge that the different individuals who made up a family would each react in a different manner to one and the same prescription. This prompted us to retrieve the dimension of the *subject.* . . . One needs to constantly bear in mind both the individual and the system of which he is a part. In other words, the individual cannot be considered disjoined from the family, nor the family disjoined from the individuals that constitute it.[76]

---

[74] The interview is cited by Matteo Selvini, ed., *The Work of Mara Selvini Palazzoli* (New York: Jason Aronson, 1988), p. 96. Emphasis in original.

[75] Similarly, see Michael P. Nichols, *The Self in the System: Expanding the Limits of Family Therapy* (New York: Brunner/Mazel, 1987). As opposed to the MRI insistence that insight is not necessary to change, Nichols argues that change may be short-lived without it.

[76] Mara Selvini Palazzoli, Stefano Cirillo, Matteo Selvini, and Anna Maria Sorrentino, *Family Games: General Models of Psychotic Processes in the*

Other advocates of a psychoanalytic approach to the family would agree. The final sentence in the above quotation stands as a fitting summary of one strand of the development of a family systems view. In the early stages therapists, steeped in individualistic habits of thought, needed to learn how to give the family its due. Later, some family therapists would recognize the need to bring the individuals back into the systemic picture.

Given its intrinsically relational understanding of the self, object relations theory is particularly well-suited to such a corrective. Object relations family therapists make several closely related assumptions. First, the quality of a child's interactions with caretakers is crucial to the development of her personality. Second, these early emotional experiences can be unconsciously internalized, forming a part of her developing self-image, as well as her understanding of others and the world at large. Third, these *internalized object-relations,* because they function like an emotional template, influence how she participates in current relationships, including those in her family. Fourth, they also influence the quality of the therapeutic relationship. In a manner reminiscent of second-order cybernetic theory, object relations family therapists include themselves as part of the unconscious emotional system in the therapy room.

One does not have to subscribe to object relations theory to recognize what family therapists of different orientations have long assumed: that individuals internalize and are shaped by experiences in their families. Richard Schwartz's *internal family systems model* is built on this premise,[77] and similar ideas can be found in approaches from Satir to narrative therapy. It is the contribution of the object relations approach to remind us that systems are not matters of outward interaction only, but include an inner world as well.

*Contextual Therapy*

Hungarian-born Ivan Boszormenyi-Nagy was yet another psychoanalytically-oriented psychiatrist studying schizophrenia and the family in the 1950s. His thinking was strongly influenced

---

*Family* (New York: W. W. Norton, 1989), pp. 260, 263. Emphasis in original.

[77] Richard C. Schwartz, *Internal Family Systems Therapy* (New York: Guilford Press, 1995).

by both object relations theory (particularly the work of W. R. D. Fairbairn) and the philosophical anthropology of Martin Buber. Nagy's approach to family treatment, which he calls *contextual therapy*, adds a unique dimension to systemic thinking that is seldom appreciated by the family therapy mainstream.

As early as 1958, Nagy was already practicing family therapy with psychotic patients at the Eastern Pennsylvania Psychiatric Institute. Through his contacts with other early figures in the movement, like Bowen, Ackerman, and Wynne, Nagy developed an appreciation for the systems view. Throughout his work, however, he sought to maintain

> a perspective on the reality that the individual himself also represents a systemic level of his own, being a whole as an existential and psychological unit. . . . There is a simple individual perspective, then there is a systems perspective, and finally a multiple individual perspective. The individual is not just a psychodynamic system, but also an existential, ethical entity.[78]

This last statement points to Nagy's key contribution—the notion of *relational ethics*.

There are four dimensions to relational reality.[79] The first is the dimension of *objectifiable facts*, which includes genetic and physical factors, as well as the circumstances of one's history. Second is the heading of *individual psychology,* under which we consider such things as a person's goals and motivations, unconscious defenses, and character structure. The third dimension consists of *transactional patterns*. Here, as we have seen, is where family systems theory moves beyond the limitations of individual psychology. Nagy, however, like Palazzoli, criticized the tendency of family therapists to anthropomorphize the system and ignore the individual. The third dimension transcends the first two, but does not replace nor exclude them.

---

[78] From an interview with Nagy in Ammy van Heusden and Elsemarie van den Eerenbeemt's Balance in *Motion: Ivan Boszormenyi-Nagy and his Vision of Individual and Family Therapy* (New York: Brunner/Mazel, 1987), p. 6. The original edition was published in Dutch in 1983.

[79] See Ivan Boszormenyi-Nagy and Barbara Krasner, *Between Give and Take: A Clinical Guide to Contextual Therapy* (New York: Brunner/Mazel, 1986), chapter 4.

Nor does the transactional perspective exhaust relational reality. There is a fourth dimension, which Nagy called *the ethic of due consideration* or *merited trust,* or simply, relational ethics. The following questions suggest the tenor of the concept:

> What is every man's due in his family? What does a child deserve? What do his parents owe him? How do parent and child evaluate the justness of their quid pro quo? How much gratitude will any child owe his parents?[80]

Answers to some of these questions are suggested by object relations theory, which has a strong normative element. The vulnerable child must have a certain quality of relationship to develop normally; this places an implicit ethical demand on parents to offer appropriate care to their children.

Nagy takes this further. The "context" of "contextual" therapy is an ethical one, a demand for justice, fairness, and trustworthiness in relationships that is intrinsic to human existence:

> The ethical balance of give and take between relating partners implies a fair return, though it includes instances of exploitation too. The dynamic here has to do with the fact that people have been cared for and owe care in return. The personalized human order that relating partners form between them is composed of at least two equal and opposite parts: The one has to do with the consequences of having benefited from other people's care. The second has to do with the obligation to offer due consideration in return, and to posterity as well.[81]

Here he draws upon Buber's notion that there is a "human order" of justice against which we can incur existential guilt.[82] When others have extended care to us, we incur a debt that must be balanced. This is the basis of the *loyalty* of children to parents—a loyalty that must be acknowledged even in conflictual

---

[80] Ivan Boszormenyi-Nagy and Geraldine Spark, *Invisible Loyalties: Reciprocity in Intergenerational Family Therapy* (New York: Brunner/Mazel, 1984), p. 68. The original edition of the book was published in 1973.

[81] Nagy and Krasner, *Between Give and Take*, p. 37.

[82] Buber, "Guilt and Guilt Feelings," *Psychiatry*, 20 (1957): 114-129.

parent-child relationships. Each family member has a perception of the *ledger*, an existential accounting of the balance between giving and taking, against which claims of fairness are made. Much of the process of therapy consists of the therapist helping each person in the family to express these claims and hear the claims of others.

There is a strong intergenerational emphasis in contextual therapy. In his concept of the family *legacy*, Nagy posits that each generation has "an obligation to help free posterity from crippling habits, traditions and delegations of previous generations."[83] This is complicated, however, by the fact that debts of fairness can also be passed from one generation to the next. A child, for example, instead of receiving due care from her parents, may be *parentified*, meaning that she is inappropriately pressed into service to be the emotional caretaker for one or both parents. This existential violation will leave her with a *destructive entitlement*, by which she knows the adults in her life to be indebted to her, but is no position to do anything about it. By the principle of the *revolving slate*, injustice will find a new victim: since she cannot retaliate against her parents, she may instead parentify her own children, and the cycle is repeated.

Historians of family therapy universally recognize Nagy's place in the development of the field. Contextual therapy, however, has made comparatively little impact on mainstream theory or practice. This is unfortunate, because of all available theories of family treatment, contextual therapy is the strongest example of an explicitly ethical/religious framework. In this light, Nagy's contribution points toward a more transcendent understanding of systems, rounding out the integrative view which concludes this chapter.

*Conclusion: An Integrative View*

The family therapy movement had its major origins in the 1950s, and rose to prominence quickly. Family systems, not individuals, were the new locus of pathology and intervention. This simple idea spawned new interventions with remarkable results. But the field continued to grow and evolve at great speed, moving through one ideological change after another. Ironically, we have reached a point where it is difficult to know what families

---

[83] Nagy and Krasner, *Between Give and Take*, p. 418.

have to do with "family therapy"—the very idea of "family" itself has become suspect as a culturally-bound social construction. "Family therapy," at least in its postmodern form, is no longer about treating families, but about the philosophical commitments of the therapist. Here, for example, is one bullet-point summary of the essentials of a social constructionist approach to training, published in a family therapy journal:

- There is no one right way to live, act, or be a family.
- Clients are the participant creators of their own new meanings, within the safe space provided by the therapist's respectful inquiry.
- The therapist may offer options and suggestions, but it is the responsibility of the client system to articulate its own stance to life.
- The therapist is not an objective observer but a co-participant. His/her own human reality is part of the therapeutic conversation and hence s/he must be ready to change and learn.
- Though the therapist is a non-expert and a non-knower in respect to client reality, s/he, through her appropriate expertise and competencies, plays an indispensable role in creating the trusting environment where new stories can be told and begun to be lived.[84]

In a sense, it is the meaning of the term "system" that has evolved. When family therapy first began, the system was the family. This gave way to the notion of a treatment system that included the therapist, which had the effect of highlighting therapist subjectivity. It was a small step from there to reinterpreting the system in terms of an interaction of ideas and meanings. The above list of ideological commitments represents a postmodern definition of systemic therapy, but it is no longer about families.

What does this say, then, about the value and possibilities of a family systems epistemology? In attempting to answer this question, I will break the term into its component parts and discuss them in reverse order, examining the use of the term

---

[84] Peter Cantwell and Sophie Holmes, "Social Construction: A Paradigm Shift for Systemic Therapy and Training," *Australian and New Zealand Journal of Family Therapy*, 15 (1994), 20.

"epistemology" in the family therapy literature, the understanding of what constitutes a "systemic" approach, and the place of the family in therapeutic theory and practice.

First, there are two broad ways family therapists have spoken of epistemology in the literature.[85] One regards the limits of what we can know. This usage is closest to the meaning of the term in philosophy. Through biological, sociological, and historical arguments, constructivist, constructionist, and postmodern authors make a compelling case for humility. Psychotherapy is a legacy of modernist culture, animated by the conviction that even the domain of life that we categorize as psychological can be controlled by technical means. Within this larger cultural metanarrative are more local ones; each school of therapy constitutes a practical subculture in its own right.[86] If, as Foucault insists, power and knowledge are inextricably entwined, then therapists are ethically bound to acknowledge the socially-constituted origins of their discipline. The recognition of a therapist's social power, coupled with the relativization of therapeutic expertise, is good cause for exploring more collaborative forms of practice.

The other use of the term is more general. As suggested at the beginning of the chapter, family therapists have generally used "epistemology" to refer to habits and paradigms of thinking. To shift to a systemic epistemology meant to rethink pathology and treatment in terms of relational systems rather than individual psychology.

Behind the debate about therapeutic epistemology, however, we can discern the presence of its philosophical partner: *ontology*, the inquiry into being and existence. Our commitments about how therapists should think are inseparable from assumptions about what *is*. Early family therapists did not simply argue that cybernetic metaphors were more useful in creating change. They often declared individually-oriented theories to be wrong-headed, whereas cybernetic theories were a truer description of the nature of problems. Later critics rightfully pointed out the modernist arrogance of this stance, preached circumspection, and developed approaches that were deemed

---

[85] For a similar argument, see Held and Pols, "The Confusion about Epistemology and 'Epistemology'" (q.v. note 2 of this essay).
[86] See, for example, Robert T. Fancher, *Cultures of Healing: Correcting the Image of American Mental Health Care* (New York: W. H. Freeman, 1995).

more respectful of clients. Yet they too had to adopt some ontological stance, some claim about reality.

This is the irony of postmodern challenges to modernist presumption. The arguments make heavy use of the term "epistemology," and advocate a relativistic approach: the therapist cannot speak authoritatively about a client's reality. At the same time, the arguments themselves rest upon their own reality claims. Postmodernists are incredulous toward metanarratives, but adopt a metanarrative interpretation of history that justifies their incredulity. Even radical constructivism, which poses a strong challenge to objectivity, rests on the results of a series of experimental studies. How do we make sense of the experimental data? How can we use them as the basis of a rational argument for constructivism? Either the experimenter must have at least limited objectivity, or the experimenter's subjectivity must be bracketed for the sake of the argument itself. The theory and its pragmatic implications fall into a self-referential vortex if one assumes that the experimenter's conclusions are nothing more than products of his own biological structure.

Maturana and his colleagues have argued that we need to limit the notion of objectivity, and rightly so. We must also remember, however, that this makes little sense if we do not also limit our skepticism. As philosopher Peter Kreeft has argued, arguments against a so-called "absolutist" stance are often paradoxical: the absolutist is usually willing to recognize limitations to her absolutism, but the relativist is absolute about her relativism.[87] Often, this is because of unacknowledged reality claims that are presented as epistemological arguments. What the field needs is clearer philosophical accounting.

These comments are meant to be suggestive; this is not the place for a full philosophical analysis. My own conviction is that we must give social construction its due, and pay full attention to how what we think we know is given to us in the social interplay of language and narrative. This said, we must also take care not to let our epistemological explorations determine our ontology. Berger and Luckmann, for example, did a masterful job of framing their treatise as a sociological inquiry. I do not know how they would have responded to the statements in a narrative therapy text that "Realities are socially constructed," and "There are no

---

[87] Kreeft, *A Refutation of Moral Relativism* (San Francisco: St. Ignatius Press, 1999).

essential truths."[88]  At the very least, we must be clear and consistent about what we mean by "reality/realities" and "truth" so as not to confuse epistemological with ontological claims.

Second, we must address what is meant by "system." As we have seen above, the content of the term has evolved over time, from a cybernetic metaphor for family interaction to a meaning-centered interpretation of the social context of therapy itself. Here again, implicit ontological commitments enter the picture: the system *is* this or that, and implications for practice follow.

Originally, however, the systems approach had a metatheoretical intent: that is, instead of specifying the content of a theory, it recommended an approach to theory-building. Modern science had pursued a reductionistic path, breaking each problem into smaller and smaller units. Against reductionism, systems theory promoted a holistic approach, which emphasized relationships and context. We do not understand the whole by summing the characteristics of its parts: we must include the pattern of relationship between the parts, and the fact that the whole is itself part of a still larger unity.

There is a difference, then, between adopting a systemic approach at the level of metatheory, and specifying the content of a system at a more midrange level of theory.  The changes in theoretical content tempt one to consider one theory to be wrong and its competitors to be right. Instead, we might consider all theories to be partial descriptions of a much more complex whole. Instead of asking, "Is the family *really* an information processing system, or an emotional system?" we should ask, "Must the family be *only* one or the other?"

Third, is there still a place for the family in psychotherapy? There should be little doubt about the importance of the family in childrearing and personality development.  The difficulty is in the possibility of the kind of "holistic reductionism" which Palazzoli criticized above.  The movement away from the strict family emphasis of earlier views is, I believe, more a reaction against this kind of reductionism than it is a pronouncement about the importance of families per se.  The family continues to demand our attention.  At the same time, however, we must exclude neither the unique contributions of the individual nor the role of larger social contexts.

In keeping with these observations, a comprehensive

---

[88] Freedman and Combs, *Narrative Therapy*, p. 22.

family systems theory should distinguish between two broad dimensions: what I would call a *multilevel relational anthropology* and a *systemic theory of change*. In this way, theorists are encouraged to give explicit attention to what unique justifications are appropriate to each dimension, and how the dimensions are related to one another.

*Dimension One: A Multilevel Relational Anthropology*

One dimension emerges from the need for an explicit ontology of persons.[89] To be fully consistent with a systemic view, this ontology should have two characteristics. First, it must recognize the multiple levels and contexts of human existence. Bowen theory attempts to do this, with concepts that span from the individual to society.[90] Nagy's model of the four dimensions of relational reality does something similar. Overall, one can see the variations in systemic theory and application over the decades as attempts to describe different levels of a vast social complex, including individuals, nuclear families, extended families, neighborhood networks, churches, and cultures.[91]

Second, it should define personhood as intrinsically social. Selfhood is not bound within an individual's skin. Though we must recognize the relative independence of the human as a biological organism, a systemic view demands that organisms be understood in their ecological context. We need an explicit ontology that posits relationships as constitutive of personhood, not as external impingements upon personhood. Again, different

---

[89] See chapter eight of this volume for a theological ontology of personhood. Within the family therapy literature, Paul Dell has also argued the need for an explicit ontology in his article "Understanding Bateson and Maturana." He asserts that Bateson never explicitly developed an ontology (I disagree), and that Maturana's structure determinism fills the void.

[90] One of Bowen's eight interlocking concepts was societal emotional process, in which he described the relevance of the concept of differentiation to large scale social processes. While suggestive, this is probably the least developed of the concepts.

[91] For example, see Ross Speck and Carolyn Attneave, *Family Networks* (New York: Pantheon, 1973); Edwin Friedman, *Generation to Generation: Family Process in Church and Synagogue* (New York: Guilford Press, 1985); John Schwartzman, ed., *Families and Other Systems: The Macrosystemic Context of Family Therapy* (New York: Guilford Press, 1985).

theories suggest some version of this. Buber's anthropology, which stands behind contextual therapy, asserts that what is truly human is found in the relational realm between, not within, individuals.[92]   Some object relations theorists posit a similarly relational anthropology.[93]   Postmodern therapists, of course, already argue that selfhood is a social construction.

Thus, an outline for a multilevel relational anthropology can be gleaned from various approaches to family therapy, on the metatheoretical assumption that each theory is a partial description of a more complex reality. Some theories, of course, will be incommensurate with each other, but not at every point. The task is to avoid reducing the complexity of human existence to a single system level. A review of the theories discussed in this chapter suggests several directions for inter- and intra-level dialogue:

• Constructivists give individual biological coherence a privileged status in their theory. Bowen's evolutionary theory points us to the rootedness of emotions in the structures of the brain. To what extent do individual biological factors pose either constraints or potentialities to higher levels?

• More than one theory assumes that aspects of a person's relationship history are internalized, as unconscious mental structures, or life narratives. How might these different views of internalization be related? And how are these internalized aspects related to one's present social context (e.g. through projective identification or processes of social construction)?

• The family continues to be one social context that is of keen interest for therapists and researchers alike. How much of the family's contribution is biological (i.e. genetic), and how much is social? How are the different aspects of the family social environment (e.g. transactional patterns, mediation of the culture through language, construction of personal narratives) related?

---

[92] See, for example, Martin Buber, *The Knowledge of Man: A Philosophy of the Interhuman*, ed. by Maurice Friedman (New York: Harper & Row, 1965).

[93] Theorists differ in their political allegiance to Freud, and thus vary in the extent to which their anthropological assumptions are intrinsically relational.   See Jay R. Greenberg and Stephen A. Mitchell, *Object Relations in Psychoanalytic Theory* (Cambridge: Harvard University Press, 1983).

- The family environment, in turn, is embedded in larger social contexts, each with cultural and socially constructed norms and rules. How does each context mediate larger contexts?[94] Which contexts are most relevant to which outcomes?
- Contextual therapy pushes a systemic ontology to consider more transcendent issues. To some extent, of course, morality and religion are socially constructed. But if human selfhood is intrinsically relational, to what extent does this include a relationship to God? Does the notion of relational justice imply a theological dimension to Nagy's existential anthropology? In our understanding of persons and relationships, what do we sacrifice by excluding this dimension of human existence, whether for ideological or methodological reasons?

These observations and questions suggest ways in which the insights of different theories might be integrated into a more comprehensive anthropology that includes multiple perspectives. A commitment to a systemic approach at the metatheoretical level means that we are not wedded to any particular partial view, but work instead to disclose how partial views may be interrelated.

*Dimension Two: A Systemic Theory of Change*

The modernist ideal would be for the practice of therapy to be fully grounded in an empirically validated psychology. The actual state of affairs, of course, is usually quite different. Though therapeutic practices are generally consistent with an underlying theory, they are not logically necessary; there may be other ways to translate a particular theory into practice. Moreover, theory and practice are circularly and not linearly related: adjustments to theory may follow, rather than precede, innovations in therapeutic method. Whatever our explicit ontological commitments, they are not likely to correspond one-to-one with techniques of change.

By the very nature of their socially-defined role, therapists are interested in change. They are paid to make change happen. But as this chapter demonstrates, therapists vary greatly in their understanding of how this should be done, ranging from strategic

---

[94] I recognize that the metaphor of social contexts as a series of nested boxes is inaccurate; contexts overlap and interpenetrate in complex ways, particularly when one considers how people inhabit multiple groups with shifting memberships. Still, I believe the question to be of heuristic value.

manipulation to the not-knowing provision of a conversational environment.

The gradual elision of the family from family therapy suggests that we need something more akin to a systemic theory of change. Working from within the confines of their own partial theories, therapists have defined and redefined the nature of both problems and their solutions. Within a modernist framework, therapists take successful case histories as confirming the validity of their clinical hypotheses. Postmodernists rightly propose a less objectivist understanding: therapeutic success tells us only that an intervention is useful, not that its underlying hypothesis is correct. Success does not prove the rightness of a theory; it only fails to disprove it.

Having recognized the illusion of pure objectivity, however, should we claim that all objective knowledge is impossible? Is the system of interest *only* a meaning system, or are there other relevant system levels? Consider the following example. A new medication is subjected to a clinical trial, and as frequently happens, a placebo effect is found. Clearly, a meaning system is involved, which may include socially constructed expectations internalized by patients and doctors, and the subtle cues that are passed between them. But should one therefore conclude that there is no pharmacological effect? On what basis would we decide?

Postmodern therapists, recognizing and rejecting simplistic claims to therapeutic objectivity, have responded with relativist principles of practice. Therapists have no expert knowledge, save the commitment to postmodernism itself, and the ability to engage in truly egalitarian conversation. Therapeutic goals rest upon the client's preferences, not the therapist's definition of normality. For therapists who adopt a postmodern stance, these are not simply abstract intellectual principles, but moral commitments based on a particular understanding of reality.

But if it is reasonable to assert that there is seldom a one-to-one necessity in the relationship between theory and practice, then we should question whether a postmodern orientation necessitates the kind of practices described. It is right to be wary of wielding power in uncritical and potentially arrogant ways, but why assume that all uses of power are oppressive? Can there be an intentional use of therapist knowledge that is not disrespectful of clients? Should therapists accept every client preference, every self-stated goal, at face value? And if not, by what logic would we resist? I cannot give incontestable answers to these questions; I wish only to suggest that accepting all or part of the postmodern critique does not necessitate a not-knowing approach to therapy.

A systemic theory of change begins with the assumption that a change at one level of a system can affect other levels. Clinical depression may be treated with medication at the level of brain chemistry: this may have an actual pharmacological effect, or create change through a placebo effect at the level of meaning. Individual and family therapies likewise may address different levels, by changing one's behavior patterns, relational responses, thought processes, or narratives. Most likely, treatment will be most successful if multiple approaches are used. Does this mean that one approach is more correct than the others, and that we must use several to find the right one? Or is it a synergism of approaches that is needed?

It is easy to assume that change in the intended direction confirms one's theory and principles of intervention. Occasionally, however, change happens in ways that we do not expect, or for reasons that we do not notice. For this reason, we need both an explicit ontology of sufficient complexity, and an accompanying theory of change that is sensitive to multiple levels of explanation.

Family therapy has traveled a long distance since its inception. Forms of first-order training and practice are probably still the norm, but over time, postmodern critiques will continue to gain in influence. The continued pursuit of a complex relational ontology and systemic theory of therapeutic change is a reasonable response to this development. Both represent a metatheoretical commitment to a systems approach that is capable of subsuming a diverse array of perspectives without giving in to a radical relativism. Therapists will continue to make ontological commitments and act upon them. It is important to make those commitments explicit and ask by what criteria we might judge between them. If it is in fact possible to have any degree of objectivity in clinical work, then such an approach may serve individuals and families better than declaring all commitments to be of equal value.

# Appendix[1]

[1]Adapted from L. A. Hjelle and D. J. Ziegler, *Personality Theories: Basic Assumptions, Research, and Application*, 3rd ed. (NY: McGraw-Hill, 1992), 20ff., & Watson, *The Great Psychologists*, 11ff.

*To what extent*:

1. Should psychological phenomena be explained in natural terms or with an appeal to a transcendent source of knowledge?

**Naturalism** . . . . . . . . . . . . . . . . . . . . . . . . . . **Supernaturalism**

2. Do we gain knowledge from sense experience or from innate ideas?

**Empiricism** . . . . . . . . . . . . . . . . . . . . . . . . . . . . **Rationalism**

3. Should psychological knowledge begin with particular observations or general principles?

**Inductivism** . . . . . . . . . . . . . . . . . . . . . . . . . . . **Deductivism**

4. Is human behavior controlled from within or from without ?

**Freedom** . . . . . . . . . . . . . . . . . . . . . . . . . . . . . **Determinism**

5. Is human reason perspicacious and potent or governed by instinctual forces?

**Rationality** . . . . . . . . . . . . . . . . . . . . . . . . . . . **Irrationality**

6. Should humans be studied as whole persons or by analyzing their parts?

**Holism** . . . . . . . . . . . . . . . . . . . . . . . . . . . . . . **Elementalism**

7. Is human nature innate or conditioned?

**Constitutionalism** . . . . . . . . . . . . . . . . . . . . **Environmentalism**

8. Can humans change?

**Changeability** . . . . . . . . . . . . . . . . . . . . . . . . **Unchangeability**

9. Are humans mainly influenced by internal or external factors?

**Subjectivity** . . . . . . . . . . . . . . . . . . . . . . . . . . . . **Objectivity**

10. Do humans primarily act or react?

**Proactivity** . . . . . . . . . . . . . . . . . . . . . . . . . . . . . **Reactivity**

11. Are humans motivated more by tension-reduction or self-actualization?

**Homeostasis** . . . . . . . . . . . . . . . . . . . . . . . . . . . **Heterostasis**

12. Can human nature be known or is it a mystery?

**Knowability** . . . . . . . . . . . . . . . . . . . . . . . . . . **Unknowability**

13. Are persons universal or unique?

**Nometheticism** . . . . . . . . . . . . . . . . . . . . . . . . **Idiographicism**

14. Are "mind" and "matter" one or two substances?

**Monism** . . . . . . . . . . . . . . . . . . . . . . . . . . . . . . . . . . **Dualism**